New Realities of Secondary Teachers' Work Lives

New Realities of Secondary Teachers' Work Lives

an international comparative study of the
impact of educational change on the work lives
of secondary school teachers in nine countries

EDITED BY
Pam Poppleton & John Williamson

SYMPOSIUM
BOOKS

Symposium Books
PO Box 204, Didcot, Oxford OX11 9ZQ, United Kingdom
the book publishing division of wwwords Ltd
www.symposium-books.co.uk

Published in the United Kingdom, 2004

ISBN 1 873927 14 2

© Symposium Books, 2004

Typeset in Melior by Symposium Books
Printed and bound in the United Kingdom by Cambridge University Press

Contents

Preface

This book describes the research undertaken by members of the Consortium for Cross-Cultural Research in Education (CCCRE) from 1993 to 1999 in a study entitled 'The Impact of Educational Change on the Dynamics of Teachers' Work Lives'.

This was a comparative study which collected data from nine different countries in order to uncover the range of changes worldwide; to study teachers' reactions to change in the various countries participating and to draw conclusions about the respective roles of innovation, restructuring and reform in different contexts. Placing these processes in international context would enable, first, the implications of change for teachers to be more fully understood, and help teachers to develop a cross-cultural perspective on their work that would encourage the development of a sense of international professional identity. Second, it could offer useful information to policy makers and community leaders as they consider action for their own educational systems.

In an age when politicians, in particular, look to developments in other countries to help solve their educational problems, it is vital to avoid making judgments on the basis of limited historical, cultural or political circumstances elsewhere. For these and other reasons, we wished not only to collect data about the various systems but also to fill in the framework with some account of what the teachers themselves experienced. Our study was designed to be small scale within each country but large scale in deriving data from semi-structured interviews based on schedules carefully designed to have an identical core of items in each country. Each researcher undertook to administer the schedule to 50 secondary school teachers drawn from schools in neighbourhoods with diverse socio-economic characteristics. It was not always possible to achieve this number though interviews were recorded and transcribed and, in all, data were available from a total of some 500 teachers worldwide. In each country, *quantitative measures* were derived from coding the interview responses under headings agreed by all researchers after extensive consultations. All these steps in the research process were discussed between colleagues at annual meetings, implemented in each country and coordinated centrally.

Qualitative data were provided by the discovery of themes and patterns of response from the interview transcripts when interviewees were encouraged to explore reflectively the impact on their work lives of the various changes reported. The two strands of evidence, qualitative and quantitative, were scrutinised for compatibility before the full stories could be told and findings compared within and between countries. The final acts of comparison enabled the process of translating similarities and differences into implications for policy and practice in introducing and implementing change in education systems

The book is organised into three sections. *Part One* contains accounts of the single-country studies, *Part Two* reports the comparative data analyses and gives tables for both within-country and between-country data, and *Part Three* draws both sets of findings together to arrive at some conclusions on the impact of change on the teacher's working life.

Consortium Members Participating in This Research

Allen Menlo & LeVerne Collet, University of Michigan (USA)

Tsila Evers, Universities of Michigan and Ohio, Cincinnati (USA)

Pam Poppleton, University of Sheffield (United Kingdom)

John Williamson & Rick Churchill, University of Tasmania, (Australia), and University of Southern Queensland, Toowoomba (Australia)

Lya Kremer-Hayon & Zehava Rosenblatt, University of Haifa (Israel)

Nóra Arató, University of Michigan (USA) and **Mariann Szemerszky**, Institute for Educational Research (Hungary)

Noel Hurley, Newfoundland Schools, formerly of the University of Windsor, Ontario (Canada)

Theo Wubbels, Utrecht University (The Netherlands) and **Hans Vonk**, Vrije Universiteit, Amsterdam (The Netherlands)

Kan Shi & Huadong Yang, Chinese Academy of Sciences (Beijing)

Johan Booyse & Cassie Swanepoel, University of South Africa, Pretoria (South Africa)

INTRODUCTION

The Comparative Background to Educational Change

PAM POPPLETON & JOHN WILLIAMSON

INTRODUCTION

The research reported in this book is an international, comparative study of secondary teacher perceptions of educational change. 'Change' is interpreted in the broadest sense, from new approaches to the teaching of a particular topic through whole school policy initiatives to legislative changes brought in by state or national governments. Change is thus used to refer to innovations at classroom or school level as well as to reforms of the whole or parts of the education system of a country.

The study took, as its starting point, the teachers' identification of the educational change that had most significantly influenced their working lives. It explored, by semi-structured interviews, how teachers perceived their roles and practices in the management of change, whether these varied according to the nature of the change, according to whether the origins were internal or external to the school; how the changes were introduced, implemented and monitored; and the extent and nature of the impact of the change on their work lives, including relationships, professional development, student learning, their own feelings, and finally, how they felt about contributing in any way to future changes of a similar nature.

It was also a comparative study in order to study reactions to change in different countries the better to understand:

- the role played by the socio-political context into which changes are introduced,

- how centrally determined objectives are incorporated into schools' programmes of development,
- how innovations come to be initiated and implemented,
- the teachers' perceptions of their role in change and resource and training needs under different working conditions, and
- the part higher education institutions can play in meeting these needs.

This brief account of the nature of the study will be elaborated later when the methodology is described more fully but, for now, we turn to the origins of our enquiry.

THE CONSORTIUM FOR CROSS-CULTURAL RESEARCH IN EDUCATION

The impact of recent educational change on the dynamics of the teacher's working life is the second study to be undertaken by members of the Consortium who are drawn from 9 of the countries comprising the total membership of 15 at the present time. The Consortium was founded in 1984 as a result of a long-standing partnership between the Universities of Michigan (USA) and Sheffield (England) in the course of which some hundreds of education students and staff had exchanged places over a period of twenty years following the Second World War. In the process of these visits collaborative projects were forged and some long-term research opportunities created which are pursued today in a much wider international context. At its inception, members decided to concentrate on the problems and processes of secondary schooling that were becoming uppermost in the minds of teachers and the general public in the mid-80s, when Germany became the third partner. Accordingly, academics at the three universities of Michigan, Sheffield and the Johann Goethe University in Frankfurt initiated an inquiry into *Aspects of Care in Secondary Schools*, which later broadened to become a study of *Work Perceptions of Secondary School Teachers: international comparisons* (Poppleton, 1990). A full account of the study, extended to nine countries, now exists under the title *The Meanings of Teaching: an international study of secondary teachers' work lives* (Menlo & Poppleton, 1999).

Why the concentration on teachers in general and secondary teachers in particular? The two decades preceding the turn of the twentieth century were outstanding in the volume of educational reforms worldwide. The forces of globalisation, the information revolution and growing awareness of the economic and social gaps between rich and poor countries generated a climate in which frantic 'borrowing' attempts between countries were made as each searched for solutions to its problems. The World Economic Forum publishes annual 'League Tables' in which the relative ranks of countries on various indices of academic, industrial and commercial success are consulted by politicians to exhort their citizens to ever greater accomplishments in the cause of national pride and governmental competence. Some of these tables compare educational systems by quoting achievement levels in basic subjects (for example, mathematics, science, literacy, reading) as well as ratings made by selected samples of the populations about the status of schools and teachers which became accepted as basic data by politicians in search of further reforms.

At the same time new expectations and demands about education were being voiced by governments, parents, educators and the public at large. Comparisons of the educational achievement of pupils such as that between the USA and Japan (Spaulding, 1989) and England and Germany (Phillips, 1987) had been made more visible by the establishment and research studies of the International Association for the Evaluation of Educational Achievement (IEA). UNESCO also laid the foundation for the systematic collection of international statistics of education at about the same time and, as the flow of information increased and was made public, anxieties mounted about failure to meet international standards in enrolment, wastage, the financing of education and, consequently, in the development of the science and technology that would underpin national achievement ambitions in the years ahead.

Anxieties soon escalated into a culture of blame. Reasons for the weaknesses displayed and failure to raise standards began to be seen as a failure of schooling and, especially, a failure of teaching. It was never better expressed than in Britain when the then Minister of Education stated that 'Teaching is too important to be left to teachers' (Baker, 1987) and initiated a series of changes which led to the Great Reform Act of 1988. In the USA, the publication in 1983 of 'A Nation at Risk' heralded a series of reform efforts aiming to make schooling more effective, but, in contrast to England, by empowering teachers in providing them with formal decision-making authority and redesigning their work (Murphy, 1992).

It was in this context that the CCCRE developed [1] and members chose, by reason of their special responsibilities, to concentrate on secondary education as the main focus of concern. They agreed to undertake comparative research into common issues related to the professional work and education of teachers that had implications for policy and practice in the member countries, as well as advancing basic knowledge. It was the IEA achievement data in particular that harnessed the notion of 'natural variation' between geographic units to examine 'issues that could not be studied well within the confines of one school system' without resorting to difficult and costly experiments (Purves, 1989).

For each stated issue, they would compare conditions within and between countries so that each country's practices might be better evaluated and ensure that the comparative findings would be interpreted by those from the country or countries involved so that they could be placed in context. This would be a collaborative research programme to examine the impact of educational change on the dynamics of the teacher's work life based on the teachers' own perceptions of the changes taking place so that they would be able to evaluate the changes, and their own responses to them, with greater understanding. Active participants came from Australia, Canada, the People's Republic of China (PRC), England, Israel, Hungary, the Netherlands, South Africa and the USA.

WHAT COUNTS AS CHANGE?

Our first question sets the scene for an exploration that lasted six years and extended over the nine different countries in America, Europe, the Southern Hemisphere and the Far East. At the beginning we discussed and defined some provisional issues in order to frame a research project. Some of the issues that emerged in that process are described below.

Change as Reform

Educational reforms are generally seen as features of whole systems, and the trends outlined above have driven them in one or more of several directions, among which the main tendencies have been the introduction of national curricula, schemes of national assessment, new management structures for schools, heightened accountability to a new 'parentocracy' (Brown, 1990) [2], more stringent controls over the funding of universities, and greater publicity and openness about the state of schooling, including, in some cases, the construction of league tables which place schools in rank order on the results of GCSE and A-level examinations. The latter has proved to be particularly resented by schools and teachers. In Britain, these potentially demeaning measures (to schools and teachers), and similar national reforms, have been underpinned by ideologies that have moved schools, colleges and universities away from the public service ethos of state education towards the competitive market requirements of managerialism (Ball, 1999). Similar developments have occurred in the form of major reform movements in countries such as Australia, Canada, New Zealand and the USA. 'Educational institutions are not merely affected by the market – they are themselves a market' (Cowen, 1996). Major strategies involved in this transfer of power from traditional administrative systems such as local government have been the creation of non-governmental organisations or 'agencies' that oversee the implementation of reforms. In England and Wales examples would be the Office for Standards in Education (OFSTED) and the Teacher Training Agency (TTA), the implementation of which 'has had to rely on the efforts of teachers acting under unprecedented levels of control and bureaucratic procedures'

(Mortimore & Mortimore, 1998). England has not been unique in this respect, though it may have travelled further along this road than most.

Change as Restructuring

Developments in many other countries have not been so all-embracing. In Europe particularly, they have taken the form of restructuring efforts rather than reform, have tended to be mainly concerned with evaluation systems, operating on a regional basis with varying degrees of national vigilance, and are more likely to be based on internal than external procedures (Hopes, 1997). An exception to this generalisation has been the development of school/institutional partnerships in initial and continuing teacher training where internal and external contributions work hand in hand.

In America, restructuring has been regarded as phase 2 of a reform process in which power and authority are redistributed to teachers, parents and other stakeholders (Murphy, 1992) as policy changes are put into effect. The target has been the development of new forms of school organisation and management reflected in the change from principal as manager to principal as facilitator and from teacher as worker to teacher as leader (Murphy, 1992). The school has now become the main focus of this phase (Green, 1987). The belief that the school and teachers, in particular, are the main agents in bringing about higher standards and greater effectiveness is the basis of the school improvement movement in both England and the USA (Firestone & Rosenblum, 1988; Seashore-Louis & Miles, 1990; Nias, 1989).

A good example of restructuring occurred in the UK in the 1980s when an attempt to improve England's poor record of industrial training compared with other countries was targeted by the introduction of TVEI (the Technical and Vocational Education Initiative) into the curriculum of secondary and further education (Badley, 1986). Initially regarded with some suspicion, a well-managed programme of implementation was handled by the local education authorities, in conjunction with teacher training institutions and industrial concerns, to bring about recognition of work experience as a fundamental element in the curriculum. However, presenting a recent draft report on the results of 44 local authority inspections, the Chief Inspector of Schools [3] said, 'Our position has always been that the successful school is successful because of the effectiveness of its own management and effective schools should have ... the freedom to manage their own destiny'. Conflicts between the power of the state, the local/regional authority and the individual school are a significant feature of educational policy formulation in the late twentieth and early twenty-first centuries and one that bears heavily on the working lives of teachers.

Change as Innovation: schools and teachers

Teachers themselves have an important part to play in introducing innovations in the teaching process and in the informal processes of schools that may eventually lead to wide-ranging reforms.

That was certainly the hope of the 'teacher as change agent' movement of the 1970s and '80s in which the role demands on the change agent included a range of leadership, facilitator and communication skills (Badley, 1986). At the same time, and in conjunction with that analysis, additional skills were being defined by the 'teacher as researcher' movement (Rudduck, 1991), in which the examination of the teacher's own practice 'allows the teacher to explore it in depth, to gain new insights, to set new goals, and to achieve new levels of competence and confidence'. However, few governments have had the confidence to define precisely the teacher's role as change agent. If, and when, it happens, it is generally dependent on the initiative of an individual and a particular school.

The increasingly diverse role expectations for teachers in the 1990s make for a somewhat confused picture of the roles played by individuals in the school (Neave, 1992) and in the change process – for example, the difficulties faced by teachers in OECD countries in coping with the increasingly complex expectations held by parents, caring agencies and politicians. Consequently, teachers have been treated in ways that diminish the value of teaching both as occupation and social practice. Such concerns are not found in Western countries only. Yano (1997) commented on the situation in Japan, 'Teachers are currently confronted with a variety of problems which they do not know how to cope with'.

Other interpretations of the teacher's role widely canvassed in the literature are those of leader versus facilitator (Rudduck, 1991) and passive instructor versus active decision-maker (Fullan & Stiegelbauer, 1991; Hargreaves, 1994). It is within the school that teachers are most likely to be cast in the role of implementers of change rather than initiators and they come at the end of a long process of implementation from government to local authorities to schools, to heads or principals, to senior staff and, finally, to teachers. The interdependence of these players will define the type of change being considered.

These three forms of educational change – reform, restructuring and innovation, are not mutually exclusive and we should expect to find examples of all three in the different countries involved in the research. Without having clear expectations about the incidence of each form in each country, however, the aim was to look at the situation through the teachers' eyes and to discover what, for them, had been the change which had exerted most impact on their working lives, for 'Educational change depends on what teachers do and think – it's as simple and as complex as that' (Fullan & Stiegelbauer, 1991, p. 117).

14

METHODOLOGY: STAGES OF THE RESEARCH

The research was not primarily perceived as a policy-oriented study in aiming to produce clear-cut policy recommendations for the introduction and management of change, though neither was it seen as irrelevant to that aim. The more cautious view is that policies designed to produce changes are necessarily formulated and implemented in particular circumstances that might not necessarily exist elsewhere. Nevertheless, it was hoped that a cross-country investigation would tease out implications that could be helpful to those intending on considering the adoption of practices that appeared to be more successful than those presently in use.

A Conceptual Framework to Guide Data Analysis

The aim of this section is to take the reader through the various stages of the research project in order to gain a general understanding of what was done, without, at this point, going into technical details, which are given in Part Two.

Procedures

First, to gain access to what teachers do and think we have to ask them to report and evaluate their experiences, and to do so, moreover, in ways that can yield comparisons both within and between countries. The strategy most generally employed in comparative studies is the survey since it can be designed to have a standard format that ensures that every person responds to exactly the same question as every other. The survey is ideal for gaining information but requires the researcher to conform to a number of rules governing the construction of the survey instrument (test or questionnaire), who shall be asked to respond (the sample), how they shall be selected (randomly or systematically on some criterion), the method of administration (by post or through personal contact) and a number of other requirements designed to ensure that variations in responses are not due to random influences. Such requirements are even more important in the case of an international comparative study because of factors such as the difficulty of achieving equivalence of meaning in different languages when translation is necessary.

Designing an Interview Schedule

Bearing these factors in mind, Consortium members considered designing an interview schedule that would (a) incorporate questions in a number of areas thought to be relevant to assessing the impact of change on the work life, (b) enable members to obtain one hundred per cent responses from a smaller number of teachers, and (c) offer

15

Introduction

interviewers the opportunity to probe meanings and expand explanations at will. Both qualitative and quantitative techniques of data analysis would be employed.

In the course of intensive discussions between members (1993-96), a semi-structured interview schedule was developed incorporating 12 areas presented under two major headings: *the characteristics and antecedents of change* (independent variables) and the *impact of change on aspects of the teacher's working life* (dependent variables).

Characteristics and Antecedents of Change

Q1: *Domain of change.* In view of the widespread impression of the globalisation of change and the degree of harmonisation that existed between countries, a means was sought of gaining an overall picture of the extent and nature of recent educational change in the nine contributing countries. In order not to influence respondents by the preconceptions of the interviewer, we asked them firstly, to name three examples of changes that they had experienced within the past five years and then to choose which of these had been the change of greatest importance to them in their work as teachers. The remainder of the interview concentrated on this final choice.

Q2: *Perceived origin of the change.* Where did they think that the change originated and who was instrumental in its adoption?

Q3: *Perceived objective of change.* Was it primarily designed to improve student achievement, skill development, personal-social development? Or to be of benefit to teachers, parents, the status of the school?

Q4: *Role of teacher in the change.* To what extent was the teacher involved as initiator, implementer, planner, decision-maker or not affected at all?

Q5: *Timetable for change.* Was the change introduced quickly or gradually?

Q6: *Factors facilitating implementation.* Financial, human and physical resources provided, professional development opportunities, collegial effort and support.

Q7: *Forces impeding implementation.* Lack of resources, administrative support, opposition from colleagues, lack of consultation and communication.

These characteristics and consequences of change were now incorporated into a more systematic form that showed the possible relationships between them portrayed in Figure 1. This became a first, tentative model for data analysis. Information was also collected about demographic variables such as the teacher's country of origin, age, gender, marital status and professional/career and school context variables.

16

The Impact of Change on Work Life

Q8a *The extent of impact of change on teacher's work life.* Pedagogy, a scale value 1-6, from 'none' to 'all of it'.

Q8b *Impact on the things you do.* Mentions of new teaching approaches, managing stress, greater attention to students, records, planning.

Q8d *Impact on relationships.* More/less, harmonious/strained, formal/restricted.

Q8e *Impact on use of time.* More/less under own control, time for lesson preparation, meetings/self-consciousness of time usage.

Q8f *Impact on professional development.* Positive, negative, neutral.

Q9a *Impact on student learning.* Scale value 1-6, from 'none' to 'all'.

Q9b *Nature of impact on students.* Mentions of more/less serious about learning/knowledgeable/cooperative/skilful/communication/diverse.

Q10 *Teacher's feelings about the change.* Scale value 1-6, from 'very negative' to 'very positive'.

Q11a *Teacher's willingness to participate in similar change in future* Scale value 1-10.

Q11b *Willingness to participate in any future change.* Scale value 1-3: 'yes', 'uncertain', 'no'.

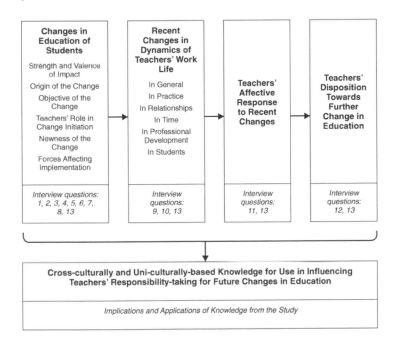

Figure 1. Conceptual framework for the Consortium's cross-cultural comparative study of the influence of educational change on the dynamics of teachers' work lives and their dispositions toward further change.

Introduction

Sampling

It should be emphasised that the interviews would draw on the subjective perceptions of the teachers rather than any 'objective' records or official statements. The accepted strategy finally agreed was to draw samples of teachers from schools that were as alike as possible in terms of school type (comprehensive, state-run, socio-economic catchments) and could, therefore, be compared legitimately. The strategy was also to draw comparable samples of teachers from schools in terms of age, gender, seniority, length of service and other demographic characteristics.

Each country was responsible for the conduct of its own interviews and agreement had been reached to aim for samples of 50 teachers from 10 schools. Schools were asked to provide a sample consisting of one recently appointed teacher, two mid-career teachers and two senior teachers occupying different roles. If possible, it was desirable that the sample would contain a balance of male and female teachers.

Collection and Treatment of the Data

All interviews were recorded and transcribed enabling them subsequently to be coded by the researchers in each country according to an agreed numerical coding scheme that took account of all responses. The results could then be presented in the form of cross-tabulations between countries and categories ready for the cross-country statistical analyses presented in Part Two. Thus, together with the single-country descriptions in Part One, a shared data set was created that would yield to both qualitative and quantitative treatments and provide a sound basis for the making of comparisons. It can now be presented in diagrammatic form to show the elements incorporated into the interview schedule and the relationships between blocks of variables that may be explored both qualitatively and quantitavely, both within and between countries.

COMPARING THE INCOMPARABLE?

Historically, comparative studies in education have concentrated on identifying similarities and differences in countries' educational outcomes that might lead the governments concerned to develop improved understanding of the factors that produce them and modify their policies to incorporate these understandings. For example, in the Western world during the 1990s, anxieties over relative standards in education were fed by the results of international surveys such as the Third International Mathematics and Science Study (TIMMS) carried out in 1997. This and other studies (Reynolds, 1998) that purport to show superior levels of performance in the Pacific rim countries have encouraged others to beg, borrow or steal the pedagogies involved

18

irrespective of cultural dissimilarities, historical trends or the politicisation of educational systems. Torsten Husen (1987) noted that 'those in England and in Germany both for and against greater comprehensiveness in education used the same Swedish studies to support their positions' (quoted in Spaulding, 1989, p. 13).

What, then, will an international study tell us that studies of change in our own countries could not? Does it tell us more than we might learn from studying our own system in greater depth? Our expectations should not be too great but normally, we rarely have the opportunity to step back and view our own systems from a wider perspective. The contribution of the different framework that comparative study provides is often beneficial. If we can do this in collaborative context we also stand to learn much more.

OVERVIEW OF PART ONE

Looking ahead to the papers presented in Part One of this volume, each of the authors of the nine chapters presents a description of the education system in their country in relation to recent changes that have taken place. The chapters have been arranged in alphabetical order depending on the country of origin, as are the tables presented in Part Two, in order to assist ease of reference forwards and backwards between the two sections. Each author also had access to the comparative analyses presented in Part Two and has been free to comment on the single-country findings in that context.

Chapters follow a pattern that allows coherence to develop. Each author first describes the relevant historical and cultural components of the country's educational system with particular reference to changes affecting teachers. This is followed by an account of the teachers' interview responses, frequently illustrated by examples of the teacher's voice and some evaluation of the effects on their work lives in terms of workloads, relationships, career hopes and patterns and personal attitudes towards change. Reference may also be made to comparisons with their colleagues in other countries from the tables presented in Part Two.

The methodology adopted makes this an empirical study with one foot in the *positivist* tradition based on notions of rational enquiry and the validity of quantitative data, while the other foot is planted in the *interpretative* mode of qualitative data that recognises the subjective nature of people's perceptions and attempts to reconstruct the meanings and perspectives that they bring to situations. In this study, the challenge is to bring these two approaches together in a coherent manner that will yield more than each method used separately.

Looking Ahead

A review of the single country studies in Part One may be structured around certain themes and issues to show where the major examples of similarity and difference lie.

The three types of change identified earlier – reform, restructuring and innovation – form a descriptive framework for considering differences in the context and content of change internationally.

Context

The authors of the chapters in Part One describe a variety of contexts, from the most macro-socio-economic-political level to the micro-classroom level. In doing so, they present the perceptions of the teachers in the study in ways that speak of the 'insider' rather than some more external or objective voice. While these are unique views on the context described, they are no more and no less than the views of the teachers who were interviewed.

A Context of Reform

The study was located in the comprehensive, or common, schools of each country, that is to say, the state-run schools with non-selective entry. Comprehensive education incorporates fundamental value judgments about equity in a context of social and intellectual diversity or, in more contemporary terms, the achievement of an inclusive rather than an exclusive society. However, this has to be seen against a background of political consensus versus diversity and, as the case of England shows, a dramatic change over the period of the 1990s marked by a significant shift to a more centralised and utilitarian system; from the needs of the child to the needs of industry and commerce. This was also the case in Australia where there were parallel developments in moving to a more vocationally-based curriculum and draconian systems of assessment. Churchill & Williamson (Australia) and Poppleton (England) show how, in each case, the majority of teachers felt their professionalism to be challenged in relation to the ignoring of the range of experience they had to offer and the degree of autonomy they could exercise over the curriculum and pedagogy. In both of these cases details of how broad political shifts have created challenges involving the state are presented from the teachers' perspectives.

Two other countries affected by political upheavals were the People's Republic of China and South Africa, for which the nominated origins of change were much more dispersed between internal and external sources though around half of the teachers respectively perceived the change to have been centrally inspired. Major problems in the Chinese educational system have been to do with funding a vast expansion in provision for the whole school age population and to enable the schools to provide a curriculum that will best prepare students for a rapidly changing lifestyle. Kan & Huadong place great emphasis on the development of a market economy that will be responsive to these aims. South Africa, on the other hand, is the newest of our countries to develop a radically different approach to educational reform and has undergone the most upheaval. Although over half of the teachers interviewed identified the source of change as central government, over one-third considered that there was still scope for teachers and schools to act flexibly in the best interests of students. Booyse & Swanepoel eloquently reveal the struggles involved in coming to terms with a multicultural, multilingual education project under the sudden transfer of power to a new government.

A Context of Restructuring

Canada is a case of restructuring rather than wholesale reform. Hurley presents an account of the introduction of a 'Transition Years' reform, and of how the many articles of collective agreements have had a debilitating influence on how educational change has been initiated and implemented in the province of Ontario. The initiative lay with the government but the implementation with the provinces.

A similar restructuring programme occurred in the Netherlands in the early 1990s, but this concerned curriculum reform right through from junior to senior secondary levels. Wubbels & Vonk show how the restructuring has affected classroom practices and, consequently, the work lives of Dutch teachers in fundamental ways. They interpret the effects in terms of the relationship between the individualism of Dutch teachers and the egalitarian, consensus society that has a high tolerance of ambiguity.

Cross-culturally, intermediate sources of change were nominated by teachers in Hungary and Israel. Emphasis is now on the local authorities, the school and its teachers. In Hungary, Arató & Szemerszky, describe how, after the decline of communism, professional independence was delegated to schools which were given the freedom to design and implement new teaching methods. This was inevitable once the Marxist curriculum had collapsed and the consequences for teachers and students are spelled out.

In Israel, the majority of changes were initiated by teachers and/or school administrators. This tendency may be the result of a good deal of autonomy being granted to religious groups, each having its own school sub-system and unique cultural heritage. Social and ethnic diversity is a characteristic that is likely to set the scene for greater teacher input in the form of innovations adopted by the school. It is, as Rosenblatt & Kremer-Hayon claim, an opportunity for a systematic turnabout in the schools' functioning. Each of these countries has experienced massive political upheavals.

A Context of Innovation

Last, but not least, Evers & Arató, describe continuous educational change in the USA since 1983, another country in which the implementation of reform has been in the hands of the states and local, rather than federal, government. It is these bodies that set most guidelines and priorities for public and elementary schools in conjunction with school boards. In these circumstances, there is far more scope for innovation in schools that cater for multiethnic, multilingual and multi-religious communities. Schools and teachers have greater freedom to design and implement their own curricula but must still recognise issues of standards.

Part One ends with a summary of the various contributions. In 'The Teacher's Voice. Examining Connections: context, teaching and teachers' work lives', Williamson & Poppleton call on the descriptions of system characteristics to draw attention to the balance between national, regional, local and school-based bodies that appear to have perceptible effects on the work of teachers. This balance is also changing as the privatisation of educational services is adopted as a solution to the problems of universal, lifelong education in the post-modern world. New alliances have strong implications for the attitudes and behaviour of teachers.

OVERVIEW OF PARTS TWO AND THREE

Phases one and two of this study look at the same database through different lenses. Phase one explored the whole range of the macro- and micro-social influences on the work life of teachers. Phase two, on the other hand, takes selected responses, now coded and aggregated, to explore cross-country similarities and differences as a guide to the role of teachers in policy-making generally.

These differences in approach may be seen in the development of the interactive model of Figure 1, Part One, which recognises the interdependence of the variables explored within each country, to Figure 1, Part 2, where a linear path of influence is assumed, from the nature of the change, through to its implications and applications. From there, Figures 2 and 3 show quite clearly that the aim is now to predict the teacher's affective response and disposition to take part in any future change from a series of multiple regressions based on the total smple.

In Part Two, therefore, the editors present a more systematic statistical analysis of country similarities and differences based on the numerically coded responses to the interviews provided by all contributors. Some of the results were foreshadowed in Part One but the qualitative data were unable to reveal the presence and extent of interactions between macro- and micro-factors. Readers will find this account demanding, but interesting, as they follow the skilful unravelling of these relationships.

The accounts given in the first two parts of the book differ in their objectives, techniques and style of reporting, but each has integrity within its own paradigm and each makes a valuable contribution to the study of educational change. The accounts also contribute to the ongoing discussions of the respective roles of qualitative and quantitative methods of enquiry in the field of comparative studies.

In Part Three of the book, the editors attempt to bring strands of evidence together to bear on the issues that were raised in the Introduction and to remind those who make and implement policy changes at whatever level that, ultimately, their success or failure will depend on the professionalism of teachers and the contexts in which they work.

SUMMARY

Despite the differences between countries in terms of size, school provision, political ideology and economic standing, there is a cultural homogeneity about secondary education that leads to notable similarities in the presenting issues in the last years of the twentieth century. Concepts that crop up frequently are standards, excellence, the market, quality, accountability, choice, diversity. From rendering a professional service, teachers are now seen to be delivering a product that will be judged in much the same way wherever in the world it may occur.

Notes

[1] Countries are (in alphabetical order) Australia, Canada, China (PRC), England, Hungary, Israel, the Netherlands, South Africa, USA. Reference to England should be read to include Wales and Northern Ireland, as the three regions come under the same regulations as far as education is concerned and are different from the Scottish system.

[2] 'Parentocracy' was the name given by Phillip Brown (1990) to 'a system whereby the education a child receives must conform to the wealth and wishes of parents rather than the abilities and efforts of pupils'. As such, it is a shift away from the 'ideology of meritocracy'.

[3] Christopher Woodhead.

Introduction

References

Badley, G. (1986) The Teacher as Change Agent, *British Journal of In-Service Education*, 12, pp. 151-158.

Baker, K. (1987) Speech to the North of England Conference, Rotherham, 9 January.

Ball, S.J. (1999) Global Trends in Educational Reform and the Struggle for the Soul of the Teacher! ERIC Citation, Accession No. 9911190125.

Brown, P. (1990) The 'Third Wave': education and the ideology of parentocracy, *British Journal of Sociology of Education,* 11, pp. 65-85.

Cowen, R. (1996) Last Past the Post: comparative education, modernity and perhaps post-modernity, *Comparative Education,* 32, pp. 151-170.

Firestone, W. & Rosenblum, S. (1988) Building Commitment in the Urban High Schools, *Educational Evaluation & Policy Analysis,* 10, pp. 285-299.

Fullan, M. & Stiegelbauer, S. (1991) *The New Meaning of Educational Change.* Toronto: OISE Press.

Green, J. (1987) *The Next Wave: a synopsis of recent education reform reports.* Washington, DC: Denver Education Commission of the States.

Hargreaves, A. (1994) *Changing Teachers, Changing Times: teachers' work and culture in the postmodern world.* London: Cassell.

Hopes, C. (1997) *Assessing, Evaluating and Assuring Quality in Schools in the European Union.* Brussels: The Directorate-General, Education, Training and Youth, European Commission.

Husen, T. (1987) Policy Impact of IEA Research, *Comparative Education Review,* 31, p. 31.

Menlo, A. & Poppleton, P. (1999) *The Meanings of Teaching: an international study of secondary teachers' work lives.* Westport, CN: Bergin & Garvey.

Mortimore, P. & Mortimore, J. (1998) The Political and the Professional in Education: an unnecessary conflict?, *Journal of Education for Teaching,* 24, pp. 205-219.

Murphy, J. (1992) Restructuring America's schools: an overview, in C.E. Finn Jr & T. Rebarber (Eds) *Education Reform in the '90s.* New York: Macmillan.

Neave, G. (1992) *The Teaching Nation.* Paris: OECD.

Nias, J. (1989) *Primary Teachers Talking: a study of teaching as work.* London: Routledge.

Phillips, D. (1987) Lessons from Germany? The Case of German Secondary Schools, *British Journal of Educational Studies,* 35, pp. 211-232.

Poppleton, P. (Ed.) (1990) Work Perceptions of Secondary School Teachers: international comparisons. Special Double Number, *Comparative Education,* 26, pp. 2/3.

Purves, A. (1989) Introduction, in A. Purves (Ed.) *International Comparisons and Educational Reform,* pp. vii – x. Virginia: Association for Supervision and Curriculum Development.

Reynolds, D. (1998) Teacher Effectiveness: better teachers, better schools, *Research Intelligence,* 66, pp. 26-29.

Rudduck, J. (1991) Practitioner Research and Programmes of Initial Teacher Education, *Westminster Studies in Education,* 12, pp. 61-72.

Seashore-Louis, K. & Miles, M. (1990) *Improving the Urban High School: what works and why?* New York: Teachers College Press.

Spaulding, S. (1989) Comparing Educational Phenomena: promises, prospects, and problems, in A. Purves (Ed.) *International Comparisons and Educational Reform,* pp. 1-16. Virginia: Association for Supervision and Curriculum Development.

Yano, H. (1997) Professionalisation of Teaching in Japan, paper presented at the 8th Biennial Conference of the International Study Association on Teacher Thinking, Kiel, Germany.

PART ONE

Secondary Teachers' Experience of Educational Change in Nine Countries during the 1990s

Teachers' Work Lives in an Environment of Continual Educational Change: Australian perspectives

RICK CHURCHILL & JOHN WILLIAMSON

AUSTRALIAN SOCIETY AND EDUCATION IN THE 1990s

Throughout the 1990s, the social, economic and political organisation of Australian society was embroiled in a continuing process of profound restructuring. In the first half of the decade, contemporary commentators, such as Mackay in *Reinventing Australia* (1993) identified the emerging society as characterised by cost reduction pressures; by the opening up of domestic markets through tariff reductions; by the failure of new technologies to deliver on the promise of job creation; by the privatisation of state enterprises; by the paradox of a highly educated workforce in a context of entrenched levels of unemployment; by conflict between the twin imperatives of economic development and of environmental concerns; by a re-examination of Australian cultural identity in a context of multiculturalism; and by an overall decline in Australians' standards of living, associated with the emergence of a three-tiered social structure consisting of a relatively small but growing class of wealthy citizens, a large but shrinking middle class, and a large and growing class of the newly poor. Nevertheless, despite all efforts and intentions to the contrary, by 1994 Australia remained less affluent and less competitive than government, and business in particular, desired.

As they collectively constituted a key arm of government, the Australian education system and the various State systems in particular were simultaneously both driven by and helped to drive a seemingly radical vision of a restructured Australia. The projected link between the nature and purpose of education and the development of Australia into a modern, competitive, globalised society was made directly in Prime Minister Hawke's now-clichéd notion of 'the clever country' in 1990 which, in turn, helped to set the agenda for the oft-cited Finn (1991), and Carmichael (1992) reports. The overall vision was one of lifelong

29

learning, with school systems projected to have a focus on developing traditional literacy and numeracy skills, vocational preparation and multi-skilling, and an orientation towards innovation, flexibility and enterprise.

From the late 1980s Australia's federal and state government departments in general, and state education systems in particular, came under significant pressure for increased productivity as a direct result of the fiscal stringencies generated by Australia's macroeconomic situation and perceived lack of international competitiveness. Hence, at the very time that Australian society was being shaped within the maelstrom of upheaval associated with what Toffler (1985) described as a change from a manufacturing society to an information society and what Hargreaves (1994) saw as the emergence of the postmodern age, education systems were coming to be increasingly accountable for their performance and for the outcomes which resulted from their endeavours. These pressures took the form of a general concern for responsiveness and for quality in educational operations and outcomes. These concerns were made manifest through cuts in government funding levels; through the decentralisation or devolution of much operational decision-making to local district and school levels; through the establishment of tighter systemic review procedures; and through federal curriculum initiatives in areas judged to be of national importance. In this latter area, the promotion of vocational preparation and the development of national curriculum statements and profiles were both significant and indicative.

At the systemic level, Australian state education authorities responded most visibly to the multitude of pressures for change through the announcement of a plethora of new policies and guidelines for teachers and schools. In April 1989, near the beginning of the period covered by this study, the Australian Education Council (a body consisting of the federal and state ministers of education, together with senior officials representing the education departments of each of the respective public service bureaucracies) issued the statement which came to be known as the *Hobart Declaration on Schooling,* in which ten common and agreed goals for schooling in Australia were proclaimed. In November of the same year, the South Australian Education Department issued a new plan for the next triennium in which a review of junior secondary education was announced and the establishment of a restructured model for the final two years of secondary schooling was affirmed. At much the same time, the Tasmanian Department of Education and the Arts identified four major goals in the then current version of its corporate plan, including an intention to improve learning programs in schools through new policies for both primary and secondary education, through encouraging students' participation in education beyond Year 10 and through measures designed to provide educational and social justice for all students.

For the remainder of the 1990s, the expectation that education systems would be responsive to a changing set of educational needs in Australia generated an ever-increasing flow of statements detailing new priorities for, and consequent expectations of, teachers and schools. By 1995, the four goals identified by the Tasmanian Department of Education and the Arts only five years earlier had escalated to 21 curriculum priorities, to which needed to be added the national agenda for the education of girls and responses to the implications of a revamped State Education Act with its attendant regulations. By 1999 when the Australian Education Council revamped the National Goals of Schooling, 1989's ten goals had expanded to 18, albeit in three categories.

The simultaneous co-existence of so many dramatic pressures on state education in Australia produced, as was the case in many other settings, a volatile situation characterised, according to Hargreaves (1995), by a number of paradoxes, each of which had significant implications for the work of teachers in schools. By the mid 1990s teachers were being expected to operate within an increasingly complex and contradictory milieu. Their work was conducted in a dissonant context, with some of the more notable paradoxes identified (Hargreaves, 1995, pp. 14-15) as including: parents failing to support the priorities they wished schools to pursue; business failing to utilise the skills it claimed to want in school leavers; parochial national curricula being developed in a context of increasing globalisation; standardised testing and common curricula being promoted in an increasingly diverse and multicultural society; and orientations both toward the future and toward a world of change being promoted at a time of increased nostalgia for the clearer choices supposedly associated with the less complex times of the past.

That the turbulent times of the late 1980s and early 1990s had produced considerable difficulties for teachers did not escape the notice of state education ministers or federal officials. However, both the ministerial members of the Australian Education Council and the Australian government saw the appropriate response to these problems as one which addressed structural, rather than personal, issues. A profound change in the structure of the teaching profession was promoted as the pathway through which to address issues related to the quality of teaching and learning:

The morale, career paths and conditions of the teaching force are of major concern to employing authorities and to the Australian Government. Award restructuring for all sectors of the economy is a key strategy of the Australian Government's agenda for microeconomic reform. The need to change workplace practices and improve the efficiency of all industries, including education and schooling, is crucial for Australia's economic future. The award restructuring process aims to achieve enhanced quality teaching, improved career and training opportunities for teachers and develop more efficient and effective schools (DEET, 1990, p. 63).

Thus the 1990s were years when the links between education and industry were to be seen as having important implications for both teachers' teaching and students' learning in Australian schools. One of the more visible signs of the expectation that education would prepare students more fully for effective participation in the workforce, while itself performing more productively in an industrial sense, was an increased emphasis on vocational preparation across the curriculum. Australia's teachers, for so long derided for their lack of experience in the 'real world' of work, became responsible, not only for quality and productivity in their own work, but for the capacity of their students to meet the vocational competency expectations of Australian industry. Yet this was only one of a multiplicity of change pressures that were impacting on the work of Australian teachers at the time.

These extra change pressures fell into three loose categories: results of government action in fields other than education; results of an ideological shift associated with changes in government; and results of policy confusion within education.

The impact on teachers of government actions in areas not directly related to education is best illustrated by the results of the federal government's decision to privatise the nation's telecommunications carrier, Testra. The funds resulting from the privatisation of, initially, a third of Telstra were, in part, directed towards a range of projects. One effect on teachers was a large-scale push for teachers to become proficient in the educational use of information and communication technologies. In some rural areas, the impact was even more far-reaching, with the local school being cast in the role of community information technology centre.

The election of a coalition, conservative federal government in 1996 was followed by a number of ideologically-driven measures: the abolition of the National Project on the Quality of Teaching and Learning; the Ministerial Council's acceptance of nationwide testing in literacy and numeracy; a shift of education funds towards independent schools at the expense of schools in the various state systems: and a forced narrowing of the curriculum and restriction on the role of teachers in curriculum decision-making associated with the imposition of specified allocated time for literacy and numeracy studies in primary schools.

From the perspective of many teachers, the 1990s were a decade of policy confusion. At the same time as the level of resources provided to state schools was increasingly restricted by Treasury, other arms of the bureaucracy required the inclusion of students with disabilities and the implementation of across-the-board testing of specified student learning outcomes. At the same time as funds for professional development of teachers and curriculum were being restricted, increased funding was allocated to the training and development of current and prospective school principals in a 'magic bullet' approach to educational improvement, underpinned by a view that, in each school, a single person (often employed on a performance-related contract) would make all the difference.

The common factor in all of this was a marked increase in the extent to which the work of teachers was to come under intense scrutiny, at both official and public levels, through the 1990s. Formal systems of teacher registration had been adopted or foreshadowed in a majority of the states by the end of the decade. In 1998, the *Report of the Senate Inquiry into the Status of Teaching* was released. It was entitled, *A Class Act, yet* very few teachers would have felt that this was an apt description of how their work was perceived in Australia.

METHODOLOGY

The study was conducted in 87 primary and secondary schools from the state education systems of Tasmania (Tas.) and South Australia (SA). A multisite, multimethod approach was adopted for the study, with 89 teachers completing a lengthy survey instrument, and 38 teachers participating in semi-structured interviews. In all, 100 teachers participated in the study: 27 of these participated via both interview and questionnaire, 11 respondents were interviewed but not surveyed and the remaining 62 participated only by completing a questionnaire. The survey data were gathered to supplement the interview data and to assist in examining the problem from a variety of perspectives and through a number of lenses. The sample of teacher respondents was not selected randomly. Rather, participants were chosen from randomly selected schools, with these being collectively representative of the types and locations of schools found within the state education systems of South Australia and Tasmania. The teacher participants, who were all 'classroom teachers' (defined as teachers who spent at least 80% of school hours instructing students), were identified through negotiations between the researcher, the respective school principals and those teachers at each school who had expressed their willingness to be part of the research process. The demographic details of the sample are detailed in Table I.

All the interviews were conducted in private at convenient times at each interviewee's school during the second and third weeks of the final term of the 1994 school year. The surveys were distributed at the same time.

	Survey (n = 62)	Survey and interview (n = 27)	Interview (n = 11)	Total sample (n = 100)
State system				
South Australia	31	14	6	51
Tasmania	31	13	5	49
Gender				
Male	23	12	6	41
Female	39	15	5	59
School level				
Primary	35	16	4	55
Secondary	27	11	7	45
Average age (years)				40.5
Time teaching (years)				16.7
Time at current school (years)				4.9

Table I. Demographic details of the sample.

In order to guard against sole-interviewer effects, two research assistants were trained to conduct half of the interviews. Thus the 18 Tasmanian interviews were shared between the principal researcher and one assistant, while the 20 South Australian interviews were shared between the principal researcher and a second assistant.

A semi-structured interview schedule, consisting of 15 main items with a number of prepared prompts or probes, was produced in an extensive pilot programme involving interviews with 13 teachers outside the study sample, review and amendment by a panel of five eminent educational researchers and, finally, modifications in response to the two research assistants' preferences for patterns of language which they found natural.

With the permission of each of the subjects, the interviews were recorded on audiotape and, later, transcribed. The draft transcriptions were then sent to the interviewees, who were invited to make any amendments that they felt were warranted.

This opportunity to amend the draft transcripts was not merely to ensure that the transcripts accorded with the subjects' recollections, it was also intended that this process would allow the interviewees a second avenue to express their views. Thus, more than half of the 38 interviewees made significant amendments – alterations, explanations, additions and deletions – to the draft transcripts. Therefore, this opportunity to amend the draft transcript resulted in data the interviewees saw as more complete and more accurate, while also constituting a form of feedback to the subjects.

The 15 items which made up the interview schedule emanated from those aspects of the classic change literature relating to teachers' reactions to educational innovations, with the more significant of these being teachers' concerns about change (see, for example, Hall & Loucks, 1978) and teachers' responses to change (see, for example, Doyle & Ponder, 1977 78). The resulting interview items dealt with the identification of particular changes seen by teachers as affecting their work most significantly in the past five years, the origin of such changes, implementation timelines, the degree of teacher influence in decision making, perceived objectives, factors assisting and hindering implementation, the range of effects on teachers' work lives resulting from such changes, teachers' feelings about the changes, and their predispositions toward future changes in education.

Data from the interviews were analysed using a modified form of open coding and subsequent axial coding (Strauss & Corbin, 1990). In the style of grounded theory, the resultant categories emerged from the data.

The survey instrument consisted of 28 items, and dealt with the same set of issues probed in the interviews. It was developed through a process involving panel review and pilot testing with a sample of 25 teachers outside the study sample. The survey was distributed by hand to those teachers participating in both the interview and the survey modes, and by mail to the teachers participating by survey alone. A response rate of 53.9% was achieved with this survey distribution procedure.

RESULTS

The teachers' responses to both the interview and the survey instruments were complex, with the data reflecting the diversity of the teachers and schools involved. Nevertheless, a number of shared themes emerged clearly from the statements which teachers made when responding to either or both of the instruments. The results are described below under headings of the three research questions.

1. Which Educational Changes Do Teachers See as Having the Greatest Impact on Their Working Lives?

The 89 teachers who responded to the survey instrument identified 79 different educational changes as affecting them significantly in their work in the first half of the 1990s (Churchill et al, 1995). The change cited most commonly was *systemic cuts to education funding*, but the introduction of *national curricula, increased accountability* requirements, new models for *assessing and reporting* on students' work and *social justice policy* initiatives were also cited by many survey respondents. While the teachers' gender, primary or secondary placement, experience, age or time in their current school had no apparent impact on their responses, teachers from the two states nominated changes in common (such as those mentioned above), along with other changes which were unique to the context of the individual state systems. Thus, the state of origin made a difference to the identity of the changes cited by teachers, but similar differences were not observed in relation to any of the other demographic characteristics of the sample.

Each of the 79 changes cited was seen as affecting, mostly, one or the other two major domains of a teacher's work. In this classification, each change was understood to affect teachers most strongly in either their direct work with students *(the Caring Professional domain)* or in their work as members of whole-school staffs and as employees of large education systems (their *Organisational domain)*. This distinction emerged from interviewed teachers' discourse about a difference between *real teaching* (work with and for students) and *paperwork* (work required by their employing system, but seen by the teachers as not related directly to their teaching or to students. The bipartite distinction is not dissimilar to that inherent in the long-established *Getzels–Guba* model (Getzels & Guba,1957) of the organisation as a social system, through which organisations are seen to have a nomothetic and an idiographic dimension.

Of the 12 changes nominated as the most significant, six were classified as belonging to the *Caring Professional* domain: the introduction of restructured senior secondary curricula, the introduction of national statements and curriculum profiles, the introduction of new models for assessing and reporting on students' progress, the inclusion of students with disabilities in the regular class, increasing difficulty in the management of student behaviour and changes in the teacher's own teaching methods. Five of the changes were classified in the *Organisational* domain: increased workloads resulting from funding cuts, new systemic personnel policies and procedures and their impact at school level, increased requirements for teacher accountability and the devolution of decision-making to school level. One change, the introduction of new computing technology, was not classified as affecting either one or other domain predominantly. When the most significant changes were classified according to this distinction between work domains and the teacher sample was divided into its various sub-groups, it was apparent that both the domains of teachers' work had been affected significantly by recent changes in education.

No differences were apparent in these patterns between any of the demographic groups in the sample. The results are shown in Table II.

Work domain	Different changes	Times cited
Caring professional	36 (46%)	219 (51%)
Organisational	37 (47%)	194 (46%)
Uncategorised	6 (7%)	15 (3%)
Total	79	428

Table II. Work domains affected by educational changes.

It is clear from Table II that to the extent that this distinction between these domains is a useful one; recent educational changes have affected the two domains of these teachers' work in almost equal proportions.

When they were asked to nominate the main objective of the one change that had affected their work *most strongly,* the survey respondents cited 32 different main objectives. These ranged from the somewhat cynical, 'Keep educational administrators in jobs' and, 'Keep students out of the unemployment statistics', through the baffled, 'This has never been explained', to the more optimistic, 'Provide success for all students' and, 'Improved educational outcomes for all'. The most common response of all, however, was, 'To save money', with this single objective being cited by 27% of survey respondents. Indeed, a clear majority of these teachers felt that the change that had affected them most strongly was designed to achieve organisational, rather than professional, ends. Thus 61% of these changes were seen as serving organisational purposes *such as managing the system better or saving money,* while only 37% of the changes nominated as having the strongest impact were seen by these teachers as serving their professional goals of *improving the quality of their own teaching and their students' learning.*

While the interviewees nominated many different individual changes as having significant impact on their work, four elements were characteristic of both the content and the tenor of the responses and these are outlined in turn.

Unfamiliar Practices Replacing Established Work Patterns

It is apparent that the teachers interviewed felt most affected by educational changes when their confidence in their work was threatened or disrupted by expectations about which they felt uninformed. When they felt that they were denied the opportunity of making sense and meaning out of new challenges, regardless of the nature of the innovation, these teachers felt the effects of changes to a considerably greater extent than they might have, had they been able to become familiar with the true nature of the expectations and procedures associated with such changes. Comments indicative of this belief were made by two teachers discussing the introduction of national curriculum profiles.

> *A lot of your so-called free time – your extra time – is taken up with just deciphering what you are supposed to be doing.*

> *I reckon they just designed them [national curriculum profiles] and said, 'Okay, we've done our job. Now it's your job to implement them – off you go!' Nobody really knew what to do.*

External Imposition

While it is common in Australia for teachers to engage in a considerable level of locally based innovation efforts, the teachers in this study described the changes which they thought affected their work most significantly as being imposed externally by central administrative authorities and governments. Thus it seems that changes which originate outside these teachers' work settings and which are presented as mandatory are seen by them as being the most problematic for their work lives.

When discussing the origins of changes and how these are presented to them, the teachers interviewed gave two types of responses. The first type of response was brief and to the point, as in the two following examples.

> *The stuff came out of the blue really. Here it was – and then we had to implement it all by a set date.*

> *It's just fed down through the system, 'Here it is, go and do it!' To me it always seems to be from high-up in the hierarchy.*

The second type of response was more lengthy, but no less explicit about the teachers' lack of perceived ownership of most innovations. The following comment was indicative of this position.

> *It was very much pushed on you. It was almost, 'Well too bloody bad – it's coming in and you've just got to put up with it'. And although it was sugar-coated a lot – they weren't that rude – you couldn't get away from the fact that the changes were being forced on you.*

Multiple Simultaneous Innovations

Both the Tasmanian and South Australian teachers expressed concerns in the interviews about the number of different change initiatives being promoted simultaneously. They felt that there was little acknowledgement of the effect of this multiplicity of innovations on teachers who already see themselves as being committed fully in the day-to-day tasks associated with working with their students. Perhaps more than anything else, teachers saw this situation as being counter-productive, in the sense that the multiplicity of demands limited the extent to which they could implement any one innovation effectively. In the South Australian context, the following comments typified the teachers' perceptions of the situation.

> *The range of change is so much, it's so uncoordinated and it comes from a variety of places. It's very, very hard: it makes things very complex, makes people very frustrated and probably doesn't work efficiently either.*

> *I just want to be a teacher for a while. Just leave me and the children alone for a while; let us be comfortable. We have been trying so hard over the last five years we haven't really let anything settle. Sometime, somewhere, they have got to stop banging the side of the chook [chicken] shed. You know, it's bombardment all of the time.*

Tasmanian teachers saw the situation in the same light.

> *You are not just talking about a change in isolation, it's in combination. If there is something else suddenly thrown in at you, as there always is, you just go into overload. So it's not really the change itself that creates that feeling, it's just the fact that it's another change in a succession of changes.*

Abbreviated Timelines

The differences in perceptions of the lengths of time that are appropriate for implementation have been discussed elsewhere, but it is apparent that these teachers believe that the implementation timelines established by others are unrealistically short. On the other hand, these same timelines appear reasonable, presumably, to the people who have the facilitation and promotion of a particular change initiative as the single focus of their current work in an education system. Not a single teacher in the sample felt that sufficient time had been available for effective implementation.

> *There was all this new jargon and no one knew what it was about. You could go to a PD [professional development] session – but then you were supposed to be doing it in the next week in your room. We have to take it on board straight away. The in-service was too intensive in too short a time and there*

was no time for reflecting, internalising or evaluating what you'd learned.

There just wasn't time to come to grips with the issues involved; there was a lack of time to work collaboratively, a lack of time to implement and a lack of PD.

2. How Do Teachers See Their Working Lives Being Affected by Educational Changes?

Both of the data-gathering instruments sought the teachers' views on how they felt their working lives had been affected by their experiences with recent educational changes. Data obtained from both the sources were highly congruent, with virtually all of the teachers reporting a more harried, demanding and stressful work context. The results obtained from the surveys are displayed in Table III.

Change effects	Teachers affected
Increased workload and stress	65 (73%)
More difficult teaching conditions	60 (67%)
Adopted new methods of work	54 (60%)
Worked harder each day	48 (54%)
Felt pressure completing tasks on time	47 (53%)
Adopted new roles and tasks	39 (43%)
Adopted a stress-management strategy	32 (36%)
Collaborated more with colleagues	31 (35%)
Reduced commitment to teaching	26 (29%)
Improved teaching conditions	22 (25%)

Table III. Effects of educational change on teachers' work.

When asked to describe how recent educational changes had affected teachers in their work, each of the interviewee's responses tended to cover similar ground. Four elements formed a common pattern in the data. Two of these four elements were welcomed by the teachers interviewed, while two were regarded as being decidedly unwelcome. The teachers reported a distinctly unwelcome *intensification* of their work, and a similarly unwanted *shift in the focus* of the core elements of their work. On the other hand, they welcomed an apparent *increase in collaboration* with their colleagues, and perceived *improvements in aspects of teaching and learning.*

Intensification of Teachers' Work

This study provides much support for the view that there has been a considerable intensification in the work demands placed on teachers in recent years. Teachers claimed that a greater amount of work was expected of them, and further, that the nature of the teacher's role had not only expanded but become more complex, encompassing a range of functions which were not expected of teachers only a decade or so ago.

The following comment is representative of the perceived increase in the amount of work required.

> We are expected to do more and more and we are getting less
> and less time, staff and money. It's supposed to be positive,
> but the classes are getting bigger and we haven't got the money
> to resource them, so how could that be positive?

The increased demands on teachers to take on new welfare and support roles were reflected in responses from teachers from both systems. Indicatively, a Tasmanian teacher said:

> Society's values have broken down and because that's
> happened we have got children coming to school who are
> hungry, who are emotionally disturbed, who have got parents
> involved in split-ups – there are enormous problems that we
> have to deal with more and more every day.

The same phenomenon was reported across South Australian settings:

> You have a lot more one-to-one contact with people which is
> non-educational – it's education-related, but it's actually
> talking about problems students bring with them from outside.
> Again, there's more time lost whenever someone says, 'Look,
> I'm having a few problems. Can I have a chat with you?'

A Shift in the Focus of Teachers' Core Work

For many of the respondents an apparent shift in focus away from their contacts with students in the classroom and toward documentation and administration was a particularly unwelcome effect of educational change. This was a recurring theme, amounting to teachers mourning the loss of that which they had long claimed as the *raison d'etre* of their role: working constructively with students. Teachers' comments included the following.

> I spend too much time hassling with the paperwork instead of
> actually teaching. If you're spending more time doing the
> written work, you've got less time to put into actually teaching
> and preparing.

> *It has changed my attitude to teaching compared to my attitude when I first started teaching. The focus then was on working in the classroom and on getting things done in the classroom. The focus now has shifted to the paperwork associated with classrooms.*

Increased Collaboration

Perceived shortcomings in systemic implementation strategies allowed the teachers in the sample to make a virtue out of a necessity, in that they turned increasingly to their colleagues for assistance when faced with insufficient assistance elsewhere. Indeed, when questioned about the factors which had most assisted teachers in their efforts to implement change initiatives, the respondents almost universally referred to the assistance they received as a consequence of discussing matters with their colleagues at their own school.

> *You become more dependent on your colleagues. If you want help, you turn to them, rather than to whoever the consultants used to be.*

> *People have seen a need to share their work – to share ideas and materials. Before that, everyone was teaching what they wanted to teach, when they wanted to teach it, how they wanted to teach it – but now we're thinking more professionally together.*

Improvements in Teaching and Learning

Proponents of systemic and pedagogical reform could take some comfort from some of the interviewees' reports of significant improvements in their teaching practices and in their students' learning experiences. These improvements were apparent in relation to clearer and more objective assessment practices, and there were reports of children participating more meaningfully and actively in determining the nature of their own learning experiences. Most typically, it was claimed that such improvements had resulted after teachers had reconstrued their role in the teaching-learning process.

> *I find myself being more a co-worker with the kids than a director.*

> *As the teacher I've become the facilitator of what the children themselves choose they want to learn about.*

42

For others, the extra hours spent planning activities and establishing clear assessment criteria were seen as worthwhile.

> *I feel more relaxed with my students because we all know what we are looking for and so it's not 'me and them'. It's much easier – I can give them good feedback all the time.*

> *While it's probably doubled the time I would normally spend on programming and assessment details, it's improved the way I assess things and made it more positive.*

3. How Do Teachers Feel about Educational Changes and the Quality of Their Working Lives?

When they were asked how they felt about the educational change that had affected them most in their work, the survey respondents reported positive, negative and ambivalent feelings in similar proportions. It emerged, however, that the domain in which the change most affected these teachers' work was the significant factor in explaining their feelings in relation to the change.

Teachers displayed a tendency to hold *positive feelings about changes affecting the caring professional domain* and a clear pattern of *negative feelings about changes affecting the organisational domain* of their work. These results are shown in Table IV.

The teachers' feelings	All changes	Changes within the caring professional domain	Changes within the organisational domain
Positive	33 (37%)	23 (49%)	7 (18%)
Mixed/neutral	24 (27%)	18 (38%)	6 (16%)
Negative	32 (36%)	6 (13%)	25 (66%)
Total	89*	47	38

Table IV. Teachers' feelings about educational change in two domains.
*Includes four changes that were not classified in either specific work domain.

The work domain which had been most affected by the current educational change initiatives was also a significant factor in the surveyed teachers' self-predicted responses to future changes in education. The teachers who had experienced a significant change in the organisational domain predicted markedly more negative responses to future changes in education, no matter what these changes might be! While part of this tendency might well be due to *a fear-of-the unknown factor,* experience with a system-driven change perceived as being unrelated to teaching and learning was associated with a distinct increase in predicted negative responses to future educational changes, while this tendency to approach future changes warily was not as apparent in teachers who had been most affected by changes at the classroom level. The relevant data are displayed in Table V.

Predicted response	The domain most affected by current educational change	
	Caring professional	Organisational
More positive	8 (17%)	5 (13%)
Unchanged/undecided	25 (53%)	11 (29%)
More negative	14 (30%)	22 (58%)
Total	47	38

Table V. The predicted response to future educational changes.

Experience of a significant change does not appear to be associated with any marked decrease in the level of suspicion with which future change is regarded. Indeed, it transpired that even for those teachers who had responded successfully to the requirements of a change about which they had been uncertain or negative initially, such achievement did not translate into positive receptivity toward future changes. Respondents explained this by stating that the pace and number of contemporary change initiatives constituted significant problems for them. There was, therefore, an entrenched resistance toward the educational changes of the future, as the teachers in this sample sought the respite they saw as necessary for them to be able to take stock of their current situation and to respond properly to existing expectations.

In the parts of the interviews that dealt with this aspect of the research, the focus was on educational change in general, rather than on specific changes nominated by the participating teachers. Perhaps for this reason, it was rare for respondents to cite precise examples in their comments. However, an *acceptance of the inevitability of change, nostalgia for the past, a sense of survival and coping* in the face of current change expectations, and considerable *cynicism* about the real motives behind, and the results of, educational innovations characterised both the teachers' feeling about educational changes and the impact which they claimed such changes had had on the quality of their working lives.

Acceptance of the Inevitability of Change

No teachers presented as opponents of educational change *per se,* nor was there any sense in which teachers expressed a view that change could be resisted fruitfully. Comments such as, 'Change is always with us', 'Change is universal' and 'Nothing stays the same forever' were common. Typically, respondents accepted that change had been and would continue to be part of their work context.

A South Australian teacher described his responses to national curriculum profiles, which were, in his view, then the most recent major change, in the following terms:

> *I'm prepared to at least look at them and give them a go. Most people have come to accept it and are now sort of working on it.*

A Tasmanian teacher was more accepting than were most of her colleagues of even those educational changes which seemed to deliver few advantages to schools, teachers or students:

> *I have always been fairly positive towards educational changes and, in fact, I even understood when we had to have funding cuts.*

Nostalgia for the Past

It is perhaps unsurprising that, consistent with the overall aging of the members of the teaching profession in Australia, a degree of nostalgia for better, or at least less paradoxical, times past was expressed by many respondents. In some of the literature this is occasionally referred to as the fond recall of a *golden age* in which the quality of teachers' work lives was supposedly so much better, and so much less tenuous and problematic, than today.

A teacher from South Australian schools made the following comment

> *I don't believe schools are the happy places to work in they used to be. Morale is nowhere near what it was in the past.*

The comment of a Tasmanian teacher is indicative of a sense of sorrow that something valuable had been lost.

> *I think we need to get back to a point where we value the people in the system and the people who are, in fact, doing the job. The love of the job has gone from what it was, and that is sad.*

Surviving and Coping

While these teachers reported difficulties in understanding and accepting new processes, procedures and expectations associated with educational changes of all varieties, many teachers had been able to surmount most of their problems and, within a relatively short time, to come to terms with the requirements of the innovations. Numerous teachers' comments indicated that, despite early fears and misgivings in the context of uncertainty and concern about their capacity to cope, they

45

typically found that this anxiety receded as they became more familiar with the innovation. Much of the initial concern expressed by teachers was, therefore, fear of the unknown. To some extent, surviving such a period of uncertainty seemed to make some teachers feel more confident about their capacity to cope with whatever a potentially unstable future might hold in store for them.

A Tasmanian teacher reflected this notion that the reality of even large-scale changes had not been as bad as she had feared.

> *My current feelings are that we are over the hump – it's a bit of a 'been there, done that' feeling. I am a bit tired, I guess, but more confident. There was a bit of trepidation in the beginning but what seemed to be insurmountable was eventually surmountable.*

In South Australia, some teachers had seemingly developed some self-protective attitudes as part of their response to change initiatives, as the following remark indicates.

> *You've got to learn to go with the flow. If you don't go with the flow, you'll go around the bend.*

Cynicism

For many teachers there was a firm belief that educational-change initiatives were often promoted by people who were more interested in advancing their own careers than in achieving improvements in education. This perception, whether fair or unfair, accurate or inaccurate, specific or general, was apparently the source of considerable cynicism in teachers' views toward educational innovations. This cynicism was compounded further by a commonly held belief that most initiatives produced little in the way of tangible benefits for teachers or students. What is more, many teachers viewed current change initiatives as transitory, in the sense that they would soon be replaced by other initiatives. Hence *tactical delay* was seen as a viable response to many change initiatives. The following response is indicative of the general feeling expressed by the interviewees.

More and more teachers are becoming increasingly cynical. saying, 'Okay, this was the flavour of the month last year, how long is it going to last?'

DISCUSSION OF THE RESULTS

During the course of discussions between members of the Consortium for Cross-Cultural Research in Education, the following propositions were put forward and are now presented in the Australian context.

1. Changes attributed to sources internal to the school are likely to have more favourable consequences for both teachers and their students than changes attributed to external sources. (More favourable consequences – stronger impact on teachers' work life, more positive effect on professional development, stronger effect on student learning, more positive feelings about the change, more interested in responsible involvement in a similar change, more receptiveness to involvement in further change in general.)

In Australia the strength of the impact of a change on teachers' work lives was not necessarily perceived as favourable. Changes perceived as having negative impacts (or unfavourable consequences) were reported as being no less strong in impact than were those changes which were perceived to have had a favourable impact overall. Changes perceived as originating from internal sources (only 16% of all nominated changes), such as the adoption of whole-school behaviour management processes, were perceived much more positively than were those changes perceived as originating from external sources, such as the results stemming from wide-ranging systemic cuts for the funding of schools.

2. Increased feelings of ownership of a change by teachers are likely to produce a stronger impact of the change on their work lives, a more positive effect on their professional development, more positive feelings about the change, more receptiveness to responsible involvement in similar change in the future, more receptiveness to involvement in further change in general, and a more strongly perceived effect on students' learning.

Only 23% of the Australian teachers in the sample perceived the main objective of the significant change as relating directly to their own work context. Similarly there was a significant difference ($p <.0001$) between the degree of influence teachers felt they could exercise in decision-making related to changes from internal, as compared to external sources. Furthermore, changes perceived as originating internally attracted a significantly ($p <.002$) higher level of commitment from these teachers than did changes which were perceived to originate from external sources.

While the overwhelming majority of Australian respondents saw themselves as 'adapters' (63%) rather than 'adopters' (3%), 'compliers' (17%) or 'resisters' (7%) in their response to educational change, involvement with internal changes (seen as more owned by teachers) attracted significantly more positive ($p <.004$) attitudes toward future changes than did involvement with changes seen as originating externally.

3. School changes regarding content and/or method of teaching are likely to elicit more positive feelings from teachers than changes concerning assessment of student learning, school experience of students, or school system management.

The teachers in the Australian sample (despite the study being conducted in the context of the development and dissemination of National Curriculum Statements and new State-based restructuring of senior secondary curricula and assessment) distinguished between matters affecting 'teaching and learning' on the one hand, and 'organisational' matters on the other. Thus context and method changes which were determined (at least partially) individually, collaboratively or locally drew significantly more positive ($p <.0001$) perceptions than did those changes to curricula and curricula structures and processes which were seen as determined outside the school.

4. School changes aimed at improving the academic experience of students were likely to elicit more positive feelings from teachers than changes aimed at improving the social or cultural experience of students.

5. Teachers who perceive a school change as having strong effects on students' learning are likely to feel more positive about the change and view their work lives as having been more strongly impacted by it than teachers who perceive the change as having weak effects on students' learning.

In the Australian study 47% of teachers felt that the changes that had affected them most in their work were *intended* to serve the interests of either students, teachers or parents, while only 31% of the same respondents claimed that these changes had *actually* served these groups' interests. Furthermore, 9% of all respondents felt that there had been no beneficiaries at all from the cited changes.

Overall, interviewees saw these as most often serving organisational purposes, such as 'managing the system better' or 'saving money', while considerably less often being designed to 'improve the quality of teachers' teaching or students' learning'.

Changes aimed at improving the social/cultural experiences of students (such as new policies in the equity and social justice field) were not perceived as positively as changes aimed at improving students' academic experiences (such as the introduction of criterion-based assessment, cooperative learning and student-centred curriculum).

6. When teachers' experience with a school change arouses their interest in taking a responsible role in further school change of a similar nature, they are likely to become more receptive to further changes in general.

The Australian teachers in the sample saw themselves, in roughly equal proportions, playing supportive (29%), compliant (28%) and resistant (38%) roles in the processes involved with educational changes. These teachers played significantly more supportive roles (p <.0001) in 'teaching and learning' changes and similarly significantly more supportive roles (p <.0008) in changes originating from internal rather than external sources.

There was a strong positive correlation (r = .55, p <.0001) between the nature of the role *(supportive, compliant* or *resistant)* played by Australian teachers in a current significant change and the nature of their likely response (more positive, uncertain or more negative) to the educational changes of the future.

Degree of commitment to the current change, satisfaction with key elements of work life and capacity to influence decision-making related to a current change were all positively correlated with the nature of teachers' predicted responses to future educational innovations.

CONCLUSIONS AND IMPLICATIONS

The interview data gathered in the study indicate that, despite teachers' discourse being still rooted firmly in the genre of Fullan's (1995) *multiple innovations* era, there are a number of new realities for teachers at work in today's schools. Undeniably, it is clear that some of these realities have been part of teachers' working lives for a number of years, and are thus somewhat less 'new' than the others. However, it is the simultaneous co-existence of all seven factors that has important implications for teachers and their work lives in Australian state schools from the time of the late 1990s. The *seven new realities for teachers at work* are as follows:

A Myriad of Change Expectations

The number of multiple, simultaneous innovations and change initiatives recognised by this study's teachers in both interview and survey contexts shows no sign of abating. The pace of technological change, and the resultant pressure on schools and teachers to keep up, can only magnify the current level and complexity of change expectations facing teachers. Devolution of much decision-making from the administrative centre to the school level has done little to ameliorate problems experienced by teachers with changes they see as being imposed externally.

Conflict between Organisational and Professional Goals

While teachers respond generally positively to curriculum initiatives and other innovations and expectations which have classroom activities as their focus, they respond negatively and with cynicism to new procedures and expectations which they see as serving the needs of the educational bureaucracy and diverting their own attention from their 'real teaching' tasks. The connections between increased accountability and documentation requirements on the one hand, and improved teaching and learning practices on the other, are not yet accepted fully in teachers' discourse.

Dissatisfaction with Education Systems

These teachers expressed considerable dissatisfaction with, and alienation from, the actions of the systems that employ them. In particular, teachers viewed the state systems' implementation expectations as unreasonable and at odds with teachers' perspectives in terms of time. Increased expectations in a context of reduced resource levels creates both problems and resentment between teachers and their employing systems. For the teachers in this study, therefore, their employers acted in ways that ignored fairness and common sense, and seemed distant from day-to-day realities associated with teaching and learning. For many teachers, the systems were failing twice over: both as poor employers and as disinterested educators.

Competition between Two Kinds of Collaboration

While Hargreaves (1994) described the *contrived collegiality* that he saw as associated with devolution, this was only one of two forms of collaboration common among teachers in this study. There is no denying that contrived collegiality is both common and transparent. However, teachers apparently afford little credibility to either the processes or the products associated with such decision-making. On the other hand, they set great value on the *mutually supportive collaboration* in which they engage in self-selecting groups. Teachers see this self-initiated form of collaboration as their most valuable source of professional assistance and as a source of personal and professional support in an educational climate characterised by low levels of esteem for teachers in the wider community.

Dissonance Associated with a Paradox of Professional Expertise and External Control

The apparent contradictions between the various expectations held of teachers in the current educational context have been well documented elsewhere (Hargreaves, 1995). While many of the paradoxes Hargreaves described were noted by teachers in this study, they expressed even more dissonance about matters related to expertise and control. At the very time when they saw themselves teaching better than ever before, they were more constrained than ever before by curriculum decisions made by others and by documentation and accountability requirements. The levels of teacher expertise and professional freedom of judgement are not seen to be balanced appropriately.

Intensification

Cuts to teacher numbers and to other resource areas which have resulted in significant increases in the amount of work required of teachers, combined with compacted timelines and a broadening in the range of roles teachers are expected to play, offer further support for the perception of an intensification in teachers' work.

Ironic Options for Distance and Immunity

As the teachers in this study aged and acquired a repertoire of pedagogic skills within which they could operate with some confidence, they laid increasing claims to professional autonomy, at least within the confines of their own classrooms. In the same time frame, in theory at least, devolution has afforded teachers considerable empowerment at the local level. Somewhat ironically, therefore, these teachers have seemingly become less susceptible to the exhortations of their superiors. They demonstrate this immunity by standing back from the implementation of many change initiatives, reserving for themselves the final decisions about whether or not innovations will be enacted at the classroom level.

These *seven new realities of teachers' work* constitute only a snapshot of the ever more complex world of the teacher at work. However, the picture of teachers' work presented in this snapshot is consistent with long-standing themes of the change literature. Furthermore, these new realities have significant implications for teachers and for teacher educators.

This Study's Results in the Light of the Literature

The results of the current study are consistent with what might be expected in the light of much of the burgeoning literature covering change in education. Three of the seminal ideas spanning the time frame of that literature from the 1970s to the end of the twentieth century (from, for example, Doyle & Ponder, 1977-8 to Fullan, 1995) and which might be paraphrased as follows: first, you *can't mandate what matters;* second, teachers *will adapt rather than adopt* innovations; and third, teachers will support only those innovations which they see as offering *practical benefits* for their own teaching or their students' learning, are all reflected continually in the tenor of teachers' responses across the whole sample of this study.

In essence, therefore, despite expressing concerns about the pace and number of educational changes with which they have to contend; despite expressing concerns about the educational worth and real motives underlying many change initiatives; and despite expressing concerns about increased workloads and stress resulting from the current educational change context, the teachers in this study emerge as survivors. What is more, they emerge as *autonomous* and *empowered survivors,* in the sense that what they do in their classrooms remains largely a matter only between themselves and their students and in the sense that they claim the right to ultimate decision-making in implementation matters at the classroom level. Furthermore, they maintain a continuing focus on their classroom activities as the core tasks of their profession.

Taken to its logical conclusion, the autonomy of the teacher's role and the empowerment afforded to those who occupy that role give today's teachers, or at least those who participated in this study, a form of immunity from what they might regard as the worst excesses of the current change context.

Implications for Teachers and Teacher Educators

Of the many implications of these new realities of teachers' work, the issue of how teachers will respond to the imperatives of the future is paramount. Surely there can be no positive outcome if teachers simply lament the myriad of change expectations, divorce themselves from organisational goals, and retreat behind the closed doors of their classrooms as part of a struggle to hold back the tide of educational changes. Surely in those circumstances, they will be engulfed eventually. If, on the other hand, teachers can use their autonomy, immunity, expertise, mutual support and their focus on quality teaching and learning to influence the future of education at the enacted level, then the work of the teacher may well merit and receive appropriate recognition.

Teacher educators could be forgiven for feeling just as battered by the prevailing elements as do many of the teacher respondents in this study. For a number of years in Australia, teacher educators have been lambasted for being *out-of-touch with the classroom* on the one hand, and for *failing to devote attention to quality research* on the other. Indeed, the pressure for change in teacher education faculties is undeniably pervasive at a time when previously secure student numbers and faculty positions might now be best described as uncertain.

At the time of writing the Commonwealth Government has released a Green Paper outlining its views on how university research should be funded. Another Green Paper was foreshadowed for 2000 to look at 'Teaching within the University sector'. Both of these Green Papers have major implications for teacher education.

Without advocating yet another quiet revolution in teacher education, it is a reasonable observation that the great majority of pre-service training of teachers concentrates on only the *caring professional* domain of a teacher's work; while the *organisational* domain is almost unrepresented in pre-service curricula. Given that almost half of the educational changes identified by this study's teachers as having the strongest impact on their work fall into the organisational category, pre-service teacher training programs should reflect a much broader conception of teachers' work.

Despite the calls of advocates of whole-school change, and of Fullan (1993) among others, that 'everyone must be a change agent', the reality evident in this study is that many teachers feel unprepared, unwilling or unskilled in and for the roles they occupy in their responses to change initiatives and directives. While there is, of course, an extensive literature dealing with the management and effective implementation of change and innumerable courses are offered at the postgraduate level to cater for potential leaders of educational change processes, there is very little available for teachers who seek the skills, strategies and understandings necessary for them to do more than merely survive in a climate of rapid and continual change. That there is little available currently to present and prospective classroom teachers presents an opportunity, and perhaps even an obligation, to teacher educators.

Teacher education programs will need to be framed in such a way that paradox is managed skilfully by their graduates. In this study, teachers present themselves as autonomous and empowered survivors who are somewhat immune from many change efforts. The paradox here is that teachers are likely to be able to maintain their sanity, keep stress at a manageable level and retain their focus on students and classroom relationships, while systemic expectations of teacher behaviour may not always be met because of the same immune system. This situation, through a feedback loop, is likely to mean that even larger doses of 'vaccine' will be required for teachers who are troubled by the tension between the two domains of their work within the education system.

If Sungalia (1991, p.16) is right that 'the quality of teaching and learning in an educational system can only be improved from within the system, from within the classroom, from within the heart and mind of the teacher who is determined to teach so that students do learn all that they possibly can', then our teachers ought to be helped to identify those practices which are critical for such quality teaching and learning. What is more, they should be empowered further to defend and protect those practices, while adding new dimensions to their pedagogical repertoires as appropriate. Teacher educators will only be able to assist future teachers in these activities if they are themselves, first, aware of the new realities of teachers' work lives in the latter 1990s; and second, able to both use and impart theories of action (such as that suggested in Smyth, 1988) appropriate for teachers operating within the dynamic complexity of the current and future educational context.

References

Carmichael, L. (1992) *The Australian Vocational Certificate Training System.* Canberra; NEET.

Churchill, R., Williamson, J. & Grady, N. (1995) The Impact of Educational Change on Teachers: work a multi-site, multi-method approach, in R. Cotter & S. Marshall (Eds) *Research and Practice in Educational Administration.* Melbourne: Australian Council for Educational Administration.

Doyle, W. & Ponder, G. (1977-8) The Practicality Ethic in Teacher Decision-Making, *Interchange*, 1(3), pp. 1-11.

Finn, B. (1991) *Young People's Participation in Post Compulsory Education and Training.* Report of the Australian Education Council. AGPS: Canberra.

Fullan, M. (1993) *Change Forces: probing the depths of educational reform.* London: Falmer Press.

Fullan, M. (1995) The Evolution of Change and the New Work of the Educational Leader, in Wong Kam-Cheng & Cheng Kai-Ming (Eds) *Educational Leadership and Change: an international perspective.* Hong Kong: Hong Kong University Press.

Getzels, J. & Guba, E. G (1957) Social Behaviour and the Administrative Process, *School Review*, 34.

Hargreaves, A. (1994) *Changing Teachers, Changing Times: teachers' work and culture in the postmodern age.* London: Cassell.

Hargreaves, A. (1995) School Renewal in an Age of Paradox, *Educational Leadership*, 52(7), pp. 1-19.

Hall, G. & Loucks, S. (1977) A Developmental Model for Determining Whether the Treatment is Actually Implemented, *American Educational Research Journal*, 14(3), pp. 263-276.

Mackay, H. (1993) *Reinventing Australia*. Sydney: Pan Macmillan.

Smyth, J. (1988) Teachers Theorising their Practice as a Form of Empowerment, *Educational Administration*, 30, pp. 27-37.

Strauss, A. & Corbin, J. (1990). Basics of Qualitative Research: grounded theory procedures and techniques. Newbury Park: Sage.

Sungalia, H. (1991) Teaching and Learning in a World of Educational Reform. Keynote address to the annual conference of the Australian Council for Education Administration, Gold Coast, Queensland.

Toffler, A. (1985) *The Adaptive Corporation*. Aldershot: Gower.

Once Bitten, Twice Shy: teachers' attitudes towards educational change in Canada

NOEL P. HURLEY

SOCIO-POLITICAL CONTEXT FOR THE CANADIAN STUDY

Canada's educational system is very much affected by the federal nature of its political system. From its creation as an independent nation in 1867 with the British North America (BNA) Act, education has been under the jurisdiction of the individual provinces. Provincial autonomy in education was reaffirmed in the repatriation of the BNA Act with the passage of the Constitution Act in 1982. This decentralised control has had profound effects on how and when changes have taken place in education. Frequently, some provinces have lagged far behind others in educational reform initiatives and new programme implementation.

Data for the Canadian study were gathered in the provinces of Ontario and Nova Scotia. The present discussion concentrates on the Ontario system and the data that were gathered there. Ontario is the most populated province in Canada and occupies 1,068,580 square kilometres. The province accounts for a little more than 10% of Canada's total area. The various regions of the province are tremendously different in terms of weather, size of population, ethnic background, and linguistic background. Northern Ontario has a scattered population with a small number of smaller cities and large towns dependent on resource-based industries. The majority of communities in the region are small and relatively isolated and the ethnic composition is mainly of Aboriginal or Native Canadians.

Southern Ontario is more urbanised with a number of medium- to large-sized cities. The most productive farmland in the province is located in the southern portion and, as a result, some of the southern counties have significant rural populations even though they are mostly urbanised. In 1991, there were 68,630 farms with an average size of 80 hectares, and about 80% of the farmland under cultivation was in the southern region (Government of Canada, 1991).

Most of the people in the southern cities are dependent on very diversified industries, mainly in manufacturing and service sectors. Ontario accounts for more than half of Canada's industrial activity. Most of Ontario's manufacturing is located in the Golden Horseshoe, from Oshawa through Toronto, Hamilton to the Niagara River. Teachers in the present study lived in the south-western part of the province and could be considered representative of the Canadian population, in that the majority of the people in the country are living under similar conditions, particularly in Ontario.

The large population of Ontario compared to that of most of the other provinces makes the initiation and implementation of change more difficult than in smaller provinces. The population is more ethnically diverse in Ontario than in all other provinces with the exception of British Columbia, which has seen a large increase in immigration from the Pacific Rim area over the past two decades. The ethnic diversity of the population and varying linguistic and cultural backgrounds tends to bring with it larger numbers of students who have special needs.

Throughout the 1990s, Canada has been governed at the federal level by Liberal governments. These governments ordinarily would be expected to develop and implement policies that fall to the left of the political spectrum. Glassford (1997) claims that the Liberal Party in Canada campaigns on the left but governs on the right. The pro-business approach and balanced budget agenda of the Liberal government throughout the 1990s support his claim. This decade has been characterised as one of government cutbacks, downsizing, an erosion of health care, and reductions to the provinces from the federal government of payments in support of social programmes.

At the provincial level the socialist New Democratic Party (NDP) was elected in Ontario for the first time in 1991. Shortly after being elected the NDP government abandoned its socialist roots and pursued an agenda that could only be considered conservative. They rolled back teacher pay levels to erase recent pay increases, they mandated mandatory time off without pay, and cancelled articles of collective agreements that has been negotiated with provincial government employees. After one term in office the NDP government was soundly defeated by the right-wing Progressive Conservative Party (PC).

The present Ontario government is pursuing a right-wing, balanced budget, and pro big-business approach to government. Public sector employees have been subjected to outright verbal attacks from the PC government, accompanied by wage freezes, amalgamations, job reductions, and a demand for more work for the same or less pay. The socio political environment as a result is not one wherein one would expect to find high morale or high levels of job satisfaction.

Another constraint impeding change in the study area is the unusual union structure and the number of teachers' unions in Ontario. The teachers' unions have been divided on the basis of gender, language, and religion. When initial data were gathered for the present study, women belonged to the Federation of Women Teacher Associations of Ontario (FWTAO), Roman Catholic teachers teaching in the Roman Catholic school system belonged to the Ontario English Catholic Teachers' Association (OECTA), and French teachers belonged to the Association des Enseignants Franco-Ontarien (AEFO). Male teachers in the public system belonged to the Ontario Public School Teachers' Federation (OPSTF), and public high school teachers were members of the Ontario Secondary School Teachers' Federation (OSSTF), the most militant of all the teachers' unions. Recently, FWTAO and OPSTF merged to form a single public school elementary teachers' union, the Elementary Teachers' Federation of Ontario (ETFO). The various unions bargain for contracts with individual school boards and, as a result, many of the articles of the collective agreements are different and so have a debilitating influence on how educational change is initiated and implemented in the province.

Much of the change that has been initiated in Ontario has been the result of long-standing attacks on the public education system. Radwanski's (1987) publication of the *Ontario Study of the Relevance of Education and the Issue of Dropouts* was one of the most widely publicised attacks on the provincial system of education. He claimed that the curriculum lacked relevance to the needs of students in the modern economy, and that the system should be reformed to make it more relevant to the sociological needs of the people. This and other publications were the 'sources of legitimation' that Firestone et al (1999) refer to as a justification for the introduction of educational change in their study of change implementation in the United Kingdom and in the USA.

Teachers in Ontario have been subjected to claims from government that Ontario students are not receiving the level or type of education they need to cope and prosper in modern society. These claims are supported by various studies that show Ontario students with lower levels of cognitive achievement than their counterparts in other Canadian provinces. Hurley (1997) argued that, in its Goals of Education, the Ontario Ministry of Education mandated that teachers should emphasise affective rather than cognitive achievement. Nine of the 13 Goals are affective in nature. Thus, even though the Ontario student cognitive achievement outcomes are not statistically different from other provinces where cognitive outcomes are the main emphasis, teachers are nonetheless roundly criticised for doing a poor job. Doing what they are mandated to do, namely, produce students who have a positive self-image, brings teachers what appears to be unfair criticism. The educational climate is one where teachers have felt under attack, under-appreciated, and discouraged by their communities.

Teachers argue that in Canada they are expected to be 'all things to all people'. Students appear to come to school with an increasing number of problems that are expected to be magically cured by the educational community. One study participant, who was discussing a suspension with an early secondary student, was defiantly told by a student, 'You can't suspend me because I have oppositional defiance disorder. Go ahead, call my social worker, call my psychiatrist'. The participant was of the opinion that family support structures that were taken for granted a couple of generations ago are no longer available to children and that 'many of the problems that we have in our schools are, I feel, the result of what we have termed dysfunctional families'. As an aside, the study participant informed us that she told the student to advise his mother when he called her that he had been suspended from school for three days.

Leithwood & Jantzi (2000, p. 2) argue that 'most school restructuring initiatives assume significant capacity development on the part of individuals, as well as whole organisations; they also depend on high motivation and commitment to solving substantial problems associated with the implementation of restructuring initiatives'. Successive studies on change implementation in Ontario (Benninger, 1996; Glassford, 1997; MacDowell, 1998; Palazzola, 1998; Salinitri, 1998: Parent, 1999; Schertzer, 2000) provide mounting evidence of an increase in resistance of Ontario teachers toward change initiatives. Current tensions, particularly at the high school level, have resulted in the initiation of job actions that have resulted in the cancellation of extra-curricular activities in many of the province's high schools. Some federation locals have even gone as far as to pressure their members to refuse to provide practice teaching placements for teacher candidates from faculties of education. Fullan & Stiegelbauer (1991) stated, 'educational change depends on what teachers do and think, it's as simple and complex as that'. This claim, when assessed in the context of the increasingly resistant perceptions of Ontario teachers, casts doubt on the prospect of smoothly implemented educational change.

In summary, it can be argued that the lot of teachers in Canada is similar to that of teachers in other countries. They feel they are faced with increasing workloads, more complex problems related to students, increasing societal expectations, diminished resources, and declining public support. Under these conditions one might expect to find teachers to be stressed and suffering from low morale.

DISCUSSION OF FINDINGS FOR THE CANADIAN STUDY

A brief review of findings for the Canadian study is given to facilitate ease of reading. Interviews were conducted in 14 south-western Ontario high schools which were located in Public School Boards and Roman Catholic Separate School Boards and in urban and suburban centres. Pupil populations of the schools ranged from 632 to 1400, with the average being 985 per school. The number of teachers in schools ranged from 38 to 93, with an average faculty size of 64 teachers. Teacher ages ranged from 27 to 56 years and the average age was 42.8. Teachers interviewed had been teaching for 3 years for the most junior and 33 years for the most senior teacher, with an average of 17.7 years. The demographic composition of participants was close to the teacher population in the south-western Ontario region and so constituted a representative sample. Data were coded using the standardised coding manual produced by the Consortium for Cross-Cultural Research in Education (CCCRE).

The most significant change identified by the majority of teachers was 'change in policy or practice regarding the kind of experiences children have in school'. The particular change that was mentioned was the Ontario Ministry of Education (1994) programme called the *Transition Years,* which was adopted from other provinces and countries and was designed to ease the transition of pupils from elementary schools to high schools. A major problem with its introduction into Ontario schools was that the programme was not developed for and did not suit the structure of Ontario schools. This is discussed later in the chapter.

The second most significant change identified by teachers was 'the novel character and experiences of students'. This change was the choice of 17% of the teachers interviewed as the most significant in their school. Some teachers referred to the 'general lack of work habits and discipline', the '(negative) attitudes of parents and students', 'students' social (mis)behaviour', and the 'attitudes of students toward school and education, they do not take it seriously'. A few teachers specifically stated that they felt the change in student attitude was the result of the change in family structures and increasing incidence of single-parent families. 'Changes in home life, that is, one parent families, a sense of insecurity, and a lack of commitment' tended to cause a 'widening of the teacher's role'.

The third change choice identified by teachers was 'changes in teaching'. Forty per cent of teachers recognised a change in teaching or instructional methods as the second most significant change that was happening to their professional work lives. These were recognised by teachers as a necessary adjustment they had to make to accommodate changes in students' characters and life experiences. More specifically, teachers felt 'students seem to be coming to school with increasing amounts of baggage caused by increasing social problems at home'.

Teachers' fourth change choice was 'changes in student experiences'. Thirty-three per cent of the teachers identified this as their third most significant change choice. This choice was consistent with their second choice, and seemed almost predictable from socio-political indicators present in the system.

Origin of Change

The Transition Years programme was initiated by the Ministry of Education in Ontario, yet only 58% of teachers interviewed perceived the Transition Years programme as having been government initiated. One would have expected nearly 100% of teachers to have been able to identify the origin of that change. Those who identified the change as being government initiated were able to identify the Ministry of Education as the initiators. Although the Ministry of Education was identified as the originator of the change, teachers felt they were given no plan for implementation. One respondent stated, 'Ministry of Education ... have a dictum, but no plan of action'. This happened in spite of the Ministry being located within one city block of the offices of Michael Fullan, who is internationally acclaimed for his career-long efforts of synthesising educational change research and making it available to practitioners.

Others saw the government actions as an ill-advised response to societal demands for a more responsive and effective educational system. A number of teachers felt the government was responding to changing family structures and the concomitant negative effects these changes were having on pupils. 'The evolution of the family, latchkey kids, parents' attitudes toward kids, a lack of respect, and the breakdown of the family' were identified by one teacher as the reason government felt pressured to do something about the perceived declining achievement levels. Other teachers argued that there were 'decreasing expectations from parents and teachers', while others said 'societal demands on family (coupled with) decreasing parental roles, and the need for more counseling' put additional stress and pressure on teachers in their schools.

Teachers also commented on the pressure they were receiving to invoke changes to the educational system as a result of global economic competition. One study participant stated that he felt there was a 'global influence towards unstreamed classes'. Another stated that she felt the Ministry of Education was forcing these changes on the school system because media reports from employers were claiming that students were not being adequately prepared for the global economy. Few teachers saw the change as originating from the school.

Objective of the Change

One-third of the study participants saw the introduction of the Transition Years programme as having mainly a social objective. These teachers recognised the need for a smooth transition from elementary to secondary school and to provide 'adjustment before labeling'. About 48% of participants saw the main reason for the change to be improvement of instruction. One teacher commented: '[the change] will provide a better balance, to state what students can actually do'; a second teacher felt that the students would get a message from the destreaming that their teachers were confident of their ability to handle the same content as other students.

Teachers' Role in the Change

Of the study participants, 44% saw themselves as the implementers of the change. Many interviewees saw themselves as having little influence on the planning and initiating of the change. This perception was supported by the comment from one teacher who said: 'We had groups coming in and telling us about it, not much input from us was requested'. Other comments included phrases such as, the programme was 'dropped on us', it was 'mandated', or we were required to 'implement it'.

Question	% response	Question	% response
Domain of change		*Teachers' role in change*	
School management	13	Resister	9
Teaching	19	No role	
Learning outcomes	2	Supporter	6
Student experiences	66	Implementer	44
		Shared decision	7
		Planner	7
		Initiator	13
Origin of change			
Teacher initiated	2	*Forces helping implementation*	
School initiated	18	Support provided	57
Community initiated	23	Resources provided	29
Government initiated	58	Professionalism	48
		Forces impeding change	
Objective of change		System resources	67
Improve education	48	Personal resources	3
Improve accountability	18	Decision-making process	59
Social objectives	33	Opposition	31

Table I. Canadian teachers' perceptions of the characteristics and antecedents of change.

Implementation of the Change

Most of the teachers (82%) stated that the change was implemented gradually. Many of the participants viewed the gradual implementation as a natural transition while others thought that time was necessary to develop implementation and contingency plans. One teacher explained that the gradual implementation included many amendments from the Ministry that saw the implementation plans change from month to month. The changing of implementation plans was accompanied by changing target dates, and then no penalties were imposed on transgressor schools or boards. One teacher stated, 'if you ignored what they were doing that the mandated change would soon go away'. This resulted in some schools not implementing the proposed change at all. In fact, that is what eventually happened to the entire programme.

Of the teachers who mentioned professional development, 48% perceived the professional development activity as being of assistance to the implementation of the change. Of those who cited professional development as being helpful, teacher comments were fairly positive. Some comments were: 'I jumped into professional development – workshops and evaluation'. 'Workshops on cooperative teaching and evaluation [were helpful in implementing the change]'. One of the participants said that professional development helped them understand the need for change. One statement that indicated this type of perception claimed that 'talking together with the teachers about what worked ... helped'.

Another of the interviewees alluded to the part played by student teachers in the implementation process. This teacher pointed out that the presence of student teachers 'allowed for experimentation' in the change implementation process. Implications for faculties of education of the role of student teachers in the implementation of educational change are discussed later in this chapter.

The second most mentioned aid to implementing the change was collegial help. One-third of the teachers mentioned that the help of colleagues was of assistance in change implementation. About 3 out of 10 teachers (29%) noted that administrative support was of help in implementing change. It is likely that in those schools wherein teachers perceived that administrators were not supportive, the implementation of the change was less successful. Those teachers who felt their principals were supportive commented that administrators encouraged them 'to change [their] attitudes toward the change' and one teacher mentioned that 'the patience of the administrator allowed them to fail [and start over again]'.

Teacher responses to their role in the implementation of the change seemed to be honest. Only 20% of teachers indicated their own enthusiasm for the change assisted in its execution. With 80% of the teachers not enthusiastic about implementing a change, and with only

13% perceiving their own skills as assets to the change process, the likelihood of successful implementation seemed in peril.

Interview respondents mentioned the lack of communication and consultation as an obstacle for change. Benninger (1996) noted that 55.6% of principals in her study perceived lack of communication as a major problem. With principals not knowing what was expected and lacking a clear direction for the programme, the school staffs were being left without clear direction, if they got any at all. One teacher commented very clearly that there 'was a lack of direction at the Ministry, school board, and school levels'.

The level of resources was mentioned as a hindrance to implementation of change by 67% of teachers. Professional development funding and professional development days that would have been used by school boards for implementation of the new programme were cancelled by the provincial government as part of their financial restraint processes. This on the surface seems to be at odds with the perception of study participants that there was little direction from the Ministry or their boards. The boards and the Ministry are the main sources of professional development in the Ontario school system.

Very few of the teachers in the original 1996 CCCRE study felt that there were too many changes. Only 13% of the participants stated that the number of changes was a problem. Later studies (MacDowell, 1998; Salinitri, 1998; Nantais, 1999) found that teachers from boards in the original CCCRE study felt in later years that they were overwhelmed by the number of changes and the speed at which these changes were being introduced. Some of the reforms that were introduced were held to be good directions in which to move, but thought by participants to be too much at once. It seemed to some that few changes had been introduced for a relatively long period of time and that many changes were deemed to be needed at once.

The public perception of the expanding role of teachers was problematic for some participants. One of the difficulties that was elaborated by one teacher was the need for teachers to be more than just a teacher; a new expectation was for teachers to be social workers as well. This was summarised by one teacher who said teachers are met with expectations 'of being so many things to the group of students'.

Some of the study participants spoke of the lack of support from outside the school as an obstacle to the implementation of the change. One teacher said there 'was a lack of support from home'. This teacher elaborated that teachers were now responsible for student social development, but that societal expectations remained just as high as always for academic outcomes.

Some teachers were convinced that the programme they were presently offering was superior to the new programme that was being implemented. This perception prevented them from implementing the

65

new programme as effectively as it could have been, because they did not support it. Frequently people are reluctant to change but are even more reluctant if the proposed change seems inferior to present approaches. One teacher said, 'I felt I was giving up a beautiful programme to give a watered down one'.

Leithwood & Duke (1999) indicated that many of the programmes developed for use in Canada, the USA, Europe, and Australia attempted to simplify the complex processes of school change and to make these processes easier for school leaders to manage. If the initiators of these changes in Ontario had followed those guidelines, the implementation of the identified change in Ontario might have been much easier and more successful. The reaction of Ontario teachers to the implementation attempt was similar to the reaction of British teachers as reported by Firestone et al (1999).

Firestone et al (1999) conducted fieldwork in two American states and in England and Wales. They attempted to clarify the implementation of assessment policy at the central, local administrative, and classroom levels. In their international research data they found support that assessment policy can be useful in promoting easily observable changes, but not what they termed 'deep modifications of teaching practice'. The change identified by Ontario teachers is best described as a deep modification to teaching practice. It was mentioned by many of the study participants that assessment techniques had to change as the approach to content changed.

Effects of Change on Teachers' Work Lives

Most teachers (58%) felt that the most significant change (the adoption of the Transition Years programme) affected their work lives by causing them to have to change their method of instruction. Many of those interviewed noted that their own methods had changed dramatically from what they were 10 years earlier. One said, 'My teaching style and attitude towards change have changed'. Another teacher remarked that because of the changes he was 'more aware of the learner'.

The second biggest effect on teachers' work lives that teachers identified was the change in content of what was to be taught. They were of the opinion that new subject areas had to be incorporated into their teaching and that because of this proliferation of content, what was taught had to be 'watered down'. This reflected the aim of the change to expose all students in the intermediate level to the same level of instruction. Many of the teachers noted that they had to teach 'to the middle' of their classes in order to reach the wide range of student abilities in each class.

The same teachers who mentioned changes in subject content also noted that teachers had to adjust student evaluation techniques. One teacher verbalised the feelings of many when she stated that they had to concentrate 'more on process and less on product', and this at a time when society was demanding higher academic outcomes. Having wide ranges of student abilities in the same class caused problems in teaching and evaluating because of the difficulty of maintaining the interest of the high-ability students while not demoralising the lower ability students. Teachers also felt the need for much greater levels of planning because of the mixed-ability groups they were now teaching. One of the positive outcomes of the change was that it forced many teachers to collaboratively plan curriculum and professional development with their colleagues as a means of coping with the demands of the new programme.

Teachers felt their relationships with their colleagues became more harmonious because of the change. They attributed this improvement in staff relations to increased discussions with others on how they were managing the change. Teacher comments were more numerous on this point than on many of the others on which they were questioned. These comments can be summarised by pointing out that teachers had a need to share with others the stresses, problem-solving approaches, and the good and bad aspects of what they were experiencing.

Effects of Change on Professional Development

Participants in the Canadian study felt that the changes had an expansionary effect on the amount of professional development they undertook. Teachers felt they had no alternative but to undertake professional development because they lacked the experience and expertise to adequately implement the change that had been mandated. This was evidenced by one teacher's comment: 'I was no longer sure of exactly what to do'. A number of teachers (57%) indicated that the change had a negative effect on the amount of professional development they were able to pursue because of time pressures they were experiencing. Inadequacy of school board initiatives in the area of the new programme was also identified by some teachers as a negative professional development consequence. In effect, many of the consultants charged with the responsibility for in-service and professional development at the board level had not received the training necessary to adequately perform their roles. Many of the interviewees mentioned having to take outside courses at universities and colleges to bring their instructional techniques into line with what was needed.

Question	Response %	Question	Response %
Impact on work lives		*Impact on student learning*	
None	5	None	3
Little	5	Little	8
Some	21	Some	21
Much	35	Much	51
Almost all	17	Almost all	9
All	17	All	8
Impact on relationships		*Impact on professional development*	
Negative	67	Negative	57
None or other	11	No effect	17
Positive	52	Positive	26
		Willingness to participate in future change	
Impact on student learning			
None	3	Negative impact	42
Little	8	No impact	38
Some	21	Positive impact	20
Much	51		
Almost all	9		
All	8		

Table II. Canadian teachers' perceptions of the impact of change on their work lives.

Effects of Changes on Students

A majority of teachers who were interviewed felt that the mandated change had an effect on student learning and experience. The greatest overall response was that change produced greater differences between students. Teachers felt that the higher ability students were not challenged under the new programme and the lower ability ones were frustrated by subject content they could not handle. A typical comment was: 'lower ability students seem to produce less, advanced students are not challenged enough'. Whether or not students could have been better off under the new programme seems to have been disadvantaged by the attitude many teachers had towards the multi-ability grouping that accompanied the de-streamed programme.

Teachers were bothered by the lack of careful planning on the part of the Ministry. Vague procedures, instructions, and goals accompanied a lack of communication on the part of the boards and the Ministry. A teacher stated the problem was 'not getting the information right away, we had to seek out what we needed to know rather than having it given to us'. Another teacher explained the programme 'was difficult to apply in the classroom'. These complaints were consistent with problems identified in the implementation of change by Fullan & Miles (1992). They referred to problem areas identified in the implementation of change, such as diffuse objectives by the originators, lack of technical skills in the implementers, and insufficient resource availability for teachers. The inadequacy and inappropriateness of the Transition Years programme for the Ontario system is discussed later in the chapter.

The negative experience with this programme left about one third of teachers apprehensive toward future change initiatives. Many of those who gave a negative response felt that more consultations are required with teachers and principals before change initiatives are delegated to schools. Many interviewees felt the Ministry of Education was at fault for not actively consulting with teachers and principals. Many of those questioned felt they were being bombarded by the number and rate of changes they were experiencing in the school system. With the number of changes that had been imposed in recent years, these teachers had become resistant to future change implementation. 'Change upon change makes one less willing to accept more', was the way one teacher summed up his attitude toward future initiatives.

DISCUSSION OF THE CANADIAN EXPERIENCE

The change identified by participants in this study was initiated at the Ministry of Education and seemed to be driven by political idealism to undertake an initiative that was politically correct. The Transition Years programme was imported into Ontario from other jurisdictions where it had been developed. In many of those provinces and countries the organisation of schools was more suited to the development of the type of transition programme attempted by Ontario. It was readily evident that students graduating from elementary schools to secondary schools experienced transitional difficulties. The unique structure of the Ontario school system required a programme developed to meet its special needs. The Ministry seemed to be trying to import a ready-made solution for a complex set of problems. Some of these difficulties are addressed in the following section.

First of all, the Transition Years programme was developed for school systems that had an intermediate school structure. Students in these schools progressed from an elementary system that was highly process-oriented, through an intermediate school that was a blend of process and product, and to a high school system that was specialised and more product-oriented. The years in the intermediate programme provided a period of adjustment wherein students moved from generalist courses completed by all students to a streamed system where students were divided by subjects and ability.

School boards in other Canadian provinces were implementing transition programmes as early as 10 years before Ontario. Most of the jurisdictions that did implement these programmes had junior high schools or intermediate schools where students in the intermediate grade level were taught in the one building. In Ontario, elementary schools went as far as Grade 8, and then Grade 9 students were transferred to usually much larger high schools. These students were doubly disadvantaged by having to deal with the issues of puberty in an environment that was threatening and unfamiliar. Many of the high schools in Ontario are organised on a factory system of schooling. These seem to be based on the premise that there are economies of scale to be derived from having as big a school as possible. 'Bigger is better' has not really met the test of school effectiveness criteria whenever school size and efficiency has been researched. Mortimore (1993) found that the smaller the high school the more effective it was. Small in his study ranged from 450 to 600 pupils. In the part of Ontario where this study was completed, school trustees and school board administrators regularly fight to close schools within this population range. Perhaps many of the problems related to Transition Years that the Ministry tried to solve with the introduction of the Transition Years programme might have been better solved by dividing the existing high schools into smaller entities. More emphasis needs to be placed on the needs of the student and less on the bureaucratic conveniences of school governing organisations.

Most of the change introduced into the Ontario system has been and continues to be top-down change. If results of recent studies on the effect of change on teachers' work lives (Palazzola, 1998; Nantais; 1999; Schertzer, 2000) continue, then it is likely that the number of resisters to change will drastically outnumber the willing implementers. The original CCCRE study reported 38% of teachers who would be less willing to participate in future change initiatives; Salinitri (1998) reported 45% as being less willing participants, and Parent (1999) reported 66% who would be less willing participants. Further evidence of these increasing problems related to the implementation of educational change in the Canadian context was the province-wide strike in Ontario to protest the recent Bill 160 and the continuation of a work-to-rule campaign in much of the province. For change to bear fruit, the impetus will likely have to come from the roots of the organisation rather than from the top down.

References

Benninger, L. (1996) Comparing Principal and Teacher Attitudes towards Educational Change, paper presented at the Annual General Meeting of the American Educational Research Association, Chicago, IL, April.

Firestone, W., Fitz, J. & Broadfoot, P. (1999) Power, Learning, and Legitimation: assessment implementation across levels in the United States and the United Kingdom, *American Educational Research Journal*, 36, pp. 759-793.

Fullan, M. & Miles, M. (1992) Getting Reform Right: what works and what doesn't, *Phi Delta Kappan,* 73(10), pp. 744-752.

Fullan, M. & Stiegelbauer, S. (1991) *The New Meaning of Educational Change.* Toronto: OISE Press.

Glassford, L. (1997) Meeting the Needs of Future Teachers: curricular changes for pre-service teachers, paper presented at the Annual General Meeting of the Canadian Society for Studies in Education, St John's, NF, June.

Government of Canada (1991) *Statistics Canada 1991 Census Data.* Ottawa: Queen's Printer.

Hurley, N. (1997) Establishment of the Ontario College of Teachers: an analysis of its effects on professional development for teachers and faculties of education, paper presented at the Annual General Meeting of the Canadian Society for Studies in Education, St John's, NF, June.

Leithwood, K. & Duke, D. (1999) A Century's Quest to Understand School Leadership, in J. Murphy & K. Seashore-Louis (Eds) *Handbook of Research on Educational Administration,* 2nd edn, pp. 45-72. San Francisco: Jossey-Bass.

Leithwood, K. & Jantzi, D. (2000) The Effects of Transformational Leadership on Organizational Conditions and Student Engagement with School, *Journal of Educational Administration*, 38, pp. 112-129.

MacDowell, C. (1998) Elementary Teachers: stress and support systems, unpublished major paper, College of Graduate Studies and Research, University of Windsor, Windsor, Ontario.

Mortimore, P. (1993) School Effectiveness and the Management of Effective Learning and Teaching, paper presented at the Annual Meeting of the International Congress for School Effectiveness, Norrkoping, Sweden.

Nantais, M. (1999) Secondary Teachers' Attitudes toward Educational Change, unpublished major paper, College of Graduate Studies and Research, University of Windsor, Windsor, Ontario.

Ontario Ministry of Education (1994) *Policy/program Memorandum 115: the transition years for grades 7, 8, and 9.* Government of Ontario: Queen's Printer.

Palazzola, N. (1998) Elementary Teachers' Attitudes towards Educational Change, unpublished major paper, College of Graduate Studies and Research, University of Windsor, Windsor, ON.

Parent, K. (1999) Teachers' Attitudes to Educational Change, unpublished major paper, College of Graduate Studies and Research, University of Windsor, Windsor, Onatario.

Radwanski, G. (1987) Ontario Study of the Relevance of Education and the Issue of Dropouts. Toronto: The Queen's Printer.

Salinitri, G. (1998) Secondary Teachers' Attitudes toward Educational Change, unpublished major paper, College of Graduate Studies and Research, University of Windsor, Windsor, ON.

Noel P. Hurley

Schertzer, D. (2000) Educational Change and Its Effects on the Work Lives of Teachers, unpublished Master's thesis, College of Graduate Studies and Research, University of Windsor, Windsor, Ontario.

How Cultural and Social Factors of Educational Change Affect Chinese Teachers' Work Lives

KAN SHI & HUADONG YANG

CHARACTERISTICS OF THE CHINESE EDUCATIONAL SYSTEM

Administrative Structure

The reform and opening up of the People's Republic of China (PRC) to world policy in 1978 has had a great impact on the current Chinese education system and has resulted in great progress. According to statistics at the end of 1995, there were 95,216 secondary schools in China, among which were 81,020 general secondary schools, 10,147 vocational secondary schools, and 4049 technical workers' schools in which about 3.8 million teachers serve full-time duties. Enrolments at secondary schools are around 22 million. The average length of schooling set for secondary education is about six years, which is higher than the average for the rest of the world. The system of nine-year compulsory education has been implemented in most areas of China and youth illiteracy has reduced to 6%. To make education more accountable, a series of education laws and regulations, such as laws of compulsory education and laws governing teachers, have been promulgated (Liu, 1992). Before 1978, only public schools were sponsored by the central government in China, yet in recent years, some private secondary schools, sponsored by individuals or the private sector, have emerged. Local government provides no financial support for them, indicating that nowadays in China, education can not only draw on funds from various private sources, but also maintain its backing from the public sector.

A sound education system can provide human resources for the economic and social development of the country. Meanwhile, it lays a better foundation in educational development for the next century. Whereas some problems still remain in the present Chinese education system, education funding from the central government is far from sufficient and education development cannot follow the needs of people in the current changing and challenging situation. For example, previous government-oriented education did not match the social demands for skill-oriented students. The State Education Ministry (SEM) gives great consideration to innovations in education, and reform in this field is under way.

Influences of the Educational Authority Policies

In China, the SEM guides the educational system and educational services are centrally controlled by SEM. Being the principal body of authority, SEM gives instructions and guidance to individual schools ranging from general school policy, to teaching goals, to curricula of specific subjects. Especially, the assessment system of local governments for teaching is based on the proportion of students entering schools of a higher grade. In addition, educational change in China takes place in a clear top-down direction. So teachers in secondary schools have little flexibility in the teaching process, and cannot choose the most useful or up-to-date knowledge for students. It also results in teachers being less enthusiastic while they are teaching. This situation is reflected in the Consortium for Cross-Cultural Research in Education (CCCRE) interviews, in which many teachers wish that more educational changes would take place in China. Nonetheless, they are just followers under the direction of the central or local educational authority.

With economic development and social transformation in China, criteria for excellence and talent are also changing gradually. For a better adaptation of students to society, SEM is planning to launch a nationwide reform to complete the transformation from an examination-oriented system to a competency-oriented one. In the course of competency-oriented education, qualified educators should help increase students' capacity for self-reliance and active curiosity, besides mobilising and encouraging students' autonomy. This is not an easy task to fulfil. Since traditional methods and the education system are closely linked in pursuit of high enrolment to universities, the new method is likely to result in a lower proportion of students entering college, which will arouse great objections from society and parents. It is also difficult to eliminate the severe competition for university entrance among secondary schools. SEM is attempting various methods to break free from the examination-oriented education system.

However, to some extent, the control of SEM possesses its own advantages in implementing educational change. So long as an innovation in teaching methods, tools or techniques is acceptable to

SEM, it will be spread nationwide. Many experts are dedicated to the introduction of new techniques and methods in education, and positive progress has been made in recent years. For instance, the textbook *Vocational Guidance* (Shi & Liu, 1994), which assists teachers with vocational guidance of students, has been used in almost all senior middle schools in China.

Economic Influences on the Education System in China

The Chinese mainland is a vast land area consisting of 31 provinces, autonomous regions and municipalities. The level of economic development varies greatly among the different regions and this also has a great impact on education. For example, qualifications of teachers in secondary and elementary schools in big cities have reached or exceeded the standard set by SEM, while the teaching quality level in some rural areas is far lower than that in big cities or coastal regions of China.

Large differences in teachers' remuneration among specific regions also exist due to the imbalance of economic development. The average salary for teachers in some secondary schools in Beijing is higher than that of university professors. However, in the remote rural schools of the north-western region, teachers are not well paid, or even worse, they usually receive their salary several months in arrears, which also leads to little enthusiasm for the teaching process. Now SEM is making great efforts to change the situation in rural areas.

Generally speaking, China is still a developing country with insufficient financial reserves. Though education expenditure has increased during recent decades, the proportion of funds for education is still low when compared to that of the developed countries. Statistics in 1993 show that China had 17.9% of the world's students financed by just 2% of the world's education expenditure.

Political and Ideological Influences

Politics and ideology have a great influence on education in China. In the past, moral education, in some degree, was replaced by political education. Now, with deepening educational reform, the two issues are being gradually separated, as is also shown in the findings of the CCCRE interviews. Many teachers in China seem not to be much concerned with their students' moral development. In fact, they usually evaluate students' moral development from the political perspective. Another of the differences in values and ideology between the Orient and the Occident is the relationship between organisation and individual development. With the changing of society in China, education more and more stresses the harmonious development between individual and society.

75

Traditional Culture and Social Influences

The findings of this study will be applied in different countries, so more attention should be paid to the cultural and social differences between the East and the West. In China, culture is a particular factor in education change. Historically, the examination-dominated education system drew great attention from society and had a far-reaching influence on the nation. Today, families and parents pay more attention to their children's education than in the past and have ambitious expectations for their children. Since the family planning policy was implemented, couples are encouraged to have only one child. The questions that parents ask of their children are not how many practical skills they have grasped at school, but what are their test scores. For example, in a survey, when parents answered the question, 'Which problems about your children are you most concerned with?' 80.5% of parents admitted that their concern focuses on the children's scores, because high marks mean a good chance of succeeding in the university entrance examination, which in turn brings a promising future after graduation, a better job and good pay. Many teachers believe that parents are one of the most important influences and sources of pressure on educational change. Though the government wishes to lighten the burden on students, teachers and students still have to face more pressure to change the traditional methods of teaching because of the national entrance examination system for college, and parents' interest in their children's marks.

China is in social and economic transition, and teachers have to face two changes. One is the still-changing economic system and growth model from the previous planned economy to a market economy, laying a solid foundation for a modernisation drive into the new century; the other is that a worldwide knowledge economy has been emerging. Economic competition in the twenty-first century will, in some way, be the competition of the quality of the human resources. So developing competent students now becomes more crucial and urgent. This necessitates the Chinese education system paying more attention to reform or innovation, adapting to changes in social and economic development.

Now the Chinese National Education Ministry has proposed the transfer from examination-dominated to competency-dominated education, with an emphasis on developing students in all directions and reforming the examination system and the education assessment model. Students have become the key focus of today's research. At the same time, research on teachers is ignored, though teachers play a very important role in education change, especially in understanding the goals of reform and fulfilling those goals. Their thoughts and attitudes will directly influence the quality of teaching and the degree of success in implementing change, thus influencing students' behaviour. Thus, further research on teachers' participation in educational change is very important.

THE RESULTS OF THE CHINESE CCCRE RESEARCH GROUP

Background

Recently, educational changes have become a common concern for teachers worldwide, but little research has directly explored the influence of educational change on teachers themselves. In China, a number of scholars think the final goal of educational change is to facilitate the students' development, and many researchers focus attention on exploring effective teaching methods for students (Lei, 1997) and an advantageous environment and curriculum for their learning (Maehr et al, 1999). A few researchers commenced study on the teachers' work life as well as those factors influencing the quality of teachers' work life and their job satisfaction (Chen & Sun, 1994; Zhou & Lin, 1994). However, few studies consider those new factors, especially organisational factors, in the changed circumstances of education which affect the work life of teachers. In the mid 1990s, educational reforms stressing improving students' quality were initiated by the SEM in the whole country. Various change plans and programmes are being introduced in many Chinese schools. It is necessary to explore various models of educational change and their characteristics to see how they impact on teachers' work lives, which is why we conducted the CCCRE research in China. The results of this research by the Chinese team now follow.

The Sample

The sample comprised 50 teachers (14 males and 36 females) from 10 middle schools in Beijing, with an average age of 34, ranging from 23 to 55 years old. The length of teaching service varied from 3 to 35 years with an average of 12 years. Of the 50 teachers 76% were married. The age range of their students was from 13 to 18. Of the 10 schools, according to the standards of the SEM, three were 'good', with superior teaching conditions and student qualities, and the other seven were 'ordinary'. The number of teaching staff ranged from 64 to 256, and the number of students ranged from 550 to 2400.

Complying strictly with the investigation manual, we interviewed the 50 participants. In addition, the interviewees were all required to answer the questionnaire in writing.

The Current Features of Educational Change in China

We explored the differences in domain, origin, objective, teachers' role, and timetable of change between China and the overall data from all nine countries.

Domain of Change

The result of a chi-square (χ^2) test shows that there is a significant difference in the distribution of the four domains of change between China and the other countries $(\chi^2 = 17.7, p < .01)$. In respect of school management, Chinese teachers reported a higher proportion of changes than any other country with the possible exception of Hungary. This may be because current educational reform in China emphasises managing schools in a scientific way and improving the student assessment system. With the merging of school establishments, there is an urgent need to change old management practices. Therefore, how to advance school management efficiency has been an important issue focused on by many schools. Meanwhile, with the development of the economy, a variety of requirements for human resource management emerge in China. Nevertheless, the evaluation of students based only on their test scores has seemed outmoded. How to appraise students objectively to meet the demands of society for various human resources has become a theme of common interest.

Origin of Change

Forty-four per cent of teachers agreed that educational change in China comes from the government (government initiated); 26% of teachers attributed it to the school (school initiated); another 26% of teachers thought that it was teachers themselves who initiated change (teacher initiated); and only 4% of teachers believed that the community was the origin of change (community initiated). Although in reporting the change initiated internally, China resembles Israel, the Netherlands and the USA, overall, a chi-square test shows that the difference is not significant $(\chi^2 = 10.9, p > .05)$. Generally, with regard to the origin of change, most educational changes in China are looked upon as initiated by the government.

Objective of Change

Improving educational quality and meeting social requirements are the two most important objectives of educational change both in China and in the overall sample. Differences in the objective of change between China and the overall data were not significant $(\chi^2 = 2.32, p = .31)$. On this scale, China was shown to have identical trends with the overall figures.

The Role of Teachers in Educational Change

Fifty-eight per cent of teachers thought that they participated in change as implementers and only 2% of teachers claimed to resist change, which indicates that most Chinese teachers welcomed educational change, but their enthusiasm has not been completely activated. A possible reason may be that the administrators always conduct educational changes and teachers are only required to act passively. No significant difference was noted between China and the all-country results. For the majority of Chinese teachers, their role in educational reform is that of implementer. Looking at all seven teacher roles, there is a higher reporting rate in the middle of the seven roles, including implementer and sharing in decision-making, yet the difference is not statistically significant.

Timetable for Change

It was reported by 71.3% of Chinese teachers that the changes in which they participated were implemented gradually, which is a higher percentage than the international sample, but the difference is not statistically significant. So for the timetable for change, the Chinese sample indicated similar distribution trends to the overall result.

We think that gradual implementation will benefit teachers' understanding of change and, at the same time, allow reformers to modify their plans and to reduce the impact of change errors.

On the analysis given above, we can draw a conclusion that, in the factors of origin, objective, teachers' role and timetable of change, there is no significant difference between Chinese teachers and their international colleagues, while in the domain of change, China teachers put more stress on the reform of school system management and the change of student assessment.

Factors Affecting the Impact of Change among Chinese Teachers

From the analysis given above, we can conclude that except for the domain of change, the other four characteristics of change exhibit no significant difference between China and the international sample. In the remainder of this study we will explore the impact of the change on teachers' work lives in China and the total sample overall.

The Impact of Change Aspects

In view of our interests and for convenient comparison among the nine countries, we have selected only three factors for analysis: change of relationship, change of time-use and change of professional development. In the coding book, these scales were collapsed into three categories: negative, positive and no effect. According to the classification, we coded the classificatory data in the original codebook into rank data: each 'positive effect' item was scored '1'; each 'negative' item was scored '-1'; and 'no effect' was scored '0'. Take the change of relationships, for example: there are 7 positive items and 4 negative items in the original codebook. If a participant in the interview reported 3 positive items and 2 negative items, the score would be '3' and '-2' respectively. Table I shows the difference of relationship, use of time, and professional development in the teacher's work lives between the Chinese sample and countries overall.

From Table I, we find that there are positive responses to items concerning relationship change, change of time use and change of professional development by the Chinese teachers, and also that there are significant differences between the Chinese sample and the international sample. We attribute the differences to two reasons. One is the difference in characteristics of the change and the other is from other factors such as culture, demography, individual cognitive style, etc., some of which cannot be directly identified in this study. According to the above analysis, we have shown that among five types of change characteristics, it is only in the domain of change where Chinese subjects show difference from the overall pattern. Next we explored the differences between the four kinds of domain and how they affect the teachers' work lives.

	Relationship[a]			Time-use[b]			Professional development[c]		
	M	SD	t	M	SD	t	M	SD	t
China	0.64	1.54		0.86	1.32		0.62	0.72	
Overall	0.02	1.58	1.77**	0.04	1.28	4.61**	0.30	0.66	3.27**

[a] Relationship: Maximum = 7/Minimum = -4.
[b] Time-use: Maximum = 6/Minimum = -4.
[c] Professional development: Maximum = 1/Minimum = -1.
** $p < .01$.

Table I. Differences between the Chinese teachers' work lives and the total sample.

(a)

	Relationship			
	m_{China}	SD	$M_{Overall}$	SD
School mananagement	0.15	1.77	-0.38	2.05
Teaching	0.07	1.68	0.33	1.32
Learning outcome	1.32	1.15	-0.39	1.89
Student experience	1.00	1.19	0.00	1.59

(b)

	Time-Use			
	M_{China}	SD	$M_{Overall}$	SD
School mananagement	0.46	1.45	0.26	1.29
Teaching	0.71	1.06	0.00	1.19
Learning outcome	1.10	1.62	0.16	1.48
Student experience	0.88	1.24	-0.20	1.34

(c)

	Professional development			
	M_{China}	SD	$M_{Overall}$	SD
School mananagement	0.30	0.85	0.43	0.65
Teaching	0.85	0.53	0.33	0.59
Learning outcome	0.60	0.84	0.28	0.75
Student experience	0.50	0.75	0.19	0.74

Table II (a, b, c). Four domains of change effects on Chinese teachers' relationships, time-use and professional development.

From Table II, we see that teaching reform has a more positive effect on Chinese teachers in use of time and professional development than on their international colleagues in the total sample, and the result is statistically significant ($M_{China} = 0.71$, $M_{Overall} = 0.00$, $p < .05$ for the change of using time; $M_{China} = 0.85$, $M_{Overall} = 0.33$, $p < .05$ for the change of professional development). For the change of learning outcome, Chinese participants reported a more positive effect than the teachers from other countries in all three aspects of their work lives. In addition, for the change of student experience, Chinese teachers reported more positive effects on using time than their international colleagues (M_{China} = 0.88, $M_{Overall}$ = -0.20, $p <$ .05). In sum, we can conclude that the domain of change is one of the factors that lead to the differences in teachers' work lives between the Chinese teachers and the total sample.

Comparing Tables I and II, it is clear that the domain of change is not the only factor to account for the difference. Other factors must exist and contribute to the total differences. How can we expose them? We think that 'other' items in the original codebook could provide us with some clues.

Other Items in the Scale

Our results show that though the CCCRE interview codebook covered most aspects of educational change mentioned by Chinese teachers, some factors were neglected. In our opinion, some of these cultural differences should be reflected in the following factors indirectly.

1. Regarding the domain of change, seven teachers (about 15%) believed that educational change is mainly aimed at teachers. For example, some schools are busy assessing the performance of young teachers. Other schools launched projects named 'teacher-training plan for the twenty-first century'. The objective of these educational changes is to improve teachers' competence, which is different from educational changes aimed at students.

2. Regarding forces helping or impeding implementation, many teachers agree that the success of educational change rests on students' families to a great extent, especially the attitude of parents to educational change. Almost all Chinese teachers reported that success of educational change was not only related to powerful influences from society and school but also from families of their students, indicating that the Chinese family is an important influence on educational change.

3. We found that many answers on the issue of impact on the use of time were similar. Most Chinese teachers agreed that they had little time to spend in preparing lessons when facing an educational change. This suggests that educational changes also have some negative effects on Chinese teachers' use of time.

4. As far as impact on relationships is concerned, many teachers mentioned that not only was communication with students increased,

but also that the relationship with the students' parents was closer after educational change.

Demographic Factors Affecting Chinese Teachers' Work Lives

In order to examine whether other extraneous factors contribute to impacts of educational changes on teachers' work lives, we examined the effects of gender, age, teaching experience and type of school by chi-square analysis and found that:

1. For relationship, use of time, and professional development, male and female teachers in China showed no significant differences in their responses.

2. Significant correlation exists with Chinese teachers between age and total teaching years ($r = .96$, $p < .05$), so we explored the influence of teaching years on teachers' work lives. In accordance with teaching years, we divided participants into two groups: more than 20 years in teaching, and less than 20 years. Through a t-test, we explored whether there were differences of relationship change, change of time-use and change of professional development between the two groups. The results are shown in Table III and indicate that no significant difference appears between them.

Years teaching	< 20		> 20			
	M	SD	M	SD	t	Sig.
Relationship	0.45	1.51	0.50	1.71	.05	0.96
Use of time	0.90	1.42	0.70	0.82	.42	0.67
Professional development	0.65	0.73	0.50	0.70	.58	0.56

Table III. Influence of years of teaching experience on selected aspects of Chinese teachers' work lives.

3. Schools are classified as 'good' or 'ordinary' according to the schools' teaching conditions and students' qualities. By chi-square analysis for two independent groups, we found that teachers' perception of educational change is correlated with the type of school. In ordinary schools it is reported more frequently that pre-/post-classroom teaching, during which teachers had to spend more time dealing with students' assignments, is affected by educational change (Table IV). This is probably due to lower levels of competency of students in ordinary schools. Teachers in ordinary schools had to pay more attention to organising every aspect of teaching to ensure progress in educational change. For example, when the classroom teaching change was carried

on in an 'ordinary' school, teachers had to spend more time in teaching students how to prepare lessons before class, how to adapt for the change in class, how to revise, etc. But in a 'good' school, because of the higher ability of the students, teachers are able to pay more attention to classroom teaching. Although the type of school affects teachers' perception of educational change, there is no significant difference of change in relationship, use of time and professional development (t_1 = 1.2, ns; t_2 = .99, ns; t_3 = .47, ns).

Pre-/post-teaching	Good	Normal	DF	χ^2	p
Mentioned	11	28			
Not mentioned	7	4	1	4.67	< .05
Sum	18	32			

Table IV. Influence of the type of school on the pre-/post-classroom teaching.

CONCLUSION

- Except for the domain of change, educational changes in China show identical trends of change with the international picture. In the domain of change, school management changes and student assessment changes are more stressed in China than in the other countries.
- There are significant differences in relationship change, time-use change, and change of professional development between the Chinese teachers and the teachers from other countries.
- The influence of the Chinese family is one of the most important factors in educational change. More attention should be paid to it in cross-cultural research.
- Gender, years of teaching and the type of schools have no significant effect on Chinese teachers with relationship, time-use, professional development in change. But the type of school influences teachers' perception of educational change.

Current Research and Perspective

It is obvious from the CCCRE interviews that the school environment (e.g. leaders, colleagues) plays an important role, affecting teachers' participation in educational change. But what is the main factor influencing teachers' participation in and incentive for educational change? Which kind of supporting environment can prompt teachers' participation in educational change? With these two questions in mind, we interviewed about 30 teachers in eight schools. We found that the different schools started their reform activities at different levels, but a common problem was that it was very hard to maintain the efficiency of the change. The commitment of many teachers who take an active part in the change in the primary stage subsided over a period of time: some gave up or resigned. We also found that some teachers who took the training class seldom used their new teaching methods after going back to work. Why? Schneider (1996) pointed out that a change of individual behaviour could seldom last if the person's environment has not been changed. Accordingly, Rouiller & Goldstein (1993) stated that the supporting organisational atmosphere is a vital influence on change. During our survey, we also found that, compared to personality, the support of other elements (such as leaders, colleagues, students and their parents) is more important. If we can identify factors affecting transfer in educational change, we will be able to formulate a supportive environment. This study on the transfer of training is ongoing.

The CCCRE cross-cultural research provides new insights for us to understand the teachers' work lives against the background of global educational change. Through comparisons of different countries, we not only found common ground in education, which is crucial in the development of education for all societies, also achieved understandings from educational changes in different countries. We expect more related studies about teachers' work lives, such as teachers' career commitments, job satisfaction and work stresses, can be carried out by CCCRE. We also believe that we will have a deeper understanding of teaching as an occupation following such further study.

Acknowledgement

The authors wish to thank Peng Wang and Haibo Yu for their help at the stage of translating Chinese into English.

References

Chen, Y.H & Sun, S.B. (1994) The Study of Teacher's Job Satisfaction, *Psychology Science*, 17(3), pp. 146-149.

Lei, S. (1997) The Objective of Ability-Oriented Education and the Strategy of Change for Elementary Education, *Study and Experiment for Education*, 2, pp. 18-21 [in Chinese].

Liu, J. (1992) Progress in Vocational Education, *Beijing Review*, 23-29 March, pp. 31-35 [in Chinese].

Maehr, M.L., Shi, K. & Wang, P. (1999) Culture, Motivation and Achievement: toward meeting the new challenge, *Asia Pacific Journal of Education*, 19, pp. 15-29.

Rouiller, J.Z. & Goldstein, I.L. (1993) The Relationship between Organisational Transfer Climate and Positive Transfer of Training, *Human Resource Development Quarterly*, 4, pp. 377-390.

Schneider, B. (1996) Creating a Climate and Culture for Sustainable Organisational Change, *Organisational Dynamics*, 24(4), pp. 7-13.

Shi, K. & Li, J.F. (1994) *Vocational Guidance*. Beijing: People's Education Publishing House.

Zhou, J.D. & Lin, C.D. (1994) Psychological Study of the Teacher's Quality, *Psychological Development and Education,* 1, pp. 32-37 [in Chinese].

'All Change': English secondary teachers' response to a decade of change, 1988-98

PAM POPPLETON

INTRODUCTION

In the outpouring of writings about educational change, its processes and effects (Miles & Huberman, 1984; Fullan & Stiegelbauer, 1991; Miles & Seashore Louis, 1992; Fullan, 1993; Hargreaves, 1994) the teachers' voice has often been missing. Since teachers are the key agents in the implementation and facilitation of change, an English research team had begun in 1991 to study how teachers felt about the ways in which recent legislated changes had affected aspects of their working life, and the extent to which centrally determined objectives were already incorporated into schools' programmes of development. This was Phase One of the study reported here, which was later extended and incorporated into a study by the Consortium for Cross-Cultural Research in Education (CCCRE), whose members were aware of educational reform movements worldwide and who sought to understand how the experiences of schools and teachers might lead to a more effective handling of change. This latter pursuit will be referred to as Phase Two.

Researchers from the nine countries taking part in the second phase of the study [1] had a broader brief than those participating in Phase One. This was to describe and examine any of the changes that teachers in these countries felt had been significant for them and their work, and to explore with them the perceived influence of the origin of the change, its objectives, the teachers' role in implementing the change, factors both helping and hindering implementation, associated changes in work style, routines and relationships, as well as their emotional reactions to the experience. Such an examination in a cross-cultural, comparative framework might yield guidelines for policy makers and school administrators who were faced with particular problems that other countries appeared to have overcome.

This chapter is primarily concerned with the English experience, which can be better understood if it is placed, first of all, in the context of recent history. The methodology of the study will then be described, followed by the first phase, 1991-92, moving to an account of the second phase, 1993-96. Data from the two phases are then compared to examine changes over time, and brief reference is made to the cross-cultural data collected in Phase Two to indicate the nature and consequences of similar reform movements elsewhere. Finally, some understandings from the study about the nature and role of the change process in major structural reforms are drawn together, with their implications for policy making.

THE CONTEXT OF CHANGE IN ENGLAND AND WALES

Up to the mid-1960s, the establishment of comprehensive schools in place of the tripartite system of grammar, secondary modern and technical schools had proceeded at a leisurely pace, until Anthony Crosland, the Labour Minister for Education in 1965, published his famous Circular 10/65 which 'requested' local authorities to produce implementation plans. It stated: 'Our belief in comprehensive reorganisation was a product of fundamental value-judgments about equity and equal opportunity and social division as well as about education' (Kogan, 1971). Its implementation required a massive programme of training to increase the teacher supply, accentuated by the raising of the school leaving age to 16 – a reform which had been in the pipeline since 1963 but progressively delayed until 1972.

This clear statement of a set of values that education should reflect, and about which there was a post-war political consensus, is extremely important in understanding the scale and magnitude of forthcoming changes and of people's reactions to them. But parallel with these developments was a growing chorus of discontent with the content of education and the standards being achieved. A series of publications known as the Black Papers [2] named 'progressive' schools and teachers as the prime cause of declining standards, the beginning of a trend that has continued until the present day. Subsequently, the 'Great Debate' in education (1976) took an overtly political form when the then Prime Minister, James Callaghan, declared that former policies had failed and that schools were insufficiently preparing pupils to 'do a job of work'. The adjustment of the labour force to the needs of the market began to replace access to education for all, as the mission for the future.

During the period of Conservative government that followed from 1980 to 1997, the consensus about education ended and was replaced by a period of conviction politics in which the concept of education as a public service was replaced by one based on technical efficiency in the market place (Mortimore & Mortimore, 1998). The parallel transition from a developmental to an instrumental view of education led one writer to say that:

> A significant number of teachers are in a state of despair
> about whether they can continue to teach in a system which
> threatens to become progressively more centralised and
> utilitarian. The fundamental questions thus concern the
> meaning and control of education in our society. (Abbs, 1987)

Under the influence of the market model, equality of opportunity was replaced by freedom of choice; teacher autonomy by accountability; and the needs of the child by the needs of industry and commerce. This marked a significant ideological shift (Riseborough, 1994) that, accompanied by a programme of multiple changes, brought about an unprecedented crisis in teaching in which teachers were leaving the profession under stress or enduring changing conditions to which they could adapt only with difficulty (Ball, 1992).

The trigger for this crisis was the 1988 Education Reform Act (England and Wales) which introduced a package of reforms, the main ones being a National Curriculum; a complex pupil assessment programme originally designed to take place at ages 7, 11, 14 and 16; delegated budgets for schools; and an enhanced role for parents on school governing bodies. The combined effect of all these changes was such as to be expressed overwhelmingly as one of *imposed change* that brought about a quickening of the pace of change, as reforms that had been in the pipeline for many years acquired statutory form.

The Education Reform Act was presented to parliament as embodying the principles of choice (for students and parents), diversity (of both academic and vocational opportunities), and accountability (to the community). In practice, the Act has brought about the restriction of choice for students; much greater variation in the quality of school provision as 'good' schools have become overcrowded by parental choice, forcing less favoured schools to close; the loss of professional autonomy by teachers; and the loss of control by the local education authorities who previously played an important supporting role for teachers in their areas. How would the teachers feel about this very complex system, centralised in some respects and decentralised in others, but with constant awareness of who pays the piper and who calls the tune?

The National Curriculum originally comprised three core subjects (English, Mathematics and Science) and seven other foundation subjects to be included in the curriculum for all pupils. For each of these 10 subjects there would be 10 levels of attainment covering the ages 5-16 and setting objectives for learning. Programmes of study would specify essential teaching within each subject area, and assessment arrangements would relate to the 10 levels of attainment. Taken together, these requirements imposed new and extremely time-consuming requirements on the schools and placed limits on their ability and flexibility to adapt the curriculum to the needs of different children. In laying down tighter guidelines it was not surprising that the National Curriculum should be met with considerable hostility. However, the immediate reaction to these reforms was not wholly unfavourable; in fact it was 'welcomed both by schools and by teachers and by the wider public, including parents' (National Commission on Education, 1993). The National Curriculum defined an *entitlement* curriculum for every child, demanding 'teaching of a satisfactory standard under conditions that allow each child to profit from it'.

Nevertheless, the additional demands placed on teachers, as well as anxieties expressed by all sectors of the education system were such that, in 1993, teachers boycotted tests for 7- and 14-year-olds, and the government set up a Committee having greater representation for the teachers and chaired by Sir Ron Dearing. The purpose of the Committee was to review the demands made by the 10-subject structure of the National Curriculum and, especially, the demands of the testing programmes. In recommending a reduction in the 10 compulsory subjects structure of the National Curriculum to three core and one cross-curricular (information technology) subject, and reducing the amount of prescriptive material, teachers could be assured of having greater scope to teach according to their professional judgement. As a result, the Dearing Review marked a milestone in the achievement of a slimmed-down structure in which teachers would once more play a role in determining the content and method of what was taught, while relinquishing their former autonomy. By 1993-94 teachers were able to speak of 'pre-Dearing' and 'post-Dearing'.

THE PHASE ONE STUDY: METHODOLOGY

Teachers' initial reactions to the 1988 reform package were explored in interviews with 10 experienced headteachers and 40 teachers from 10 secondary, comprehensive schools situated in South and West Yorkshire. Schools were chosen by catchment area to represent the full socio-economic spectrum, and varied in size from 288 students (about to merge) to 1434 (recently merged). Headteachers were interviewed individually and separately from groups of four teachers in the same schools, to determine their major concerns about current educational changes. Each school was asked to include in the group a mid-career teacher, a senior teacher and a relatively new teacher recruited in the last five years (this proved difficult, one school having had only two new teachers in 20 years). Teachers were chosen to represent different subject areas and levels of responsibility.

The form of the interviews was very open and aimed to record teachers' views on the most significant changes for them in major areas currently under review: curriculum, assessment, financial management, and teacher training (Poppleton, 1995, 1996). All the teachers agreed to the tape recording of the interviews and all recordings were transcribed and submitted to the interviewees for confirmation.

Working from the interview transcripts, the first step in the analysis of the data was to identify common themes, issues and events that gave rise to concepts having general explanatory power (Ball, 1987). They arose in the process of acquiring intense acquaintance with the data by a process of induction. In the case of the 1991 study, the comments were made as the reforms were being implemented and in a period when the major concerns of the teachers were with the practical problems of implementing the National Curriculum and its associated schemes of assessment.

In interpreting the data, we must recognise the constant interplay between the concepts that emerge from data and the pre-existing conceptualisations of the researchers, based on their understanding of the micro- and macro-contexts previously outlined (Miles & Huberman, 1984; Ball, 1987). Figure 1 shows the reactions in the teachers' own words, taken from these interviews, together with their integration into broader categories and some of the resulting implications for the schools.

Comments	Categories	Implications
working in the dark;		
moving the goal posts;	Insecurity	Crisis management
unable to control the situation.		
those who are making us do things;		
being pushed;	Loss of	Administrative
deciphering the vocabulary.	autonomy	Press
defending treasured slots;		
in-depth knowledge of	Subject	Resistance to
our subjects;	entrenchment	change
we're here for the kids.		
encouraged to teach in		
inappropriate ways;		
greater flexibility to develop	Skill development	Identify task
cross-curricular skills;	needs (pedagogy)	demands
variations in specifications		
between departments.		
an assessment-led curriculum;		
unsure of the targets;	Training needs	Work reorganistion
coping with the paperwork.	(assessment)	

Figure 1. The teachers' voice (1991-92).

Implications

Practising classroom teachers were full of apprehension and misgivings about the National Curriculum and its imminent implementation, to an extent that amounted to serious professional anxiety. This hinged upon the lack of initial consultation and involvement of teachers in the National Curriculum working parties, and was compounded by concerns about the short time scale for implementation, the lack of resources to enable quality development of new teaching materials and methods, and the overall lack of in-service training to prepare teachers with new skills for delivering the curriculum. These anxieties are often vividly expressed by the use of metaphors such as 'working in the dark', 'moving the goal posts', 'being pushed' and 'treasured slots'. Other points to note are:

- insecurity arose from an almost complete lack of detailed planning and consultation with schools before the curriculum was introduced, and there was inadequate representation of teachers on the working parties;
- the feeling of being pushed came about from a suspicion that problems of implementation came from the expression of a particular political ideology rather than any educational development. Formerly, decisions about the curriculum had rested with the local education authorities but had, in practice, been largely in the hands of the schools and the teachers themselves;
- pressures arose from lack of match between existing staff competencies (the image of the teacher as a subject specialist) and the needs of the new curriculum, including cross-curricular themes requiring greater flexibility of approach;
- inappropriateness of methods of assessment in some subjects ignored excellent developments such as the 'records of achievement' already operational in schools, made new task demands, and defined new training needs;
- a restrictive time frame for implementation, and inconsistencies of resourcing being experienced by schools and teachers were frequently mentioned.

The Headteachers

The headteachers did not seem to afford the National Curriculum and its problems quite so high a priority, and were much more concerned with the recently devolved management responsibilities for organisation, finance, staffing and development of a general school policy. While some of the headteachers did share their colleagues' concerns and articulated them eloquently, they were more likely than their teachers to stress the positive potential of the National Curriculum in terms of standardisation, consistency and balance, but also to stress the practical difficulties of implementing all the changes in a situation described as 'death by innovation'. Faced with administrative and assessment pressure from government as well as subject entrenchment and skill development needs from the teachers, the heads were turning their minds to innovative practices in order to make possible the management of a modern educational institution. According to one headteacher, new management structures would:

> *... advise the head teacher on the appropriate allocation of attention to the following points: the management of the curriculum area on a split-site school; the integration of one or more curriculum themes or issues; responsibilities for specific subjects within the curricular area ... this is really a prompt sheet for imaginative management.*

Many of the contributions made by the headteachers were dominated by a new management jargon of delivery, management procedures, and cost effectiveness, and the introduction of new incentive allowances to correspond with the key stages of the national curriculum. For example:

> *The big difference has been to get our hands on the money. The process has been quite fascinating and extremely instructive.*

However, problems were created when existing staff competencies did not match the needs of the new curriculum as a whole. Then senior managers in schools had to be very flexible in creating teams of teachers in departmental or multi-departmental structures who could be more effective in delivering the curriculum than if the approach remained the single teacher teaching their own subject only. These developments would need specific support from the senior management team, but would be likely to encounter substantial barriers arising from the image of the teacher as a subject specialist and the financial barrier of insufficient money to support the development of such methods of working, in spite of the optimism expressed above.

It seemed that we were witnessing the development and hardening of two independent sub-cultures in the schools; the management culture of the senior management teams and the classroom practitioner culture of the teachers. Nevertheless, it should be borne in mind that, while 40 of the headteachers' comments were negative in nature, 23 were positive of a kind that viewed the compulsory nature of the curriculum as helping pupils and, through the subject-led basis, gave clear expectations for teachers to work towards in those subjects which lacked a strongly organised hierarchical structure. It is clear that all aspects of the change interacted to produce a complex set of attitudes and expectations.

THE SECOND ENGLISH STUDY (1995/96)

The new secondary curriculum had now been in operation for four years and the majority of teachers had gained experience of it as it moved gradually up the schools.

For the second English study, 8 headteachers and 27 teachers – who between them spanned most of the subjects covered in the secondary curriculum – were interviewed individually from January to July 1995, in 8 comprehensive schools in the counties of Yorkshire and Oxfordshire. The interviews were recorded and transcribed as before.

Whereas in the first study, findings were presented as themes and issues raised spontaneously by the teachers themselves, the introduction of a cross-country element required a more tightly structured interview schedule than that employed in Phase One, in order to ensure that everyone responded to the *same* questions. The form and content of the interview schedule was standardised and presented in a predetermined way. At the same time, it offered researchers the opportunity to explore particular issues and themes with the teachers, leading to a database that could be analysed in flexible ways. For comparative purposes, the schedule was constructed by the team of international researchers, translated if necessary, piloted, revised, coded, and analysed quantitatively. For Phase Two of the English study, it was analysed qualitatively as before, by drawing out themes and issues. The resulting interpretations will draw on both sets of findings.

The Teacher's Voice (1995/96)

Because of the different structure of the interview schedules, it is impossible to present a breakdown of the 1995 results under the headings used in 1991. Also, by 1995, the reforms had worked their way through the system and taken over the secondary teachers' work lives. We can, however, summarise the findings under the categories that emerged as teachers spoke feelingly of their experiences. These are presented in Figure 2.

The educational changes that had most affected the teachers' work in 1991 and that remained a major source of concern in 1995, were those related to curriculum and pedagogy. They derived directly from the introduction of the National Curriculum and were, initially, a source of great anxiety and confusion, not to say hostility. By 1995, the response was much more considered and less generalised in the majority of cases. In spite of what was experienced as a massive encroachment on the teachers' time, both in school and out, recording pupils' achievement and in meetings spent on collaboratively planning curriculum development (even if it was contrived collegiality), gains had been experienced from more flexible and variable pedagogies and more collaborative ways of working. But there had also been costs arising from the inward pressure of change, loss of external contacts, and restriction of the in-service training that teachers had known in the past. Above all, the massive encroachments on time spent on administrative tasks and meetings highlighted the need for more ancillary help and work support.

Thus, the period of 4-5 years that had intervened between the two sets of interviews had brought about both greater receptiveness and greater resistance.

Comments			Categories			Implications		
we cover a greater range of activities								
the way I teach hasn't changed,								
but what I teach has			Task awareness			Curriculum planning		
schemes of work are more formalised								
need for finer planning								
a huge increase in paper work								
most time in school spent								
on administrative tasks			Work overload			Role conflicts		
horrendous growth in meetings								
a rift between younger and older								
teachers who won't change								
a lot more insular			School and teacher			Greater 'Balkanisation		
good subject teachers who can't			dysfunction					
coordinate								
more child-centred in learning								
from experience (music)								
a whole different approach when			Greater flexibility			More variable		
talking to children (science)			of teaching method			pedagogy		
more awareness of teaching								
outcomes (geography)								
I have to assess every piece of work								
in IT for every child								
I need more time for recording			Time press			Continued work		
pupil progress						organisation need		
I prioritise more, am more efficient								

Figure 2. The teachers' voice (1995-96).

The Headteachers: (1995/96) beliefs and values

As before, the headteachers nominated as the 'most important' change in their working lives one relating to changes in the financial management and governance of schools, in contrast to the teachers' preoccupation with the National Curriculum. In itself, this indicates differences in cultural contents between levels in the school hierarchy, but what about the cultural forms through which the contents were expressed?

Many contributions referred to the difference between change as a natural, continuous process, and one that is imposed. One headteacher expressed this vividly:

> *I am a person who likes change and I still feel that schools can improve enormously and so I look for any change that is going to help the working class kid – so I love change – but it must*

have a good purpose and a great aim. So – my willingness to participate in educational change will depend on what it is.

Beliefs and values were most clearly articulated by the headteachers who, irrespective of the change that had most affected them personally, had an overall view of what it had meant for the school. One, headteacher 3, who saw change as a combination of the reform requirements and his own philosophy, said:

The curriculum is therefore based on educational values and principles and this is what I mean by being actively in control. Left to my own devices I would probably have been more prescriptive, but that is not how the school works. The school is not the plaything of the headteacher.

This head was sensitive to the dilemmas of the teachers and aimed:

to invest them with a sense of control, of professional worth, of empowerment and, at the same time, to develop a sense of corporate membership and whole school values. This at a time when all central initiatives were moving power, confidence and authority from teachers ... that has been the tension in the dynamic of change – to undertake forward planning in circumstances of instability.

Another, headteacher 1, saw the problem as:

less one of continuous change but more that changes have been planned against continuously changing targets and uncertainty over government policy.

Beliefs about the *role of central initiatives* were seen as fundamental by headteacher 5:

In education generally, I would say that the change in philosophy about the role and function of schools is the primary area of change. Clearly, it has demanded all sorts of developments in the professional training area and in administration to equip people to respond to imposed change ... I do feel that my role has increasingly been pushed in directions for which most of us are not very well equipped. The professional culture of teaching over the last few years has been damaged by people's self-esteem, the way they perceive they are valued within the British society. Expectations of them amount to what many staff would see as a betrayal of values in a comprehensive school. I think all those things have made staff extremely vulnerable, sometimes confused, sometimes embittered. So I think teachers' perceptions of themselves and their colleagues and other schools have been a major difficulty ... the league table is the sharpest example of the hostile culture that teachers perceive they are working against.

Both the National Curriculum and the introduction of new forms of school management imposed new constraints on schools and teachers:

Yes, well the world turned upside down, didn't it? A strange mixture of huge expansions of freedom with a sort of perverse increase in constraints and controls ... financial freedom to an extent that hadn't happened before ... but, of course, that coincided with the most vicious reduction in the amount of money that was available so that all we seemed to be doing was managing the contraction of the system. (Headteacher 4)

Some of the constraints that made strategic compliance more, rather than less, likely were when teachers had to make changes they believed were inappropriate. They complied overtly with statutory requirements while reserving the right to maintain freedom of thought and action as far as possible. This meant for one headteacher:

I am conscious of legislation, of what I must include in the curriculum for the students but remain alert to the chance of more options ... I tried to hold on to what was important for our English education in the school and fit the National Curriculum into that rather than trying to alter what we were doing to fit the National Curriculum.

The culture of compliance is basically a culture of resistance to change in which ways are sought of maintaining professional judgement, of coping with work overload and the restrictions on social life, both within and outside the school.

The restatement of values by the headteachers reflects how comprehensive school reorganisation was a product of fundamental value judgments about equal opportunity and social division. The conflict between striving for equality and the need for excellence in the pluralistic framework of the 1990s continues in the move to a more centralised and utilitarian system and, ideologically, from the needs of the child to the demands of industry and commerce.

Imposed change had considerable impact on every aspect of the working life. Surprisingly, its effect on professional development was seen as predominantly positive, given the earlier comments. It may be seen in the context of opportunities afforded by change – especially for those who stayed in the profession and were offered inducements of additional responsibilities carrying extra pay.

PHASE TWO: THE ENGLISH TEACHERS
IN AN INTERNATIONAL CONTEXT

We move now to a more structured analysis of the English teachers'
views in the context of the cross-cultural aspects of the study. Each
interview concentrated on the one change nominated by each teacher as
the most important, and explored perceptions of the origin of the change,
its objectives, the teachers' role in the change, factors that helped and
hindered its implementation, associated changes in work style and
routines, the utilisation of time and relationships with other people and,
finally, the teachers' willingness to contemplate involvement in future
changes of a similar kind.[3]

		Percentage Responses							
	Aus	Can	PRC	Eng	Hun	Isr	Ned	SA	US
n	50	66	50	27	34	59	121	37	50
Domain of Change									
School management (Finance allocations)	18	13	29	7	27	11	9	8	18
Teaching/subject/method (Subject, method)	20	19	31	67	46	56	70	41	40
Learning outcomes (Assessment)	42	2	22	0	0	5	6	14	18
Student experiences (Ability, class size)	20	66	18	26	68	28	15	38	24
Origin of change									
Teacher ⎫ Internal	2	2	26	4	3	26	24	14	26
School ⎰	12	18	26	7	19	50	23	19	28
Community ⎫ External	2	23	4	4	23	5	3	14	16
Government ⎰	83	58	44	85	54	19	50	54	30
Objective of change									
Social objectives	30	33	42	19	23	26	24	65	30
Improve efficiency	36	48	42	39	62	54	52	27	44
Improve accountability	34	18	17	42	15	20	25	8	26
Teachers' role in change									
Resister	28	9	2	4	3	2	4	3	2
No role	4	14	12	7	15	2	1	38	12
Supporter	24	6	10	0	9	2	17	5	8
Implementer	32	44	58	48	24	28	57	30	36
Share decisions	4	7	10	11	12	19	0	11	10
Planner	2	7	2	4	15	12	21	0	8
Initiator	6	13	6	26	24	35	0	6	24

Forces helping implementation*									
Resources (finance, human, physical)	9	59	68	22	46	42	41	38	35
Support (collegial work)	70	29	90	89	54	71	80	84	75
Teachers' own professionalism	86	48	42	59	46	36	72	72	60
Forces impeding implementation*									
System resources (lack of time/finance)	67	67	85	73	48	65	52	78	60
Personal resources (surviving & coping)	83	3	23	48	16	19	70	47	36
Decision-making (too many changes)	79	59	57	30	24	27	62	75	43
Opposition, lack of consultation	19	31	36	20	32	15	25	44	23

*Interviewees were allowed more than one response to these items.

Table I. Teacher perceptions of the characteristics and antecedents of change.

We are now able to summarise the findings in the categories that emerged as the main changes mentioned. Table I lists teachers' perceptions of some of the characteristics and antecedents of the change, and is followed in Table II by a summary of the impact of these changes on the dynamics of the teachers' working life. In the following account, the quantitative data will be illustrated by extracts from the English interviews, selected in an attempt to cover the range and variety of contributions.

	Percentage Response								
	Aus	Can	PRC	Eng	Hun	Isr	Ned	SA	USA
n	50	88	50	27	34	59	121	37	50
Impact on work life									
None	24	9	0	22	27	0	3	5	24
Little	0	5	2	0	3	4	4	5	2
Some	0	21	34	7	3	3	21	8	8
Much	30	35	48	33	24	17	59	38	30
Almost all	14	17	10	22	21	38	14	24	30
All	32	17	6	15	24	40	0	19	14
Impact on relationships*									
Negative	86	67	33	53	32	28	15	33	54
No effect	4	1	22	6	43	9	41	22	41
Positive	10	52	59	42	39	78	68	59	68

Pam Poppleton

*Impact on professional development**

Negative	56	57	76	37	27	5	41	76	22
No effect	22	17	14	0	0	0	7	14	0
Positive	22	26	10	63	73	95	52	10	78

Impact on student learning

None	14	3	6	0	9	2	4	6	2
Little	20	8	8	11	9	0	23	8	6
Some	16	21	32	26	30	12	39	32	32
Much	24	51	46	37	24	25	40	46	38
Almost all	12	9	8	19	12	30	4	8	20
All	14	8	0	7	15	22	0	0	2

Teachers' feelings about the change

Very negative	16	12	4	0	6	0	3	4	10
Negative	22	20	4	11	12	0	6	4	8
Somewhat negative	16	24	12	0	6	4	12	12	10
Somewhat positive	4	20	32	30	9	14	21	32	14
Positive	28	12	42	44	56	50	53	42	22
Very positive	14	12	6	15	12	32	5	6	36

Willingness to participate in any future change

Negative impact	34	42	6	26	24	4	14	6	8
None	44	38	58	56	32	12	62	58	52
Positive impact	22	20	36	19	44	84	24	36	40

* Percentage responses are rounded to the nearest whole number.

Table II. Teacher perceptions of the impact of change on their working life.

Characteristics and Antecedents of Change

Domains of Change

As we have seen, by 1995 classroom teachers were devoting more time to the curriculum and to whole school planning that covered a greater range of activities than hitherto. All these were described under the general heading of 'teaching', endorsed as the main domain of change by 67% of respondents.

The interview responses of the English teachers differed in some respects from those of their overseas colleagues. A major theme for all teachers was the importance of changes in subject matter and/or teaching methods. In fact, an additional category of 'both' had to be added in order to code the English responses, which did not distinguish between lesson content (11%) and teaching method (4%). This is quite a different usage from that in continental Europe and other areas of the world, where to speak of the 'curriculum' is to indicate what is to be learned in the form of syllabuses based on traditional subject divisions which, in many cases, are centrally controlled by either the state or federal governments.

100

European and North American practice also tends to equate 'teaching' with instruction, but the responses of teachers in the Netherlands are interesting, as reform there focused strongly upon the transformation of teaching methods from the traditional and didactic to those more oriented to the student and learning. There, as in Britain, a high proportion of teachers (70%) nominated changes in teaching as those that were currently most affecting their work, though in opposite directions. In Britain, while the curriculum traditionally has had to serve the requirements of an external examination system, teachers had a great deal of autonomy in designing the programmes of work and the means by which they were taught. When the National Curriculum laid down tighter guidelines it was not surprising that they should be met with considerable resistance. Israel is the third country in which the majority of nominated changes (56%) fall within the area of 'teaching', though for reasons other than national reforms.

Each of the terms 'curriculum' and 'teaching' is an umbrella concept used to cover a variety of activities that may vary between schools and most certainly vary between countries, so that the interview format was important in allowing the use of these terms to be explored and elaborated.

Activities related to learning outcomes in the area of assessment and evaluation have resulted in major increments in time demands, of a kind that involved more meetings, more record keeping and more curriculum planning, though the introduction of Standard Assessment Tasks (SATS) related to each stage of the National Curriculum had not fully worked its way through the system to the secondary schools at this point.

Student experiences were the other main feature reported by all, especially the Canadians. For the English teachers, they generally involved changes in policy or practice regarding age or ability regroupings, class sizes, or scheduling, plus observed student reactions to the new curricula that graphically described how this was happening. Consequently, the English teachers were beginning to see the need for different teaching approaches and were experiencing greater conflicts between the professional and organisational aspects of their role.

Origin of the Change

The theme of imposed change is continued in responses to questions about the teachers' perceptions of its origin. In England, only 11% of changes were recorded as internally initiated; 4% being initiated by teachers as against the 85% who identified change as arising from government policy. The international data collected in this study show that five countries were involved in implementing curriculum changes perceived as being of national origin (England, the Netherlands, South

Africa) or state (Australia, Canada). The remaining countries show the perceived origin to be widely dispersed over the categories of school-, teacher- or community-initiated change. Thus, there is a fairly clear demarcation between instances of externally and internally initiated changes. Teacher-initiated changes occur most frequently in data from Israel, the USA, the Netherlands and China, though they constitute only around one-quarter of the citations in each case.

This suggests that teacher-initiated changes occur more rarely than the change literature would have us believe, or that they were on so small a scale that the teachers thought them scarcely worth mentioning, or that in circumstances of imposed change, teachers had little energy left to initiate changes themselves. Not only this, but feeling themselves to be disempowered when new and demanding skills were required, they were hardly in a position to act independently as change agents. Nevertheless, in two schools anti-bullying projects had been introduced by senior members of staff. Richardson (1990) suggests also that while teachers improve their lessons on a day-to-day basis, they, perhaps, do not regard such changes as sufficiently significant to be reported as important examples of initiation.

Objective of the Change

English teachers were divided about the objectives of the changes they had described. Thirty-nine per cent opted for the 'safe' reply of 'improving' education. A comparable number felt that it had more to do with accountability to parents and the community – issues which were being strongly debated at that time. Fewer thought that the changes had much to do with social objectives such as working to eliminate discrimination arising from gender, race or material disadvantage, though these effects were mentioned indirectly by drawing attention to a recognised need to standardise the curriculum over the whole country so that children moving to another area would not be disadvantaged. Within this framework, teachers described a more variable pedagogy encouraged by the National Curriculum, which led them to be more aware of the range of differences between individuals. It is noteworthy that the highest response rate in the category of social objectives came from South Africa, influenced by the far-reaching political reforms of the 1990s.

The Teachers' Role in the Change

Seven categories of teacher involvement in change show that the majority (approximately 59%) saw themselves as implementers or having some role in decision-making, though there was some confusion between the roles of implementer and initiator. The latter was most likely to be claimed by those who had responsibilities as coordinators of subject development plans or whole school development plans. Unlike their Australian counterparts, few saw themselves as resisters or claimed to have a passive supporting role. This may have been a consequence of the long process of habituation to calls for change in schools by a succession of politicians (there were seven different Secretaries of State for Education over a 10-year period), and certainly there were expressions of disenchantment and non-involvement by teachers, a typical one being:

> *personally, I wasted hours and hours of work doing one thing to be told about two years later that the goal posts were going to be changed and we would do it some other way. The net result is that I've lost interest and don't care a fig about it. If it had been done differently I think a lot of teachers would have supported it. (Mathematics teacher)*

Lack of active resistance may have been partly due to teachers leaving the profession, particularly those whose subject structures had been strongly affected. For example, when Home Economics became a component of Design and Technology, one teacher described it as 'A required change that was very difficult to come to terms with in that the emphasis has changed from skill development to the design element'. She continued, 'I now have no contact with other home economics teachers – if indeed, there are any. It has eroded my position within the school and the Authority'. In spite of this, she conceded that the experience had been a positive one for the students.

There was an ambivalence in which those interviewed spoke about the contradictory feelings they experienced in the face of change. For example, a science teacher who 'felt positive' about the change listed a number of difficulties it had created and ways in which it had been detrimental to learning for some students. Many respondents said that they were not against change if it is 'for the benefit of the students', but would not welcome further change because they 'had had enough'.

Factors Helping Implementation

Before the introduction of the reforms:

> *the processes of change had not been internalised; there was no curriculum development and no particular culture of active engagement with education. Teachers were good classroom practitioners and worked very hard but they had a solitary approach. (Headteacher)*

This would now be an area of radical change.

Helping sources were ultimately classified into three categories to do with the provision of resources, support provided by the school and colleagues, and one's own attitudes, competence and professionalism. Where more than 50% of responses fell into one category, they represented the implementation plan itself in Australia, one's own attitudes in the Netherlands and South Africa, and collegial help in England and the Netherlands.

We have so far dealt with the responses of teachers acting as individuals, but equally important to the teacher culture is the quality of the relationships between them and between teachers and other community groups. Because of the nature of our data, the relationships discussed here will be primarily those that take place within the school between colleagues working and socialising together.

Collaboration and collegiality were seen as key contributors to the implementation of externally imposed curriculum reform by the vast majority of teachers. These teachers were beginning to appreciate that the answer, at least partly, lay in collaborative efforts which were actually built in to the demands on departments and schools that they produce curriculum development plans and whole school development plans, for the implementation of the National Curriculum:

> *I think really, it's meant that for the whole teaching staff to be able to achieve a common approach, we've had to write very detailed schemes of work ... tightly written, with lesson plans and objectives. (Science teacher)*

It also opened up individual teachers' classrooms:

> *There are much closer relationships with colleagues, more understanding of teaching methods, a spread of new ideas. (English teacher)*

> *... we've tried to develop our planning on the basis of a whole school sense of corporate purpose that actually is a major change in the way that schools operate; something that a school's mission doesn't convey. I mean any change has been shared, but that's how we work in this school. We work as a team and we delegate. I would say that since Dearing, there hasn't been a lot of change to our schemes of work because of what's happened. (Headteacher)*

Another headteacher, when asked what helped to implement the change, replied:

> *The hard work of colleagues. They gave unstinted time to implement the national scheme within a very short time period with strict limits for implementation.*

Comments of this nature were repeated in every school in the sample. It would seem that the process of implementation of the National

Curriculum was perceived by many teachers as having strengthened both collaboration between departments and collaborative work within them, sometimes to the teachers' own surprise. Hargreaves's (1994) view is that collaboration and collegiality are key contributors to the implementation of externally imposed curriculum reform, and the outstanding influence in this respect lies undoubtedly in the statutory requirements – in this case, the activity of developing curriculum plans.

Factors Hindering Implementation

Lack of time and financial resources, combined with too many changes all at the same time, were the main constraining factors, comprising 73% of mentions (see 'System resources' in Table I). They contributed to a vast increase in workloads, particularly in the areas of administration and pupil assessment. This has been described as 'intensification' of the teacher's work. It occurs, says Hargreaves (1994), 'when teachers are expected to respond to greater pressures and to comply with multiple innovations under conditions that are at best stable and at worst, deteriorating'. There was ample evidence of these processes in the interviews:

> As far as the National Curriculum is concerned, there has
> been a huge financial outlay; in terms of equipment, things are
> very expensive. The school had to give extra money or it would
> simply not have been possible ... there were no models or
> schemes of work. So, until you knew what the scheme of work
> was it was very difficult to get equipment, but until you knew
> what equipment you had, you couldn't devise a scheme of
> work. (French teacher 1)

> Nobody's actually worked out exactly how it all fitted together
> in the sense of the time element. That also led to problems,
> because subject departments were looking for an amount of
> time that was just not feasible. (French teacher 2)

The prevailing strategies for 'fitting things together' could often be described as 'ad hoc-ery', resulting in a good deal of stress:

> I think there are times when my teaching is abysmal. I've been
> teaching a long time but I am having to skimp on preparation.
> I settle for doing some things well and others as well as
> possible. (Science teacher)

Such contributions vividly illustrate the effects of attempting to implement major reforms within a restricted time frame.

The Impact of Change on the Dynamics of the Working Life

A number of questions put to respondents asked them to rate the impact of their nominated change on various aspects of their work life, on a scale from zero to six. In some cases, these categories were condensed to three. Table II sets out the responses in the categories but, while scanning these figures, we should recall that they represent reactions to a variety of changes.

Degree of Impact

While 70% of the English teachers recorded a considerable impact on their working lives, 22% considered that the changes had had little or no effect at all. These may have been the younger teachers who had no baseline from which to judge, as they had entered teaching while the changes were in progress and would have held relatively junior positions. Also, others may have been passive 'implementers' who did what was required but no more. Similar patterns of response are to be noted in Hungary and the USA, whereas the effect for teachers in Canada, Israel, the Netherlands and South Africa is much more marked.

Dale (1988) notes that teachers are in the position of being simultaneously both the subject and the agent of change. Being required to implement imposed change makes the development of strategic compliance more likely when teachers have to make changes they believe to be inappropriate. One English school had an eye over the shoulder on a possible inspection:

> We have recently updated the (schemes of work) ... just to
> make sure that we're covered, you know. But I would say that
> it hasn't really affected the delivery of the schemes of work,
> the subject matter ... I tried to hold on to what was important
> for our school and fit the National Curriculum into that rather
> than trying to alter what we were doing to fit the National
> Curriculum.

Impact on Relationships

The ambivalence of response noted earlier may be seen again in relation to the impact of the change on relationships, where 53% thought it had been negative and 42% saw its influence to have been positive. Similar bimodal effects may be seen in Canada and the USA while, in Australia, an overwhelming proportion of respondents registered negative effects. In England, where the increase in work overload greatly reduced opportunities for pursuing informal relationships, the National Curriculum brought about greater collaboration between colleagues, but had the reverse effect on relationships between departments and between schools.

Such patterns may not have been wholly unacceptable to those teachers whose identity is derived from strong subject departments, well demarcated from each other and with vested interests in remaining that way. In the British system they are produced by early subject specialisation, that makes subject departments the most important of the subgroups within the school and the base for career building. They also define the preferred patterns of relationships among teachers. If they exhibit certain properties (i.e. low permeability and strong insulation from other groups; high permanence; personal identification and political complexion in the sense of conferring power and status), they may be described as the cultural form of *Balkanism* (Hargreaves, 1994). There is also in the literature a strong tendency to treat Balkanisation as a perjorative term and to contrast the condition with more open patterns of relationships.

How did the teachers feel that their patterns of relationships had been affected by the changes of most concern to them? The new Science curriculum was a particular source of comment:

> *Respondent 1: There are staff here who feel they have been*
> *asked to teach off-subject and are not particularly happy*
> *about it. But the school's ethos in Science, in a way, is very*
> *much into supplying the specialist teaching.*
> *(Science teacher 1)*

> *Interviewer: Are you saying that Balanced Science, which can*
> *bring departments much more into contact, has suffered from*
> *status problems?*

> *Respondent 2: Yes, it has. We have separate heads of*
> *Chemistry, Physics and Biology who are still very much*
> *single-subject oriented. They are very good teachers of their*
> *subjects but are not willing to put in that extra bit of effort to*
> *make the coordination of the system which is required.*
> *(Science teacher 2)*

However, the *subject entrenchment* expressed by teachers was more complex than it at first appeared. The National Curriculum had introduced compulsory cross-curricular units such as Information Technology (IT), Personal and Social Education, and Equal Opportunities, which became generally known as 'off-subject' teaching and challenged the attitudes and expertise of many teachers. Under these conditions, feelings of isolation were more common for teachers 'doing some IT-subject teaching and finding it very difficult to find a specialist to talk to'. In other cases, however, there was a more positive view:

*There is much closer liaison with colleagues, more
understanding of teaching methods, a spread of new ideas ...
to be on your own and insular does not lead to development
for the school. (History teacher)*

*Relationships have strengthened through the need to
cooperate and work together. Most staff are prepared to take
their share and there is an amiable, purposive atmosphere ...
we now have to produce policy statements and curriculum
development plans within departments. These are good
because it makes everyone think about issues more carefully.
But it takes up all our free time. (Headteacher)*

*It has cemented already excellent relationships with
immediate working colleagues. We've been in this together
from the start and we knew we had to get our act together.
(Geography teacher)*

A certain amount of 'encouragement' could be applied to this process:

*We set up a series of curriculum review meetings ... laid out
the perceived issues and over 50% of the staff chose to
participate (all were encouraged to do so but told they would
be in a weak position later if faced with things they didn't like)
... we have to work much more closely together than we did.
So, yes, it brings mavericks into line ... whereas we could have
lived with mavericks more easily, we can't live with them now.
(Senior management)*

In other words, collegiality is not always disinterested or aimed at
improving collegial relationships, professional development or school
effectiveness. It may be 'compulsory, not voluntary; bounded and fixed
in time and space; implementation- rather than development-oriented;
and meant to be predictable rather than unpredictable in its outcomes'.
Hargreaves (1994) has defined this set of circumstances as contrived
collegiality, which often masquerades under the cloak of collaboration
but which is actually a disguised form of manipulation for the
implementation of policy. Much of the literature conveys the sense that,
whereas collegiality is to be encouraged on the grounds of good human
relationships, it can readily be contrived to achieve centralised control.

Relationships between schools had also been affected:

*There used to be various consortiums getting one teacher
along from each school to swap ideas – even to look at
industrial links. Things like that have all gone to the wall, they
just don't happen. (Headteacher)*

Additional responsibilities arising from the National Curriculum:

> *have made the school a lot more insular. It's stopped me*
> *having opportunities to work with other schools and stopped*
> *me calling upon the experience of a lot of people within the*
> *school because they haven't got the time or [don't want to*
> *make the] effort. (Geography teacher)*

But there was evidence of variation between schools, and we found comments that concentrated on difficulties of communication and support side by side with more positive comments about the processes of collaboration and collegiality.

Impact on Professional Development

The duality of views noted in the previous section emerged even more strongly here. Along with their colleagues in Hungary and the USA, the majority of English teachers (63%) felt that the impact of curriculum change on their professional development had been positive, the remainder being negative. None thought it had no effect, but viewed it as offering opportunities for career development:

> *For me, personally, all the changes have done nothing but*
> *enhance the work I've done – I've grown, I think, over the time.*
> *I've had lots of different responsibilities – I was Head of*
> *Department, Head of Year, Director of Studies, Head of 6th*
> *Form and Curriculum Deputy. So I've actually had lots of*
> *changes. (Senior management)*

There was also evidence that the changes had, at least, not entirely destroyed the rewards of teaching:

> *I enjoy being in the classroom with the students. I enjoy*
> *teaching my subject tremendously, therefore, my main*
> *ambition is to lead my own department. (French teacher)*

> *... the job itself is not so different from what it used to be – still*
> *as rewarding in terms of enjoying being with children and*
> *looking after their welfare ... as long as you're able not to*
> *resent things. (English teacher)*

> *People say to me, 'Well, what do you think about teaching*
> *then?' and I say, 'The best way to answer that is that it seems*
> *only yesterday that I started teaching and that must be a good*
> *thing'. It's certainly been harder than I envisaged, but it's still*
> *a rewarding occupation. When I close the classroom door and*
> *I'm with children, that's the part of the job I enjoy most. But*
> *it's a much smaller percentage of the job than it used to be – I*
> *would say only 40 or 50% of the job. (Science teacher)*

For a number of teachers, change had provided opportunities that sometimes seemed quite rudimentary:

> *I attended several courses organised by the LEA (local education authority) ... in order to get informed about what I was supposed to be delivering. These were all geared to instruction in how to deliver, not to consultation or content. Advisers themselves seemed unsure of what was actually happening. (French teacher)*

However, headteachers in particular could balance their working lives between being the leading educator and an administrator or chief executive:

> *I've developed different sorts of skills, for example, interpersonal skills which give me some satisfaction. I've had to acquire a certain amount of knowledge in technical matters, legal matters, financial matters, and I've had to develop a resilience and toughness in certain ways. (Headteacher 3)*

> *I am able to concentrate far more on classroom work with both staff and students, and in acting as a kind of master teacher or support for teachers around the school. Some people get bogged down because they don't delegate – some like it. (Headteacher 8)*

Impact on Student Learning

The majority of responses clustered in the 'some' and 'much' categories. Those who endorsed 'little impact' felt that, on the whole, pupils were not really affected by the changes taking place as they had known little else:

> *They would just have the changes imposed upon them, but they wouldn't have had the freedom beforehand.*

Teachers were more aware of the effects of change on their own pedagogy in particular subject areas, believing themselves to be 'more child-centred' (Music teacher) and to adopt 'a whole different approach when talking to children' (Science teacher).

Comments of this kind were as much about experienced changes in teacher autonomy as in pupil learning:

> *We had more freedom before to follow certain paths that the pupils were interested in. That's gone. We've gone back to giving them more hurdles that they've actually got to jump through [sic]. (History teacher)*

On the other hand, not everyone saw the situation in the same light:

... we devised our own programme, the sorts of things we were supposed to be doing and how we wanted to approach it. (English teacher)

I think there is still a lot of freedom in the way we deliver it and I think there is probably variation from school to school on just how you perceive the National Curriculum personally, or as a department. (Senior management)

Teachers' Feelings about the Change

Curriculum change was sufficiently wide-ranging as to affect all aspects of work. Although much of the teachers' work in the classroom had not radically changed, the impact of greatly increased workload demands, plus shortages of equipment, texts and other resources, had produced a culture of strategic compliance on the one hand and strategic development on the other. Some of our interviewees announced towards the end of their interviews that they were seeking early retirement, while others saw greater opportunities for professional advancement and greater control of their work. In between these two extremes were teachers who strove to keep the curriculum relevant and flexible for the children they taught. On the whole, they were very aware that standardisation of the curriculum resulted in some schools having greater problems of delivery because of the 'type of pupils we have'. These are the schools where strategic compliance was most likely to be found. An unexpected finding is that in spite of the adverse attitudes that were expressed throughout the interviews, when questioned about their feelings now about the changes, 89% of respondents declared that they felt positive or very positive that the changes would ultimately be seen as having been for the better. In terms of a cognitive social psychology there has to be justification of the effort for such cognitive dissonance. 'People learn to love that for which they have suffered' (Lawrence & Festinger, 1962).

Willingness to Participate in any Future Change

When asked whether their experiences had influenced their willingness to participate in future changes of a similar nature, 26% of teachers said that they would (with reservations); 15% said they would not, while 56% of teachers were uncertain. Those in the last group spoke about the contradictory feelings that they experienced in the face of change. The general consensus was that the changes that had affected 'much' or 'almost all' of the teachers' working lives were needed, but there was condemnation of the way they had been introduced nationally.

111

The processes of change in English education continued, and by 1995 further policy developments had hit the teachers hard. Having got the provisions of the Reform Act under way, machinery was devised to ensure that the National Curriculum was fully implemented in the form of new Education Acts. These established the requirement that every school must be inspected every four years by independent inspection teams contracted to the Office for Standards in Education (OFSTED). This rolling programme of inspections involved 6000 schools per year and the reports were to be made available to the public. The net result is that league tables of schools have come to influence parental choice, so that some schools are over-chosen to the point where choice can no longer operate and some, at the other end of the spectrum, are nominated as failing schools which have to be 'taken over' by new, experienced teams of teachers and risk closure if they cease to attract entrants. This whole process marks a radical change from concern with *process* to one emphasising *output.* Predictably, it has introduced new instabilities into the lives of teachers.

CROSS-CULTURAL COMPARISONS

Reference has already been made to some of the between-country differences but, if we are to learn anything from such comparisons, we need to compare like with like and to look more closely at the dimensions of similarity and difference. Of all the countries represented in the study, Australia is the one most similar to England in the timing and nature of its reforms over the previous decade. Examination of the data in Table I, columns 1 and 4 indicate that the change of greatest importance to both groups of teachers was externally initiated. Australian schools were also coping with a new national curriculum, increased emphasis on vocational goals, the delegation of financial responsibilities to the schools, increased accountability requirements, and new ways of assessing pupils' progress.

Over 80% of respondents in both England and Australia perceived the origin of the educational change of greatest importance to them to be government-initiated but, whereas in England the nature of the change lay in the areas of curriculum and pedagogy, in Australia responses were more diverse, with greater emphasis on the achievement of social/emotional objectives. There was no evidence for impressions fostered by the media that emphasising social/emotional objectives occurs at the expense of academic excellence. In both cases, however, the introduction of a new national curriculum and testing procedures were central features, while multiple, simultaneous innovations to be achieved within restricted time frames caused concern in both countries.

When asked about what the teacher's own role in the change had been, a significantly greater proportion of the Australian sample described themselves as a 'resister' (28%), while a few in either country had not had any role. Entries in Table I show that, at the time of the data collection, 89% of English teachers were positively involved in implementation in some form, compared with 44% of their Australian colleagues. Because of their more active roles in drawing up curriculum plans, English teachers tended to see themselves as 'initiators', although the key role for both English and Australian teachers was that of 'implementer'. In other words, the majority regarded themselves as *agents of change* rather than as *change agents;* an important distinction on the reactive–proactive dimension.

The Australian teachers were also more inclined to refer to personal characteristics when noting the forces that helped (own professionalism) or hindered (survival and coping ability) implementation. According to Churchill & Williamson (1999), many felt unprepared or unskilled for the roles they were to occupy in response to change initiatives, and were particularly affected by the load of simultaneous multiple innovations that placed limits on their ability to handle any one change effectively. The English teachers, on the other hand, were more likely to refer to the lack of availability of financial, human and physical resources that never seemed to catch up with the demands of the large-scale and radical curriculum revolution that embraced so many aspects of their work. Teachers in both countries complained about too many changes all happening at the same time.

How did these conditions affect their work and working lives? One factor in common was that around 20% of teachers in each country claimed that the change had not had any effect, whereas over 70% recorded a substantial effect. Breaking this down into its constituent parts, the impact on relationships polarised. An overwhelming 86% of Australians rated the effect of change as negative, while only half that number did so in England. The impact on professional development in England was also polarised, being 37% negative and 63% positive, while 56% of Australians felt that it had been negative and 22% positive, with another 22% testifying to no effect. It is highly likely that the English pattern reflected a process of adaptation to the reforms, in advance of Australian developments.

The teachers' responses to the impact of the change on student learning were much more diffuse in both countries and the effects observed were, broadly, that English teachers felt their students were more interested and more knowledgeable than they had been formerly while Australians felt that they had more work to do, were less knowledgeable than before and were less skilled in communication. Thirty-seven per cent of each set of teachers agreed that they now observed greater differences between their students than formerly.

Surprisingly, in spite of all their initial doubts, trials and tribulations, 80% of the English teachers now felt positive about the change compared with 46% of the Australians, who were correspondingly gloomy, but only about one in five of either sample felt that they would be willing to participate in any future change. Battle weary, they had had enough.

SUMMARY AND DISCUSSION

The decade began in an atmosphere of uncertainty and confusion over the reforms that marked the transition from a developmental to an instrumental view of education. While both have existed since compulsory education was introduced, by the end of the twentieth century, the ideology of education as a public service was rapidly being replaced in Britain by the drive to achieve international excellence in every aspect of public life. The disappearance of fundamental value-judgements about equity, equal opportunity and social division mourned by Kogan (1971) were swamped by the clamour for absolute standards against which both children and teachers could be judged, but they never totally disappeared. This study has shown that, in spite of the encroachment of the market ideology, the value-judgements are still alive and well, even if they have to fight for expression in the darker corners of the National Curriculum, the headteacher's study, and through the teachers who ask about change: 'Will it be of benefit to the children?' Headteachers generally had a developed view of the role of central initiatives and their implications for both students and teachers. They were particularly sensitive to the hostile culture surrounding the comprehensive schools, and concerned about the culture of inertia and isolation within them pre-Dearing.

The findings confirm that, over a short period of time after a radical change is introduced, people tend mainly to register symptoms of shock, believing that it will never happen or, if it does, will be less disturbing than they anticipate, and this may well appear as inertia. In the case of the English reforms, however, curriculum change was so wide-ranging as to lead to feelings of great instability. Although the need for a national curriculum was widely recognised, and although much of the teacher's work in the classroom was not greatly changed, certain conditions such as the merging of some subjects, the use of unfamiliar and time-consuming tests and record-keeping, the reduction of in-service courses, the need to include cross-curricular teaching and information technology, all ensured that the impact of these workload demands, plus shortages of equipment, texts and other resources, produced a culture of strategic compliance and contrived collegiality on the one hand, and strategic development on the other. Attitudes began to polarise. At worst, teachers welcomed the prospect of early retirement and, at best, they saw greater opportunities for professional advancement and greater control of their work. In between these extremes were teachers who strove to keep the curriculum relevant and flexible for the children they taught.

What evidence is there that the processes of reform themselves brought about lasting changes in the teachers' cultures? They certainly appear to have brought about changes in attitudes, such that the majority of the English teachers interviewed came to feel positive about the curriculum changes and positive towards change in general, provided that it would benefit the students. There is at least one good reason for this, and it is methodological. In the period between the two studies a significant number of teachers had left teaching, feeling demoralised, deprofessionalised and disillusioned. Only four out of the 35 interviewees in 1995 were aged 55 or over and three of them were leaving teaching. It was clear that we were talking to the survivors of change, who were either younger, or more resilient, or who had encountered fewer difficulties in schools where a collaborative culture already existed. The gradual disappearance of a substantial proportion of the sample in any change study is a hazard which cannot wholly be avoided or controlled, though there may be special measures that can be used to estimate the extent of the probable influence exerted by the change.

Teachers' cultures do not exist in a vacuum but are themselves subject to the social/structural changes taking place in the wider society. Theoretically, this suggests that a change in the teachers' cultures will only be long-lasting if the structures are there to support it. When change is imposed on the schools, its success is highly dependent on this factor, e.g. the science teachers involved 'needed opportunities for collaborating with their peers and for upgrading and maintaining their own subject knowledge'. On the whole, teachers were very aware that the standardisation of the curriculum resulted in some schools having greater problems of delivery than others 'because of the type of pupils we have' and because of the shortages of staff with the required competencies. These are the schools where strategic compliance was most likely to be found.

A second structural factor is the legislative nature of the reform programme itself. When change is imposed on the schools, its success is highly dependent on legal compliance that, in this case, took the form of a tightly controlled inspection programme. In line with the change away from consensus politics and a public service ethos, new structures were developed to oversee the implementation of the reform programme. OFSTED has already been mentioned as an example of the powerful new English authorities which are answerable directly to government and which bypass the existing, locally based authorities. OFSTED has the responsibility for carrying out school inspections, identifying weaknesses and strengths in each case, producing reports that are publicly available, and providing the data upon which school league tables are compiled. For schools that were doing their best under social handicaps, this last measure has proved to be the last straw for many teachers, who feel that their professionalism has been betrayed.

The major components of the teachers' cultures have been identified and illustrated from the data, but this is necessarily an incomplete picture. There are almost certainly more factors contributing to the teachers' perceptions of curriculum change than have been mentioned; for example, considerable cynicism about the political origins of the National Curriculum and its associated ideology. If these have not been given a more prominent place, it is not because they lacked expression nor because they are believed to be unimportant in the changing social and economic culture of the country, but because the analysis adopted of the teacher culture rests basically on relationships and their stability in time of radical, systematic change.

CONCLUSIONS

We set out to explore the nature and role of the change process in major structural reforms. There is a view that 'Attempts to impose change on teachers, teaching and the nature and processes of schooling have been notoriously unsuccessful' because they have failed to acknowledge '(a) that teachers are, first and foremost, people and (b) that schools are social institutions' (Sikes, 1992).

Perhaps this statement should be modified to refer to 'first attempts'. Change processes have been successfully imposed in Britain in the face of global, structural and economic changes that demanded the maximisation of work skills in the context of social institutions, but change processes have been mediated throughout by teachers and headteachers, who have had to confront and maintain both standards and values.

The teachers spoke eloquently of the predicaments, uncertainties and stresses sustained in their working lives during the critical early years of the reforms and, again later, when they were able to evaluate them more positively. This should not, however, obscure the grief and pain suffered earlier, nor excuse policy makers from considering the negative consequences of trying to change the world in seven days. That remains someone else's prerogative.

Policy Implications

Some implications of these studies for those involved in decision-making are:

- The challenge for those who wish to introduce major structural reforms of the education system is to achieve change by setting short-term goals without demanding unrealistic time constraints. Failure to do so will most likely result in a culture of surly compliance that will delay any movement towards change.

- Imposed change of this magnitude is never a single event, but a continuing process in which the end-point is always being redefined. Intervention in a process once under way needs to be of the order of the original effort and double the cost.
- The change process described here is still continuing, in a teacher culture that has grown increasingly hostile to the serial devaluation of the profession by politicians and the media. The processes of reform need to be imbued with a moral dimension that can be articulated and communicated in a way that is understood by all involved.
- Comparisons across time and countries revealed some surface similarities alongside some quite wide disparities in reaction to specific aspects of apparently similar changes. The problem of what might or might not work in other cultural contexts remains unresolved and can probably only be resolved by the careful testing out of alternatives.
- The role of research applications in policy making is not a straightforward linear process in which a problem is defined, questions are asked, investigations are mounted, results published, and policies revised and implemented. The real sequence of events is much messier than this and the role of research is to reveal critical factors that can ameliorate situations and sensitise the public to define and express its concerns. Research in the short term may be misleading and, wherever possible, the process should be followed through over a longer period of time.

Notes

[1] Australia, Canada, China (PRC), England, Hungary, Israel, the Netherlands, South Africa, the USA.

[2] Black Papers were 'a series of publications emanating from the political right, which played a significant part in shifting the terms of educational debate in the 1970s' (Finch, 1984).

[3] Three demographic variables included in the data collection and analyses were the teacher's age, gender and marital status. They were selected because complete information for all samples was available. Of the three demographic variables included in the study (teacher's age, gender and marital status), the only one to show statistically significant correlations with the seven criterion variables in the English data just discussed, was age. The older the teacher, the greater was the reported impact on the working life (which could be either positive or negative) and on feelings about the change, but the smaller the impact on the teacher's professional development. The reasons for these effects have to do with the disturbance effect on accustomed practices and routines, the threat of a

possibly foreshortened career, and dislike of the priority being given to management and administrative matters over and above the professional and caring aspects of teaching. Above all, long-serving teachers cherished the high degree of autonomy that they had experienced (or thought they had experienced in the past), and were now to be subject to a greater degree of public scrutiny.

Acknowledgements

The author wishes to acknowledge contributions made to these studies by Robert Pullin (1989-92) and Felicity Armstrong (1995-96), and in particular Sue Parsons, the production manager of this book, who was became very ill and died during the final stages of production.

References

Abbs, P. (1987) Training Spells the Death of Education, *The Guardian,* 5 January.

Ball, S.J. (1987) *The Micro-politics of the School: towards a theory of school organisation.* London: Methuen.

Ball, S.J. (1992) Changing Management and the Management of Change: educational reform and school processes, an English perspective, paper presented at the annual meeting of the American Educational Research Association, San Francisco, 21 April.

Churchill, R. & Williamson, J. (1999) Traditional Attitudes and Contemporary Experiences: teachers and educational change, *Asia-Pacific Journal of Teacher Education and Development*, 2(2), pp. 43-51.

Dale, R. (1988) Implications for Progressivism of Recent Change in the Control and Direction of Education Policy, in A. Green (Ed.) *Progress and Inequality in Comprehensive Education*, pp. 39-62. London: Routledge.

Finch, J. (1984) *Education as Social Policy.* London: Longman.

Fullan, M. (1993) *Change Forces: probing the depths of educational reform.* London: Falmer Press.

Fullan, M. & Stiegelbauer, S. (1991) *The New Meaning of Educational Change.* Toronto: OISE Press.

Hargreaves, A. (1994) *Changing Teachers, Changing Times: teachers' work and culture in the postmodern world.* London: Cassell.

Kogan, M. (1971) *The Politics of Education.* Harmondsworth: Penguin.

Lawrence, D.H. & Festinger, L. (1962) Incentive, Dissonance, and Justification, in *Deterrents and Reinforcements*, pp. 127-163. Stanford, CA: Stanford University Press.

Miles, M. & Huberman, A.M. (1984) *Innovation Up Close: how school improvement works.* New York: Plenum.

Miles, M. & Seashore Louis, K. (1992) *Improving the Urban High School: what works and why?* London: Cassell.

Mortimore, P. & Mortimore, J. (1998) The Political and the Professional in Education: an unnecessary conflict?, *Journal of Education for Teaching*, 24, pp. 205-219.

National Commission on Education (1993) *Learning to Succeed*, Report of the Paul Hamlyn Foundation. London: Heinemann.

Poppleton, P. (1995) Teacher Education and the Market Economy in Britain: the teachers' views, in R. Hoz & Silberman (Eds) *Partnerships of Schools and Institutions of Higher Education in Teacher Development*, pp. 175-188. Haifa: Ben Gurion of the Negev Press.

Poppleton, P. (1996) The Changing Structure of the Secondary Teacher's Work: an international perspective, in J.H. Coetzee & T.G. Smith (Eds) *Education and Change*, proceedings of an international conference, University of South Africa, pp. 353-359.

Richardson, V. (1990) Significant and Worthwhile Change in Teaching Practice, *Educational Researcher*, 19(7), pp. 10-18.

Riseborough, G. (1994) Teachers' Careers and Comprehensive School Closure: policy and professionalism in practice, *British Educational Research Journal*, 20, pp. 85-104.

Sikes, P.J. (1992) Imposed change and the experienced teacher, in M. Fullan & A. Hargreaves (Eds) *Teacher Development and Educational Change*, pp. 36-55. London: Falmer Press.

Teachers in Transition: Hungarian perspectives

NÓRA ARATÓ & MARIANN SZEMERSZKY

INTRODUCTION

The year 1989 marks the beginning of the period when Hungary fundamentally transformed its primary and secondary education systems. In the early 1990s the central government's previous role in education was dismantled and since that time there has been a process of re-creation. Presently public education is under a three-tier management system, with central government, self-government, and institutional levels. The Ministry of Education is the focal point of central government efforts for education. Regional governments – constituted by counties and the capital city – and municipal governments (2400 local governments out of the 3100 local and 20 regional ones) maintain educational institutions. Each one operates under six mandates from the central government: to establish (or dissolve) educational institutions; to control the budget; to appoint principals; to exercise judicial control over the institutions; to approve pedagogical programmes and local curricula; and to evaluate the efficiency of the institution.

The following trends have characterised the transformation process from 1989 to the present:

- decentralisation and increased local autonomy;
- diminished national funding and an increase in the variety of funding sources;
- continued low status and low salaries for educators;
- decrease in the size of the school-age population;
- increased numbers of schools;
- increased competition among schools for students and among students for schools;
- increased disconnection between vocational education and the needs of the new economy;
- increased structural diversity;
- increased curricular diversity.

The Hungarian School of the 1990s

Before the recent changes, the pattern of education in Hungary was only 8+4 years – eight years of primary with four years of secondary education. The first eight years were further subdivided as 4+4; that is, four years of elementary plus four years of upper primary education. Hungary has now expanded on this pattern by adding two other patterns of 6+6 years and 4+8 years. These three patterns reflect the opportunity for schools, students and parents to choose which structural combination of years seems more appropriate for their needs and aspirations.

Changes in the System of Education

The transformation of the educational system in Hungary began in the early 1980s, even before the transition to democracy, when it was recognised that interested and active participants in the educational process should assume responsibility for education, instead of delegating this task to 'outsiders' who do not actively participate in the educational process. The transformation accelerated in the second half of the 1980s with the Public Education Act, ratified by the Parliament in 1985. This law delegated professional independence to schools and invalidated the centrally administered curriculum. Schools became responsible for initiating educational experiments and implementing new teaching methods, albeit with prior ministerial consent. The Act also made provisions for the staff, schools, councils, parental organisations, and student assemblies to have the right to express their views and opinions, to propose changes, and to participate in the decision-making procedures concerning education.

Weeding out the jungle of old legal rules resulted in a radical decrease in the number of laws, articles and regulations on education by the end of the 1980s. At the same time, centrally issued orders gradually gave way to rules and orders promulgated by individual institutions. Changes for school management and teachers came in several waves. First, the national 'procedure manual' was removed and schools were given the responsibility and obligation to introduce their own organisational and operational rules. Second, there was the new notion of ownership and independence with the concomitant delegation of supervision and guidance of the schools to the schools themselves. Prior to 1987 the supervision of the schools was legally unsettled. Prior to the 1985 Act, various laws and central government decrees and instructions had regulated the school systems without clarifying the responsibilities of immediate participants. Further, only one national supervisory institution had the right to instruct, intervene, or change regulations. A ministerial decree of 1987 (Szüdi, 1998) finally clarified the issues for which the local education agencies (district boards of education) would be responsible. The order also released the schools from a role dependent on the 'maintaining' authorities at the national level.

The Law of Public Education

The 1993 Law of Public Education, which was modified in 1996, brought a final and non-reversible transformation to the school system in Hungary by clearly defining the licences, tasks and task-sharing responsibilities among those institutions which operate and serve public education. For the first time in the Hungarian education system, students' and parents' rights and obligations also were proclaimed in law. The following provisions were made by the General Education Act and the Vocational Training Act:

- Providing education for the school-age population was defined as a local task. Therefore, local governments became responsible for running local schools. For example, each of Budapest's 22 districts became responsible for providing, maintaining and developing its primary and secondary institutions of education.
- Providing religious education became obligatory when requested by students.
- The centralised curriculum system was invalidated, along with the public school inspectorate. In its place, a two-tier system was established in which the National Core Curriculum now provides basic principles and core requirements for each age group, while schools develop their own detailed curricula.
- Schools were required to develop their own pedagogical programmes, approved by local supervising authorities, while school achievement would be measured by regional or national pedagogical service institutes, by institutions of higher education, and by private institutions. Achievement lists for secondary schools, with admission rates to the competitive university system, are required to be published regularly.
- Each school is to set up an advisory board consisting of representatives of local authorities, parents and teachers.
- The modification of the Law in 1996 outlined services to be provided by schools (for example, class size, number of teachers to be employed, and number of daily classes). The Minister of Education would provide the framework of the curricula for different school types and would determine requirements for examinations.
- Salaries and related expenses were to be granted and paid for by the national government. However, local authorities had to use their own income, in addition to state subsidies, to maintain the school system. State subsidies were to come in block grants, while the per capita quota would be discontinued.

In sum, the 1993 Law of Public Education terminated the centrally orchestrated educational system and teachers' superordination, and declared equal rights for students, teachers and parents. The real change for Hungary is likely to occur when parents' and students' organisations become aware of their rights and are able to put them into practice.

Teachers and the Social Dynamics of the 1990s

Before the negative budgetary changes that happened in the 1990s, which reached public education relatively late, local authorities had been able to compensate for the diminishing financial resources that came from the central government. However, when the financial crisis did reach public schools, it was aggravated by steep demographic changes – a radical decrease in the number of school-age children and a consequent decrease in the need for teachers. The seriousness of the population decrease was well demonstrated by the following:

> *To simplify a complex issue, the demographics of Hungary at present are characterized by the following data: in 1994, 116,000 children were born (11.3 per thousand inhabitants) and 148,000 people died (14.4 per thousand). Owing to the difference in these figures, the population decreased by 32,000 (3.2 per thousand), which means that the Hungarian population decreases at a more rapid rate than the population of any other country in the world. (Andorka, 1996, p. 21)*

From a financial point of view, the most difficult years for Hungary were 1995 and 1996. A very stringent crisis management arrangement, the 'Bokros package' named after the Minister of Finance, was introduced on 12 March 1995 and contained severe financial measures. This financial and economic package aimed at the stabilisation of the national budget. However, this programme was loaded with what many see as senseless, irrational, and irritating elements, some of which later were considered unconstitutional by the Constitutional Court (Szüdi, 1998). For the Socialist–Liberal government, knowledge and intellectual capital were at the bottom of the list of things to be taken care of and, thus, they fell victim to all kinds of economising needs that followed from the principle of uniform withdrawal of state resources from all areas. In the mid-1990s, culture, the sciences, and education were neglected because the Social–Liberal government did not believe that the development of education and research would provide the necessary breakthrough in economic growth, nor would it close the economic gap that existed between Hungary and her neighbours. Higher education experienced a more than 40% budgetary cut, pushing these institutions to the sidelines of their operational boundaries. Research suffered the same drastic measures. With respect to secondary education, this period was characterised by school closures, terminated services, dismissals of teachers, and an aggressive coverage of these events in the media. In addition, the real value of teachers' salaries decreased dramatically, not even reaching three-quarters of average per capita GDP (1998 data) (Szüdi, 1998), which was the usual measure of the relative value of teachers' salaries. Among all western European countries, the proportion of adults claiming that the teaching profession was not prestigious was by far the highest in Hungary.

The introduction of tuition fees into the traditionally free-of-charge university system – a measure cancelled in 1998 with the advent of a new election and a new government – led to social unrest. Prior to 1994, university admission had been solely merit-based and selective, and need-based grants had been extended to eligible students. The disappearance of the industrial basis for vocational training made the situation even more dramatic. Social differences deepened due to increased unemployment and to a decrease in the real value of salaries.

On the other hand, conflicts based on ideological differences diminished. Self-governing educational management and local financing began to stabilise, partly because of increased institutionalisation and partly because of the implementation of the National Core Curriculum.

Since the number of students decreased, a favourable student/teacher ratio was created in Hungary, because the excess number of teachers was not reduced immediately. Several new developments also kept the need for teachers high, including the sudden rise in the number of independent schools, changes in the school structure, the expansion of high school education, the introduction of the 1992 Law on the legal standing of civil servants, and the 1993 decrease in the required number of weekly classes to be taught by public school teachers.

General Education Statistics for Hungary in the 1990s

In 1999 Hungary spent only 3.9% of its GDP on education, as compared to the average Organisation for Economic Cooperation and Development (OECD) annual rate of 5-6%. While education spending in Hungary rose from 5.9% to 6.8% between 1990 and 1992, it has been decreasing ever since. According to a report by the Ecostat Institute for Economic Analysis and Information Technology (2000), three factors have had major effects on the school system from 1989 to 1999: globalisation, pre-admission to the European Union, and the post-communist transformation of the Hungarian society and economy. Over that decade, 97-98% of school-age children participated in primary school education, with a significant shift from vocational schools to comprehensive secondary schools, corresponding with trends in other OECD countries. In 1999, 69% of secondary school students were in comprehensive schools, while 27% pursued vocational training. In 1989, the respective

125

figures were 48% and 45%. However, it should also be noted that 68.5% of people in the 15-19-year-old age group attended secondary schools, as opposed to 77.2% of those in the relevant age group in other OECD countries. The changes in higher education were even more significant. The number of full-time students doubled in that decade, with an even steeper rise if part-time students were taken into consideration. In 1999, 17.6% of the 18-25-year-old age group attended college (an increase from 10.7% in 1990).

DISCUSSION OF FINDINGS OF THE HUNGARIAN STUDY

Since teachers bear most of the burden of educational changes, it is important to examine and describe their perception regarding changes in their work lives. A total of 34 interviews was conducted in nine high schools located in different parts of Hungary (all of them outside of Budapest), in city and village centres. Thirty-four teachers were interviewed: 23 were female and 11 were male, and teacher ages ranged from 35 to 45 years. Five senior teachers, who had been practitioners in their schools for at least five years, and therefore had a broad overview of changes in their schools, were selected from each school. The teachers represented various subjects: 19 were teachers of the humanities, 10 were science teachers, and five were shop teachers. A semi-structured questionnaire discussion was held with each individual teacher. Data were coded using the standardised coding manual produced by the Consortium for Cross-Cultural Research in Education (CCCRE).

The Nature of the Most Important Change

After the 1989 transition to democracy, the first measures the new government promulgated about education related to freedom of speech, conscience, and religion. Therefore, the fact that the most significant change identified by the sample of Hungarian teachers was 'subject matter changes' echoed these relevant concerns of the whole Hungarian society. Eleven (32.3%) of the teachers stated that 'subject matter changes' were the most significant changes of the past few years. This was because changes in the humanities and social sciences were still some of the most important areas of educational reform in Hungary. Several periods of Hungarian and world history were taught for many years from a deeply biased ideological perspective. These need to be re-evaluated, cleansed of their propaganda, and then taught more objectively.

The information-age explosion and the unique political changes of the 1990s, and the interaction of these two phenomena in Hungary since 1989, was a second major change identified by the teachers. The regular application of computers to the classroom and the introduction of computer science in the curriculum were quite challenging for both teachers and students. A third major change mentioned by six (17.6%) of the respondents was structural changes in terms of adding the new 6+6 years and 4+8 years patterns to the school systems. Both teachers and students had to adjust to new age-related groupings for students in both primary and secondary institutions of education. Other structural changes included changing class sizes and changing scheduling.

Debates about the different core curriculum proposals forced schools – while competing for students and therefore for their own survival – to outline a new profile. Besides the traditional four-year secondary school structure, a six-year secondary school structure was also established, when children move to secondary education after the sixth grade at age 12 instead of 14. The particulars of the admission procedure were developed along with a new curriculum and other requirements.

Other areas mentioned included significant changes concerning students ('new generations are less and less suitable for independent study' and 'students bring less from home'); students' interests; issues concerning applied methods and textbooks; and the possibility of altering subject matter content even during the school year. Statements such as 'one was allowed to change the teaching material even during the academic year' alluded to the greater freedom gained by teachers in doing away with central plans, while 'teaching history in the German language' indicated the boom in bilingual education, something vastly different from, say, the USA counterpart. In Hungary, students compete to be involved in secondary school education in English, German and Spanish when most of the subjects are taught in the respective foreign language. Therefore, in such schools students complete their high school education in five years instead of the standard four. Many teachers agreed with the typical statement that there now was a 'greater freedom in selecting the subject matter and methods' and that 'there are more tools available, such as video players'. A few other respondents touched upon changes regarding the ownership of schools, increased independence, and a freer atmosphere, as indicated by the comment that 'the principal was democratically elected' (Teacher 32). In addition, methodological experimentation led to great satisfaction:

> Due to the transformation it became possible to engage in education with a new approach, for example by teaching integrated humanities–linguistics, literature, and culture. We have prepared our own curricula and examination requirements to be taken at the end of the second year.
> (Teacher 15)

One teacher commented that 'It became possible to engage in group teaching' (Teacher 13).

127

The Perceived Origin of the Change
and Teachers' Role in the Change

More than half of the interviewed teachers in Hungary believed that the major changes affecting their jobs were initiated by the school in a number of ways and for a number of reasons. For example, one mentioned that a dialogue between the central authorities and local educational administrators developed:

> *The school has changed its profile based on the suggestion of*
> *the school management and after consultations with the Board*
> *and the Ministry of Education. (Teacher 12)*

Or the change was seen as the product of the need to replace the old, discredited socialist ideology:

> *Educators of the school initiated the change. The Marxist*
> *curriculum had collapsed and since there was no national*
> *trend, a local change was initiated. (Teacher 18)*

When computer science education made its way into the public schools and computer literacy as a requirement was accepted, a new phenomenon emerged – applying for grants. There evolved the opportunity to lobby private and government foundations in order to raise money for the school, and to write applications/proposals for grants in order to raise money for equipment and computer training for teachers. Suddenly, the capitalist notion of fundraising emerged. As described by one teacher:

> *Following the national trend closely, the school management*
> *has presented us the opportunity to write a proposal to the*
> *World Bank for funding to sponsor training. (Teacher 17)*

Other respondents saw that the school initiated the changes out of necessity:

> *The change occurred because the whole school system*
> *disintegrated – due to the change of regime – which made it*
> *possible to establish new types of schools. (Teacher 14)*

Some schools developed an environment where creativity was encouraged:

> *Small working groups of teachers headed by the principal*
> *could claim ownership of designing the change. (Teacher 15)*

The notion of 'everybody on his/her own' soon emerged, thus expelling the long-existing tradition of casting blame on the 'system'. One respondent noted:

*It is a very complex question and the initiators cannot really
be identified. Teachers initiated discussions with one another.
Hence we discussed superimposition while the school
management would consider parental feedback. (Teacher 26)*

Two 'new' factors of the education process actively emerged, as one
teacher noted:

*It was a self-initiated change with the help of students and
parents. (Teacher 25)*

Second in significance in terms of the perceived origin of change was
initiation from the government, which was the role of national
institutions. Nearly 6% indicated that the central government played an
important role in the changes. A typical comment was that the
'Government initiated the introduction of information science' (Teacher
19).

Considering their well-described, active role in the implementation
of the change, many teachers felt justified in viewing themselves as
initiators, planners, decision makers, and implementers of the recent
changes. For example, four teachers commented similarly that:

*I was an initiator. I have created the technical conditions and
developed the substantive and methodological sides of
education by myself. In the meantime, I have also engaged in
taking training courses at the university. (Teacher 19)*

The Objectives of the Changes

The most frequently stated objective of the changes reported by the
teachers was the need to increase students' knowledge. Ten teachers
(29.4%) declared that changes were essential in order to keep pace with
technical and scientific developments. However, reaction to political and
then ensuing societal changes also played an important role, according to
seven (20.5%) of the interviewees. While describing the objectives of the
changes, several teachers also mentioned integration with, and
adjustment to, European standards. Language teachers referred to a
needed 'adjustment to the global hegemony of the English language' as a
major objective, and 'the increased importance of acquiring the highest
level at national language proficiency examinations' in order to enhance
university admission opportunities. The selective university admission
system offers extra credits for medium and high degree proficiency
examinations, out of the three levels of basic, medium, and high.

When talking about the speed of the implementation of reforms, 23
(82.1%) of the teachers stated that changes were implemented gradually
through the years:

> *We have developed, improved, and adjusted to central*
> *guidelines gradually. It was true for the past and will be true*
> *for the future as well. (Teacher 19)*

One teacher gave a slightly different slant to this process:

> *It has been implemented with the understanding that it will be*
> *changed. (Teacher 18)*

Flexibility was recognised to be of the utmost importance. One respondent stated:

> *It has been a flexible curriculum made up of parts which*
> *could be further developed. Practice will show when we need*
> *to modify. Hopefully, the basic ideas and frames will hold*
> *true. (Teacher 14)*

Only a few teachers reported drastic or dramatic changes that were implemented without any prior preparation and consultation with the staff. One said:

> *Since it came from above, I was expected to execute it*
> *immediately. (Teacher 11)*

Circumstances Assisting or Hindering the Changes

It is important to acknowledge that, in an atypical unison, almost all the teachers reported experiencing help and support from the schools and local authorities. For example, as one teacher acknowledged:

> *both personal inquiry and being urged by the school*
> *management, in addition to financial support to raise*
> *resources for the technical background. (Teacher 19)*

Speaking about the introduction of teaching history in German, one respondent noted:

> *I had to recognise its necessity. I was actively involved in*
> *developing the details. (Teacher 12)*

Speaking about the introduction of English special classes, one teacher said that:

> *For a while we received some money to buy books, listening*
> *materials. The Principal supported our establishing exchange*
> *connections with foreign countries. (Teacher 25)*

When it was appropriate, interviewees readily acknowledged help from colleagues and students. Finally, the assistance most frequently mentioned by the teachers had more to do with the development of their own personal competence, in terms of their professional skills, as well as their own empathy towards the initiated change, and the importance of their own earlier experiences in effecting the changes.

The most frequently mentioned impediment to change was the lack of financial resources. Speaking about the introduction of computer science in the curriculum, one teacher described the circumstances in this way:

> *It necessitated a significant amount of professional development and was extremely time-consuming. Too little financial resources to follow up on technical development were given. (Teacher 19)*

One respondent noted the problems caused by:

> *financial factors and now the fact that three of the English teachers were fired. (Teacher 25)*

Another described a:

> *lack of financial rewards. I will not innovate from my own resources – although I would have ideas – because it is not supported financially and my turncoat colleagues are jealous. (Teacher 6)*

However, speaking about teaching history in German, one respondent claimed that thorough preparation for the changes seemed to have been missing altogether:

> *We did not have any experience. There was no example whatsoever in the area for a similar change. We were left on our own. (Teacher 12)*

Effects on the Working Life of the Teachers

When asked to describe how recent educational changes had impacted teachers' work and the things that they do, 23 (67.6%) of the interviewees reported that the changes had affected much or almost all of their work life, while 8 (23.5%) interviewees reported that all of their work has been affected. Many of them (14, or 41%), felt that their work had become all-consuming, with preparation for classes needing more time and energy. However, teachers also admitted that teaching had become more interesting, and interaction with students had become more dynamic. One said, 'It encouraged me to make some effort' (Teacher 20) and another, 'I have increased my professional responsibilities' (Teacher 32). A few teachers even spoke about better-prepared and more inquiring students, and expressed satisfaction about the methodological and subject-matter-related innovations. Consequently, the changes have positively affected the professional development of many of the teachers. Two-thirds reported that they were professionally more informed and more open towards further innovations. For one teacher this was a major shift:

> *I was thoroughly motivated to participate in further training exercises. I sought out new materials to teach and even took a computer course. (Teacher 17)*

Another respondent stated that:

> *teaching needs continuous professional training and a teacher needs to be up to date about the news of technical development. It is really time-consuming. (Teacher 19)*

Only one teacher experienced negative effects professionally, although two mentioned recent major changes taking place in their professional fields.

Impact on Time-Use

Almost 50% of the teachers declared a need for more classroom preparation time and only one respondent associated the recent changes with gaining time spent on school-related issues. The rest of the teachers perceived the transformation and rationalisation of work time as positive developments, since they allowed for a better prioritisation of work and more relaxed individual work time, as well as for less time spent on discussions and meetings. Absolutely no effect on time-use was reported by 11.5% of teachers.

However others' comments varied: 'Preparation time has grown' (Teacher 19). 'I have more work, but it did not cause any serious problem' (Teacher 25). 'I began to read more professional literature', said Teacher 31 after realising that the diminished interest of students in physical education allowed him to extend his preparation time. Complaints were also expressed: 'I have longer work-time and spend more time at school without any special purpose' (Teacher 6), and 'I need more time for preparation and free time has been radically decreased' (Teacher 12).

The Effect of Change on Students

Asked to assess how much of students' learning and experience at school have been affected by the educational changes, most teachers perceived a greater impact on students than on their own teaching. The transformation and innovations were reported by 90.9% of the teachers as affecting students' work life, while a minority detected only a small or insignificant impact. For example:

Students are very well informed, follow the news, and
understand the world of politics and economics. I have
improved relations with the parents as well. (Teacher 25)

Thirteen teachers listed a number of positive changes they noticed among their students, including increased inquisitiveness, more openness, and more activity. Nine other respondents mentioned that their students have become more informed, versatile and cooperative, and have acquired better communication skills. Only a few responses reflected negative perceptions, seeing some high school students becoming less interested (in a subject), more alienated or groundless, or undertaking more work than they could accomplish.

Impact of the Changes in Relationships

Twelve teachers (35.1%) did not detect any significant changes at all in their collegial relationships. This is compared to one of them who detected more strained relationships and conflicts with colleagues, and another who experienced more harmonious relationships with colleagues than before. One teacher described the impact of the change in relationships: 'Positively, because I became more open' (Teacher 31). Speaking about the introduction of teaching special English classes, one said, 'I have developed a closer relationship, mainly with those who also teach in special groups' (Teacher 25).

As for enhanced interpersonal relationships, teachers successfully adjusted to the practical necessities brought about by the changed circumstances. The adjustment process initiated more communication and discussion among them, something perceived as very positive and invigorating:

I have become a bit isolated professionally. I regularly help my
colleagues and the school management in computer
applications. (Teacher 19)

Reaction to Future Similar Changes

During the 18 years, there have been several profile changes,
which always is a challenge for the pedagogue. After a while
one gets tired of it. It is only with our active participation that
we are able to offer our best for the sake of the children.
(Teacher 12)

This remark summarised the general attitude of the Hungarian teachers. All in all, respondents' reactions to participating in future changes were dependent on their experiences and impressions of this earlier set of changes. As reported by one teacher:

133

> *I have a positive view due to results achieved. Active*
> *participation in the changes influences one's attitude*
> *positively as well. (Teacher 19)*

Another said:

> *It is time to confront our own interests and tackle our*
> *problems. So far we have always accepted everything.*
> *(Teacher 31)*

A third declared:

> *The special English class was implemented, I had good*
> *experiences, and therefore, I would be glad to shoulder further*
> *roles. (Teacher 25)*

Many of the teachers indicated a strong willingness to assume responsibility in future changes as supporters rather than opponents. Only one of the Hungarian teachers mentioned that she was not willing to take any responsibility in any future process of educational change. On the other hand, 16 interviewees made statements indicating an attitude of passive cooperation with future changes/reforms. None of the teachers would decline participation in future changes as long as they were thoroughly informed, and most of them would assist in promoting the success of future changes by contributing their own ideas. As noted by one teacher:

> *It would make some difference to see what the essence and*
> *goal of the changes are, and with whom I should work*
> *together. (Teacher 6)*

Fewer – only one-third of the respondents – would participate actively in changes or contribute with evaluations. Only a few would assume active roles such as membership of the supervisory committee. Clearly, their participation would depend on the nature of the expected changes. In addition, one-fifth of the interviewees demanded that teachers be involved actively in the implementation of such changes. Fifteen (44.1%) reported a positive effect of participation in the current changes on their willingness to participate in future changes. On the other hand, eight (23.5%) reported a negative effect.

CONCLUSIONS

In 1995, the teachers in our study identified different aspects of educational changes that significantly affected their work life. These major changes related to pedagogical subject matter, to the structure of education, and to qualities of their students. They identified improving and expanding students' knowledge and adjusting the teaching curriculum to political and societal changes as the main objectives of the recent changes. The teachers also highly valued the fact that the recent changes forced them to become more informed and better prepared in their professional fields, and they perceived the resulting rationalisation and prioritisation of their teaching specialties as added bonuses. None of the teachers indicated a complete unwillingness to participate actively in any future changes.

Clearly, the major political and economic changes that occurred in Hungary during the 1990s, a period of dramatic change as the country underwent the process of transition to democracy, had an impact on every aspect of life – from the economy to the issue of increasing crime rates to the nature of education. Three qualities characterised Hungarian public education in this period as it adjusted to the transition: crisis, accommodation and stabilisation. From the late 1980s through the time of our study in 1995, Hungary's public education experienced both crisis and accommodation. The crisis was caused by the collapse of a centrally planned economy and society, where the educational system was a core component of that central control. The new governments of the 1990s launched reforms that decentralised education, moving much decision-making authority and responsibility to the local government level and to the schools themselves. When asked about the major changes in their schools, without exception the response of the Hungarian teachers was that they were part of the ongoing change and transition in the larger society. This was the point of origin for all the major reforms.

The results of the reforms depended on the skill of local and school officials and teachers to adapt to the new external political and economic environment in the country. Schools that dealt most successfully with the changes were those that had school principals or other officials or teachers who actively contributed ideas, time, or enthusiasm to exploiting the new opportunities offered by public education, while schools with officials or teachers who passively accepted the changes but did little to embrace the new opportunities lagged behind.

After a period of change and adaptation, one would expect that institutions and officials move into a stabilised pattern of interaction among teaching colleagues, various governmental levels, and with students and parents. In Hungary this stabilisation process could have been expected to occur by the mid-1990s. It did not, and the main reason for this was less to do with the lack of adaptation by lagging schools (although this surely was a problem), than by a new crisis that overcame the educational system. The social changes that occurred in the earlier moves towards democracy finally caught up with the education system by the mid-1990s in the form of a renewed financial crisis. The effects on Hungarian public education of the drastic cut in the national budget for education, plus the recession of the early 1990s were delayed because local governments provided much of the financial shortfall. However, by the mid-1990s they could no longer afford to do this. This new financial

135

shortfall interrupted the process of stabilisation of the recent reforms that were just starting to happen, throwing the education system again into renewed difficulties and uncertainties. Since our study was conducted in 1995, this fact must be kept in mind in considering our findings.

Further, the economic recession and crisis in the national budget meant a drastic cut in the level of resources for both school infrastructure (buildings, equipment, and supplies) and teacher salaries. Local governments were able to provide funds to cover these cuts to a major extent, but only until the mid-1990s. After that, the reforms introduced had to be dealt with within a context of declining financial resources.

While the Hungarian public's traditional high expectation of its well-regarded educational system has not changed, the system itself did change – its structure, subject matter, methods, technical background, and major participants. Due in part to a decrease in the size of the student body and in the number of teachers, education has diversified and teachers are motivated to develop professionally and methodologically; something that seems to appeal to them.

When asked about changes within the schools, without exception all spoke about the effects of external political and financial factors. Illuminating all teaching changes (or non-changes) cannot be done without describing the relationship between the social environment (i.e. societal, economic, and political relations) and the school. The relation between the school and the circumstances appeared to be a core problem in schools where no internal innovative and restructuring process had been initiated. Economic and educational policy uncertainties make these institutions more defenceless than those that strive to become independent and hasten to respond to changes and expectations.

References

Andorka, R. (1996) Demographic Changes and their Main Characteristics, in Pál Péter Tóth & Emil Valkovics (Eds) *Demography of Contemporary Hungarian Society.* New York: Columbia University Press.

Ecostat Institute for Economic Analysis and Information Technology (2000), in *MTI In-depth Weekly Analysis,* 11 August. Budapest: Mikroszkóp. Available online at: http://www.securities.com

Szüdi, J. (1998) A változás iskolája [The school of change], in *Élet és Irodalom* [Life and literature], Budapest, Hungary, 15 May.

The Impact of Change on Teachers' Work Lives: the Israeli experience

ZEHAVA ROSENBLATT & LYA KREMER-HAYON

THE ISRAELI EDUCATIONAL SYSTEM

The Israeli educational system can be characterised by two main and contrasting features: one is the heterogeneity of the student body, and the other is the centralised nature of the educational administration.

The first feature, heterogeneity of the student body, is represented in both school structure and students' background. Israeli schools are divided along national (Jews, Arabs), religious (secular, traditional, ultra-orthodox), and ideological (kibbutz, urban) lines. Each of these groups has its own school sub-system and maintains its unique cultural distinction. Accordingly, diverse emphases and different interpretations of educational themes also characterise each. These differences often become sources of tension, since each unique group is backed up and supported by political stakeholders who frequently assign more importance to partisan interests than to educational considerations.

In addition to national, religious, and ideological differences in students' backgrounds, heterogeneity is also the result of heavy immigration to the country. As a 'melting pot' nation, Israel has been absorbing unprecedented numbers of immigrants from various countries since its establishment in 1948. Thus, students joining the Israeli educational system come from various backgrounds (of which the most recent are former USSR republics and Ethiopia), sometimes with large socio-economic and cultural gaps.

This pluralistic framework poses serious educational challenges to Israeli democratic society. Perhaps the most prominent is an inherent conflict between striving for equality and the need for excellence. Striving for equality stems mainly from an egalitarian ideology, which traditionally has been a prime goal of Israeli governments (Gaziel, 1993). The 1968 educational reform was a step in this direction, designed to promote under-achieving groups, such as children of immigrants from developing countries. Strategies applied by the educational system to reduce social gaps among ethnic groups included administrative measures, such as support for weak students; pedagogical means, such as experimentation with didactic measures; structural measures, such as ability groupings; and enrichment programmes with intensive focus on hard-core disadvantaged communities (Adler, 1989). Yet deep-rooted ethnic gaps between Jews and Arabs, uncompromising disagreements between orthodox and secular groups, and social distance between new immigrants and Israeli-born students still prevail (Mar'i, 1989; Kremer-Hayon, 1998), although they are relatively contained in order to achieve, at least on the surface, national consensus (Elboim-Dror, 1989).

Paradoxically, this complex system is managed by a highly centralised administration – the second feature of Israeli education. The Israeli educational system is tightly coupled, hence characterised by the awkwardness and at times the inefficiencies of a large bureaucracy. A wide range of issues, such as educational policy, teachers' employment regulations, and decisions regarding curriculum-setting and teaching materials, are settled and controlled centrally.

Despite its centralised nature, the Israeli educational administration recently has been experimenting with innovative structures such as school-based management (Vollansky & Bar-Elli, 1996) and open (rather than locally determined) school registration (Goldring & Shapira, 1993). These decentralised structures reflect an educational policy designed to enhance overall achievement and excellence, while still maintaining the principles of equality and balance (Kremer-Hayon, 1998). Inherent inconsistencies and potential conflicts, then, characterise the Israeli educational system.

These characterisations served as the background for the present study on change among Israeli school teachers. The constant need of teachers to adjust to demographic, ideological, pedagogical, and technological changes provided a fertile ground for research on change patterns and impact of change on teachers' work lives.

The methodology used in the Israeli research site will be summarised in the following section.

METHOD

Fifty-nine Israeli school teachers participated in the study. Of these, 38 (64%) were female; the average age was 42.4 and average professional and school seniority was 22.4 and 13.8 years respectively. These teachers represented schools in the northern part of Israel. The average size of the student body in these schools was about 710 students.

The participating teachers were interviewed using open-ended interview schedules, developed jointly by members of the Consortium for Cross-Cultural Research in Education. The schedule of interview questions was the same for all teachers interviewed and was followed precisely. Each interview was taped and transcribed. The questionnaires contained various questions about the ways that educational change affected teachers' work lives (see below). Every interview started with a question about changes in the teacher's workplace that most influenced him/her. The change perceived by a given interviewee as having the highest impact was chosen to inspire the succeeding questions, which referred to various characteristics, antecedents and consequences of change on teachers' work lives. Data related to open-ended questions were coded according to a common codebook and content-analysed based on paragraphs as analytical units.

For purposes of analysis the variables used were grouped under two headings: (1) change characteristics and antecedents, and (2) impact of change. They are listed next by the order of the questions posed to the interviewees.

Change Characteristics and Antecedents

Q1: Domain of change (change content)
Q2: Origin of change (change initiator)
Q3: Objective of change (change goal)
Q4: Teacher's role in change (involvement level)
Q5: Timetable for change (continuous or gradual)
Q6: Forces helping implementation (internal and external)
Q7: Forces impeding implementation (internal and external)

Impact of Change

Q8: Impact of change on teachers
8a: Impact of change on work lives
8bc: Impact of change on things you do
8d: Impact of change on relationships
8e: Impact of change on use of time
8f: Impact of change on teachers' professional development
Q9: Impact of change on students
9a: Impact of change on students' learning and experience
9b: Nature of impact on students
Q10: How teachers feel about change
Q11: Impact of change on future participation
11a: Impact of change on participation in similar changes
11h: Impact of change on participation in any other change

RESULTS

Change Characteristics and Antecedents

Results referring to questions on characteristics and antecedents of change are presented in this section and summarised in Table I.

Study Question	Categories	Respondents	
		n	%
Q1: Domain of Change	Teaching	32	56.1
	Student experience	16	28.1
	School management	6	10.5
	Learning outcomes	3	5.3
Q2: Origin of change	School initiated	29	50.0
	Teacher initiated	15	25.9
	Government initiated	11	19.0
	Community initiated	3	5.1
Q3: Objective of change	Improve education	27	54.0
	Social objectives	13	26.0
	Accountability/efficiency	10	20.0
Q4: Teachers' role in change	Initiator	20	35.1
	Implementer	16	28.1
	Shared decisions	11	19.3
	Planner	7	12.3
	Supporter	1	1.7
	No role	1	1.7
	Resister	1	1.7
Q5: Timetable for change	Use gradually	40	72.7
	Use immediately	15	27.3
Q6: Forces helping implementation	Support provided	39	70.9
	Resources provided	23	41.8
	Professionalism	20	36.4
Q7: Forces impeding implementation	System resources	17	51.5
	Implementation and/or decision-making process	7	21.2
	Personal resources	5	15.2
	Opposition	4	12.1

Table I. Characteristics and antecedents of change.

Q1: Domain of Change

The main domain of change revolved around issues concerning teaching. Typical teaching-related issues mentioned were computerisation of teaching materials and changes in standard tests (*n* = 32, 56.1%). The second largest category concerned students' experiences, such as changes in the student council (e.g. replacement of a member) (*n* = 16, 28.1%).

Other changes were related to school management, such as the establishment of a 'management advisory board' [1] ($n = 6$, 10.5%). The lowest ranking group of changes was related to learning outcomes, such as changes in evaluation methods ($n = 3$, 5.3%). The overwhelming majority of the changes in Israel (89.5%) centred on micro-level school functions (teaching, students' experience, and learning outcomes), and only 10.5% were related to macro-level school management.

Q2: Origin of Change

Schools (principals and other position holders such as vice-principals, programme coordinators) were perceived as initiating the largest number of the changes ($n = 29$, 50%), while communities were least involved in change initiation ($n = 3$, 5.1%). About one-quarter of the respondents (in particular, classroom teachers) saw teachers as initiators ($n = 15$, 25.9%). Government initiation was relatively low ($n = 11$, 19%), which is a surprising result for a centralised system. Thus, most of the changes (75.9%) in Israeli schools were initiated internally (teachers and school administration), in contrast to most other countries, where the majority of changes were initiated externally. To emphasise the importance attached to the origin of the change, one of the respondents used the metaphor 'pregnancy', denoting a lengthy and critical initiation phase.

Q3: Objective of Change

As in most other countries, the main objective of change in the eyes of Israeli teachers was to improve education ($n = 27$, 54%) through the improvement of academic development and quality of teaching. The next objective was socially related ($n = 13$, 26%), such as the promotion of more value-driven behaviour among students (e.g. behaviour reflecting values related to human relations, friendship, integrity, and loyalty). Only 10 (20%) respondents indicated accountability/efficiency (such as the need to fit curricula to changing environmental demands) as a change objective.

In addition, the Israeli respondents mentioned other objectives as expected by-products of the planned change. For example, teachers said that the change would make the school healthy, move the school forward, refresh it, introduce methods and order, and take maximal advantage of abilities and resources. In many cases change was viewed not as a local and defined programme but as an opportunity for a systemic turnabout in the school's functioning and effectiveness.

Q4: Teachers' Role in Change

The majority of respondents to this question viewed themselves as assuming active roles in change, mostly as initiators ($n = 20$, 35.1%). Change initiation, for Israeli teachers, meant proposing ideas for change. In this sense, Israeli teachers were exceptional compared with all other countries, whose teachers almost unanimously mentioned implementation as their major role. For Israeli teachers, implementation was the second most prominent role ($n = 16$, 28.1%). Next came sharing decisions ($n = 11$, 19.3%), followed by the role of planning ($n = 7$, 12.3%), and lastly the role of supporting ($n = 1$, 1.7%). One teacher indicated no role involvement and one reported actual resistance.

When the role in the change was viewed as a form of change ownership, 38 (66.7%) Israeli teachers were classified as high owners (initiators, planners, sharing in decision-making), 17 (29.8%) were classified as medium owners (implementing, supporting), and only 2 (3.5%) were classified as low owners (no role, resisters). High ownership, for example, was exemplified in one teacher's statement that, following the change, 'I started to feel that I can influence and lead to value change in students and some teachers'.

Q5: Timetable for Change

Most of the changes reported were implemented in a continuous, gradual manner (72.7%). A similar pattern was reported in all other countries. One Israeli teacher said: 'I saw to it that the change would be introduced gradually to ensure success ... I think that sudden departures are dangerous'. Another teacher said: 'We introduced the change in a gradual manner to avoid anarchy'.

Q6: Forces Helping Implementation

The Israeli teachers indicated that changes were supported ($n = 39$, 70.9%), referring to help from school, state administration, colleagues and students. In the case of school administration, 'support' was described as 'attentive' to needs and refraining from pressures for speedy progress. The principal's personal persistence and goal orientation was also mentioned as a supporting force. It was stated by 23 (41.8%) teachers that resources were provided (mainly financial and human), and 20 (36.4%) teachers mentioned professionalism (mainly their own attitudes) as a major helping force. In most other countries professionalism was mentioned as the second most important source of help. An example of professionalism is seen in one teacher's comment that the change matched her professional philosophy.

Q7: Forces Impeding Implementation

Seventeen (51.5%) Israeli teachers saw system resources (mainly financial) as the main hindrance to change. Another example of system resources was the provision of relevant training to change agents. Implementation problems (such as students not being ready for change), and decision-making forces (such as too little planning) were noted by seven teachers (21.2%). Five teachers (15.2%) mentioned personal resources, such as lack of time and their own incompetence. Only four teachers (12.1%) mentioned actual opposition as an obstacle to change. Israeli teachers were less evenly spread on this question than teachers in most other countries, with lack of system resources playing a relatively large role in impeding change in Israel.

Impact of the Change

Results referring to questions on the impact of change on teachers' work lives are presented in this section and summarised in Table II.

Q8a: Impact of Change on Teachers' Work Lives

When asked how much of their work and work lives as teachers had been affected by the change, Israeli teachers ranked the impact of change as 5.16 (n = 56) on a 1 (lowest) to 6 (highest) scale. Israeli teachers seemed to be comparatively more affected by change than their counterparts in the other countries investigated (the mean impact on work lives in the other countries was 3.96 (n = 461). Obviously, the impact of change could take different forms. While one teacher said, 'I felt I'm becoming a powerful person', another confessed that he is becoming a 'robot' under the pressure of implementing change.

Q8bc: Impact on Things You Do

Change affected mostly (n = 25, 55.6%) interactive teaching, including teaching content and methods. For example, teachers reported increased use of instructional aides, and being more flexible in teaching by constantly looking for new ways and methods. Change also affected, albeit to a lesser degree (n = 11, 24.4%), pre-/post-teaching (that is, teachers' emphasis on students' evaluations and records, and better planning). Unlike most other countries, only a few Israeli teachers saw change as affecting their coping abilities (n = 4, 8.9%). One of these teachers said: 'I started daring to ask questions and fearlessly stating my opinions'. Five (11.1%) indicated no change on things they did.

Zehava Rosenblatt & Lya Kremer-Hayon

Study question	Categories	n	%	Mean	Range
Q8: Impact of change on teachers					
8a: Impact of change on work life			56.0	5.16	1–6
8bc: Impact of change on things you do	Interactive teaching	25	55.6		
	Pre/post-teaching	11	24.4		
	Personal (teacher)	4	8.9		
	coping	5	11.1		
	No change				
8d: Impact of change on relationships	More positive	36	67.9		
	No change	4	7.6		
	More negative	13	24.5		
8e: Impact of change on use of time	Better time use	41	69.5		
	More prioritisation	3	5.1		
	No change in time	6	10.2		
	use	9	15.2		
	Poorer time use				
8f: Impact of change on teachers' professional development	Negative	3	5.3	2.89	1-3
	Positive	54	94.7		
Q9: Impact of change on students					
9a: Impact of change on students' learning and experience		59		4.66	1–6
9b: Nature of impact on students	Positive impact	36	72.0		
	More differences	1	2.0		
	Negative impact	10	20.0		
	No impact	3	6.0		
Q10: How teachers feel about change		56		5.09	1–6

Q11. Impact of change on future participation				
11a. Participation in similar changes		58	27.57	1–30
11b. Participation in any other change in the future	Negative impact	2	2.8	2.80	1-3
	No impact	6	12.2		
	Positive impact	41	83.7		

Table II. Impact of change on teachers' work lives.

Q8d: Impact of Change on Relationships

Generally (n = 36, 67.9%), the change had a positive effect on relationships (of which most relationships were with staff [n = 29] and some were with students [n = 7]). For 13 teachers (24.5%), change negatively affected their relationships (referring to staff), and only 4 (7.6%) reported no change. Apparently, staff relationships were more important for Israeli teachers than other types of relationships. The improvements in staff relationships were attributed to an increased number of staff meetings and, as stated by one teacher, to 'frequent need to consult with other teachers'.

Q8e: Impact of Change on Use of Time

Most (n = 41, 69.5%) of the Israeli teachers, as shown in Table II, acknowledged that change improved their use of time (attributing it to more control of time). Three (5.1%) teachers reported better prioritisation, bringing to 80% teachers reporting improvement. Only nine (15.2%) teachers reported poorer time-use (less control), and six (10.2%) experienced no change. Compared with teachers in other countries, Israeli teachers held the most positive views concerning time-use. The following statement illustrates this positive attitude: 'The change helped me to use time to my satisfaction. I was able to use up extra time from which I had suffered ...'. Yet regardless of the way time was used, most teachers reported that the change was very time-consuming. As one teacher stated, 'I spend a lot of time in school, then I bring my work home, recruiting my family members also'.

Q8f: Impact on Teachers' Professional Development

An overwhelming majority of the Israeli teachers (n = 54, 94.7%) said that change affected their professional development positively, while only three (5.3%) reported negative effects. On a scale of 1 (lowest) to 3 (highest), the Israeli mean was 2.89, compared with the mean of 2.05 (n =

459) for teachers from other countries. One of the Israeli teachers said that change was a 'lever' for his professional development, and another teacher said that his knowledge and expertise were refreshed as a result of the change, since he 'had to go through training'.

Q9a: Impact of Change on Students' Learning and Experience

On a scale of 1 (lowest) to 6 (highest), the mean impact of change on Israeli students' learning and experience was 4.68, higher than that in any other country (the mean score of all other countries was 3.78, $n = 460$).

Q9b: Nature of Impact on Students

Most Israeli teachers ($n = 36$, 72.0%) acknowledged positive impact of change on their students, attributed mostly to the students' interest ($n = 19$), cooperation ($n = 8$), knowledge ($n = 5$), and others. For example, one teacher said that as a result of a change in election rules to the student council, even scholastically 'weak' students 'bloomed', having new opportunities to express themselves. Another teacher felt that change exposed students to 'more openness and flexibility'. Ten (20.0%) teachers reported negative impact, attributed mostly to more competitiveness due to pressure to express untried skills and abilities. Only three (6.0%) teachers reported no impact, and one teacher indicated some difference.

Q10: How Teachers Feel about Change

On a scale of 1 to 6 (where 1 is 'very negative' and 6 is 'very positive'), the mean score of Israeli teachers' feelings about the change was 5.1 ($n = 56$). This score was higher than the scores of all other teachers of other countries (mean 4.29, $N = 460$). Considering the dynamic nature of the Israeli educational system, characterised by rapid and major changes, this finding perhaps reflects a high level of change acceptance on the part of Israeli teachers.

Q11a: Participation in Similar Changes

On the question of whether teachers would be willing to participate in similar changes in the future, Israelis scored 27.57 on a scale of 1 to 30, where 1 was 'less willing' and 30 was 'more willing'. Israeli teachers had a higher tendency than any other group of teachers to become engaged again in similar changes (general country mean 23.07, $n = 388$).

The willingness to participate in future changes was qualified, though. One teacher said that she would be glad to cope with similar changes only if she could be involved in planning and design of the change.

Q11b. Participation in any other Change

Most of the Israeli teachers ($n = 41$, 83.7%) said they would be willing to participate in other changes in the future. Six Israeli teachers reported no impact on their willingness to participate, and few ($n = 2$, 4.1%) admitted to negative impact. Compared with other countries' teachers, Israelis had the most positive inclination to participate in future changes. On a scale of 1 (lowest) to 3 (highest), Israeli teachers scored an average of 2.80, higher than in any other country (general country mean 2.18, $n = 452$).

One teacher stated unequivocally that he saw 'every change as a challenge'. Another teacher qualified his willingness to participate: 'I am willing to undertake any role in change, as long as I am convinced that it contributes to my school, because not every change fits every case ... I am against change for the sake of change'.

Interrelationships among Indicators of Change

Table III presents the significant interrelationships among the study variables. Results show that impact of change on teachers' feelings (Q10) correlated positively with the impact of change on their work life (Q8a) and professional development (Q8f), and also with the impact of change on students' learning (Q9a). Students' learning was also positively associated with impact on teachers' work life (Q8a). The inclination of Israeli teachers to participate in similar changes (Q11a) was positively and strongly related to professional development (Q8f) and impact of change on teachers' feelings. Willingness to participate in any other change (Q11b) was correlated only with professional development (Q8f). Clearly, professional aspects of change among Israeli teachers are linked with their feelings toward change and their active orientation toward change. The two variables yielding most of the correlations with other variables were impact of change on professional development (Q8f) and impact on teachers' feelings (Q10). These observations imply that Israeli teachers were emotionally involved with change in their work, and that their professional development was an important factor. The practical implications are that these two variables – teachers' feelings and teachers' professional development – need to be considered in planning for change.

Question	Impact on teachers' work life (Q8a)	Impact on professional development (Q8f)	Impact on student learning (Q9a)	Impact on teachers' feelings (Q10)
Impact on student learning (Q9a)	0.54 (.00)			
Impact on teachers' feelings (Q10)	0.50 (.00)	0.31 (.02)	0.41 (.002)	
Willingness to participate in similar changes (Q11a)		0.57 (.00)		0.29 (.03)
Willingness to participate in any changes (Q11b)		0.54 (.00)		

Table III. Zero-order correlation coefficients among study variables (r, *p*). Only significant results (*p* < .05) are reported.

Summary of Results

The profile of Israeli teachers in change points to positive attitudes, strong involvement, and orientation towards academic improvement. The changes that affected teachers were mostly teaching related. These changes were originated internally by school administrations and, to a lesser degree, by teachers, and they proceeded gradually and continuously. The roles taken by Israeli teachers in change were those of initiators and implementers. They were generally supported by school and state administration, but were impeded by too few financial and other resources. The impact of the nominated change on work life was mostly apparent in the areas of teaching content and methods. In addition, change affected positively teachers' relationships with staff members, use of time, professional development, and their students' learning. Finally, Israeli teachers felt highly positive about the changes they were involved in, and were willing to engage in future changes.

In comparison to teachers in other countries, Israeli teachers were unique in their tendency to initiate changes, their highly positive feelings, and their emphasis on students' learning as a prime change outcome.

DISCUSSION

In general, the results of this study show that the attitudes of Israeli teachers toward change were positive, and, moreover, were sound and contributed to schools' effectiveness. The link between positive attitudes to change and change effectiveness has been largely confirmed in organisational literature. For example, Sparks (1988) found that improving teachers were more willing to experiment in classrooms. Moreover, Rosenblatt et al (1993) showed that the positive attitudes of all stakeholders (including teachers) in a declining school district were critical and helped to turn around the organisational crisis. In another study, Waugh & Godfrey (1995) found that receptivity to educational change depended, among other things, on teachers' participation in decision-making, and on perceived support from senior staff. Indeed, Israeli teachers tended to take active roles in change, to be willing to participate in future changes, and to feel supported by senior administrators. It is therefore concluded that the attitudes and change-related behaviour of the Israeli teachers contributed to their schools' well-being.

The highly positive feelings of Israeli teachers toward internal school change can be viewed perhaps from the perspective of the Israeli work-culture framework. In a multinational study, Israeli workers were found to be more work-centred than workers elsewhere (Harpaz, 1990a; see also Kremer-Hayon & Goldstein, 1990), and consistently to hold high work-ethic standards (Harpaz, 1988). Israeli teachers were also found to value work interest over and above other work values (Harpaz, 1990b; Zarhi & Elizur, 1996). These characteristics might explain the high tendency and ability of Israeli teachers to introduce and implement changes at work. Findings indicated that Israeli teachers were focused on their work and on striving both to improve their work environment and to adjust their own skills.

Notwithstanding their generally positive attitude toward change, Israeli teachers still felt that the educational administration fell short of fully supporting changes in schools. When asked about forces helping implementation of change, only 41.8% of them mentioned resources provided, compared with 51.5% who viewed system resources as impediments to implementation (Table I). Administrative and capital resources apparently do not match the human resources in the Israeli educational system.

Some of the changes in the Israeli educational system might be explained by the unique challenges it faces. As noted, the Israeli educational administration struggles with seemingly conflicting trends to provide equality and at the same time to promote excellence. The results indicate that the most typical domain of change in Israel is teaching related, and that the emphasis on teaching methods and professional development might reflect the perceived need constantly to search for ways to bridge gaps among different groups. Indeed, as Adler (1989) argues, pedagogical changes might provide answers to differences in needs and ability levels. In future studies, however, it will be important to explore whether teachers' emphasis on academic achievements as the main objective of change is directed toward under-achieving segments of the student population.

In spite of the centralised nature of the Israeli educational system, the Israeli teachers showed a relatively high level of initiation and involvement. This tendency might stem from the democratic roots of the Israeli political culture and from strong union protection, which provides Israeli teachers with almost absolute job security (Rosenblatt & Ruvio, 1996; Ruvio & Rosenblatt, 1999). These two factors, coupled with a tendency within the Israeli educational system to contain conflicts (Elboim-Dror, 1989), seem to imply that teachers' involvement with change was authentic rather than superficial.

The high involvement of teachers in particular, and school administrations in general, in educational change emphasises the marginal role of community involvement (only 5.1% of the originators of change). Parents in Israel have traditionally played an insignificant role in schools, in spite of legislation that allows parental involvement. In a recent observational study of Israeli school principals, very little interaction was observed between principals and parents (Rosenblatt & Somech, 1998). This reality is gradually changing in Israel with the establishment of experimental community schools, the expansion of school choice (Goldring & Shapira, 1993), and the increase in political power of parents' organisations. However, these changes are too fresh and too recent to have been reflected in the current study.

Finally, Israeli teachers exhibited a significant degree of professional flexibility in response to change. Changes affected their teaching methods, improvement in their students' evaluations and planning, better use of their time, and higher professional development. It remains to be explored whether this flexibility spills over to their students, so that these students can themselves flexibly adapt to future changes.

CONCLUSIONS

The reality of Israeli school education implies a drastic need for change. Unique contextual factors related to inconsistent student backgrounds, coupled with global environmental factors related to technological and social trends, require that teachers initiate, cooperate with, and implement educational changes. The Israeli teachers studied here seemed to respond well to this challenge. They showed positive attitudes, participated actively in change efforts, and effectively adopted skills and methods needed. Change seems to contribute to teachers' professional development and self-efficacy, in spite of the fact that it also has its toll on their time and energy. Finally, judging by their comments, government and school administration have not sufficiently matched teachers' readiness for change with support and resources needed for effective response to change.

Note

[1] Management advisory boards include a number of senior teachers who are either appointed by the school principal or elected by the school teachers' body. This board has a number of advisory functions that vary from school to school depending upon the school needs and role definitions.

References

Adler, C. (1989) Israeli Education Addressing Dilemmas Caused by Pluralism: a sociological perspective, in E. Krausz & D. Glanz (Eds) *Education in a Comparative Context: studies of Israeli society*, ch. 3. New Brunswick, NJ: Transaction Publishers.

Elboim-Dror, R. (1989) Conflict and Consensus in Educational Policy Making in Israel, in E. Krausz & D. Glanz (Eds) *Education in a Comparative Context: studies of Israeli society*, ch. 4. New Brunswick, NJ: Transaction Publishers.

Gaziel, H. (1993) *Education Policy at a Crossroads between Change and Continuity: education in Israel in the past decade.* Jerusalem: Institute for the Study of Educational Systems.

Goldring, E.B. & Shapira, R. (1993) Choice, Empowerment and Involvement: what satisfies parents? *Educational Evaluation and Policy Analysis*, 15, pp. 396-409.

Harpaz, I. (1988) Variables Affecting Non-financial Employment Commitment, *Applied Psychology: an international review*, 37, pp. 235-248.

Harpaz, I. (1990a) The Meaning of Work: summary and relevance for Israeli society, in *The Meaning of Work in Israel: its nature and consequences*, ch. 14. New York: Praeger.

Harpaz, I. (1990b) The Importance of Work Goals: an international perspective, *Journal of International Business Studies*, 21, pp. 75-93.

Kremer-Hayon, L. (1998) Political and Cultural Influences on Educational Change in Israel, paper presented at the American Educational Research Association meeting, San Diego, CA.

Kremer-Hayon, L. & Goldstein, Z. (1990) The Inner World of Israeli Secondary School Teachers: work centrality, job satisfaction and stress, *Comparative Education*, 26(2/3), pp. 285-298.

Mar'i, S.K. (1989) Arab Education in Israel, in E. Krausz & D. Glanz. (Eds) *Education in a Comparative Context: studies of Israeli society*, ch. 7. New Brunswick, NJ: Transaction Publishers.

Rosenblatt, Z., Rogers, K.S. & Nord, W.R. (1993) Toward a Political Framework for Flexible Management of Decline, *Organization Science*, 4(1), pp. 76-91.

Rosenblatt, Z. & Ruvio, A. (1996) A Test of a Multidimensional Model of Job Insecurity: the case of Israeli teachers, *Journal of Organizational Behaviour*, 17, pp. 587-605.

Rosenblatt, Z. & Somech, A. (1998) Work Behaviour of Israeli Elementary-School Principals: expectations vs. reality, *Educational Administration Quarterly*, 34, pp. 505-532.

Ruvio, A. & Rosenblatt, Z. (1999) Job Insecurity of Israeli Secondary-schoolteachers: sectoral effects, *Journal of Educational Administration*, 37, pp. 139-158.

Sparks, G.M. (1988) Teachers' Attitudes toward Change and Subsequent Improvements in Classroom Teaching, *Journal of Educational Psychology*, 80, pp. 111-117.

Vollansky, A. & Bar-Elli, D. (1996) Moving toward Equitable School-based Management, *Educational Leadership International*, January, pp. 60-63.

Waugh, R. & Godfrey, J. (1995) Understanding Teachers' Receptivity to System-wide Educational Change, *Journal of Educational Administration*, 33(3), pp. 28-54.

Zarhi, R. & Elizur, D. (1996) The Structure of Work Values for Religious and Non-religious Teachers, *Proceedings of the Fifth Conference of the International Society of Work Values*, Montreal, August.

The Impact of Change on Dutch Teachers

THEO WUBBELS & HANS VONK

INTRODUCTION

In this chapter we present the design and results of the Dutch study on changes in teachers' work lives. As a background for the results, we first present some information about the Dutch educational system at the time of data collection, its foundation and structure, and the characteristics of the teaching force. Because the study looked at teachers in secondary education, we focus on the characteristics of the secondary teaching force and then present information on recent developments in secondary education.

THE DUTCH EDUCATIONAL SYSTEM AND THE TEACHING FORCE

The Founding Principles of the Dutch Educational System

Freedom of Schooling

The freedom to found schools, to organise them, and to define the religious, pedagogical or other conceptions on which they are based is laid down in the Constitution. This right may be exercised within the context of educational laws, which define the structure of education, the outline of the curriculum and the foundation criteria, such as the minimum number of students, the distribution of schools founded on the same basis in a particular region, and the norms for granting. The result is a wide variety of schools at all levels. Two main categories can be distinguished: public-authority schools (+40%) on the one hand, and private schools (+60%) on the other. The latter category can be subdivided into schools based on a religious conception, such as Roman Catholic schools; schools founded by the various Protestant denominations; and more recently, Muslim and Hindu schools and a variety of private non-denominational schools which include Montessori, Dalton (Parkhurst) and Steiner (Waldorf) schools. All schools, whether public or private, that meet the requirements set by the government are financed on an equal basis. The great number of competent authorities – more than 6000 – best demonstrates the variety in the educational system. For public-run schools the competent authorities are the municipalities in which they are situated and for private schools the board has the same function.

Central Government Control

The central government defines the education policy and controls education by means of regulations and legislation, taking the provisions in the Constitution into account. This is done directly by imposing qualitative and/or quantitative standards to be met by the educational process in the schools, for example, by central school examinations. More indirectly, this is done by means of regulations concerning the finances and additional resources the schools receive and other conditions schools have to comply with, such as the qualifications of its teaching staff. The central government's chief responsibilities lie in the spheres of organisation, funding, inspection and examinations. Furthermore, their responsibilities also include the legal status of teachers: certification, career development and remuneration (Ministry of Education and Sciences, 1989).

The Structure of the System

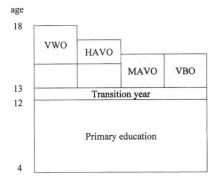

Figure 1. Structure of the Dutch educational system in 1996.

The structure of the system in 1996 is demonstrated in Figure 1. In the Netherlands compulsory education spans 12 years, from age 4 to 16, followed by two years' part-time education. Primary education starts at the age of 4 and ends at the age of 12, during which the students are placed in successive age groups (groups 1 to 8). Apart from the transition year or period, secondary education is based on the principle of streaming; that is, it consists of (i) preparatory vocational education

(VBO, 4 years), (ii) junior secondary general education (MAVO, 4 years), (iii) senior secondary general education (HAVO, 5 years) and (iv) pre-university education (VWO, including the Gymnasium, 6 years). As a consequence of the trend during the last decade to concentrate schools, the majority of schools currently represent the whole range. All secondary education starts with either a transition class (Form 1) or a transition period (Forms 1 and 2), after which the cohort is subdivided into streams on the basis of the cognitive abilities of the students: students who will attend VBO, students who are able to attend secondary general education (MAVO and/or HAVO), and those eligible for pre-university education (VWO). In principle it is possible to move from one level to another; usually this is a move downwards, and only infrequently a move upwards. If streaming up takes place, this happens usually after students have completed the examinations for one level and decide to continue their studies at a more advanced level.

Characteristics of the Teaching Force in Secondary Education

General Characteristics

Of the total number of teachers in secondary education, 70% are male and 30% female (Berkhout et al, 1998). Males still dominate in the sciences: mathematics, physics, chemistry, information technology and the other technical subjects. Tables I to III present information gathered in the same recent survey (Berkhout et al, 1998) on the composition of the teaching force by age, work experience in years of service, and level of initial education and training.

Teacher age group	21-35	36-50	51-65
Percentage of secondary teaching force	16	32	54

Table I. Composition of the teaching force by age (secondary education) (source: Berkhout et al, 1998).

In the Netherlands the average age of secondary school teachers is on the increase, which is a matter of great concern for several reasons. In coming years the number of students in junior secondary education will increase (United Nations, 1993) and, subsequently, those in senior secondary. In the same period, a considerable efflux of teachers is expected while, given the decreasing numbers of trainees in teacher education programmes, the influx of new teachers will be insufficient. Also, in coming years, a considerable shortage of teachers is expected (Vonk, 1996). In mathematics, the sciences and foreign languages in particular, the first alarming signs of this development can already be observed.

Years of teaching experience	0-5	6-10	11-25	26-40
Percentage of secondary teaching force	12	12	54	22

Table II. Work experience (in years of service) (source: Berkhout et al, 1998).

Table II shows that a large proportion of teachers in secondary education is well experienced, which usually means that they are in the middle of their careers. This stage in a teacher's professional life is characterised by reorientation on the job and by stepping back a little. One cannot expect this group to embrace changes with as much enthusiasm as the group of teachers who have less than 10 years of experience.

University degree in a subject + additional TE	Higher professional education	Part-time higher professional education
39%	39%	22%

Table III. Level of initial education and training (source: Berkhout et al, 1998).

Table III shows that the teaching force in the Netherlands is well trained.
    Another issue looked at in the 1998 survey is the teachers' motivation for choosing the profession. The motivation 'vocation' outscored all others. Vocation was scored by 64% of the teachers under 35 years of age, by 60% of the 36-50 age group, and by 55% of the senior teachers. The sub-group of teachers with a university background scored lower on vocation as their prime motivation for choosing the profession than the others; finding a job was their prime motivation.

Conditions of Service

Teaching staff in the Netherlands have a strong legal position. Teachers in public-authority schools have a legal position similar to that of central government civil servants, which is regulated by the RPBO (Legal Status Education Decree). Staff of private schools are employed on civil law contracts, but compliance with the RPBO is a prerequisite for receiving a government grant. So, if a school wishes to be funded by the central government, the school board must include RPBO provisions in its staff employment contracts. As a result, the difference in legal status between the various groups of teachers is very limited.
    The conditions of service laid down in the RPBO include the requirement that competent authorities have to draw up regulations, e.g. determining the order in which staff may be made redundant if staff numbers have to be cut, and about holiday leave during school holidays.
    The salaries and other remunerations of teachers employed by schools funded by the central government are determined by the central

government. Teachers are remunerated according to the post they hold. Each post requires a qualification as laid down in the RPBO and carries a salary determined by the salary scales embodied in the Civil Servants' Pay Decree 1984. In comparison with the conditions of service in other European countries two issues attract notice: teachers' workload and salary.

Dutch secondary teachers actually teach 954 hours per year, while the average workload in other OECD countries is + 750 hours per year (Organisation for Economic Cooperation and Development [OECD], 1995, p. 182). In addition, the teacher–student ratio is 18.8 in the Netherlands, while the average in the other European Commission (EC) countries is 14.6 (OECD, 1995, p. 180; EC, 1995, p. 40). Dutch teacher salaries are below average (OECD, 1995, p. 188) in comparison with teacher remuneration in other European countries, taking the standard of living into account. Since 1995 schools have gained more responsibility and freedom in hiring staff, setting work conditions, and offering competitive salaries.

RECENT DEVELOPMENTS IN SECONDARY EDUCATION

During the last decade, a number of major changes have taken place in secondary education, which deeply affect the work life of teachers. Some of the changes are still in the implementation phase. The changes concern restructuring the governmental management of the education sector, and far-reaching curriculum reforms for junior secondary and senior secondary education.

Governmental Management of the Education Sector

A characteristic trend in educational policies of the last two decades is the 'withdrawal' of the central government from having first responsibility for all affairs in public life that can be dealt with by the private sector. This policy is also valid for the education sector. In contrast with the last 150 years, the government today governs 'from a distance'. That policy is based on the conviction that market forces will stimulate both the effectiveness and the quality of schooling, and the efficiency of the governance of schools. This new way of governing education has led to a strong decentralisation of the responsibilities in three domains: financial management, staff policies and quality control.

Financial Management

Schools are funded on the basis of the number of students attending that type of school, the average length of time the students attend the school, the average class size, and the teachers' salary scales. Apart from that, the so-called 'overspending regulation' is in force, which results from the equal funding policy of public-authority and private schools. Municipalities (the public authority) which spend more on publicly run schools than the grant they receive from the government during a particular year have to pay an amount to the privately run schools equal to the extra amount spent on publicly run schools.

Until recently, schools were financed on the basis of a reimbursement system. Currently, a 'norm-based system' is gaining ground. In this system, a set of school variables is brought together in one formula on the basis of which the grant for a particular school can be calculated easily. Apart from teacher remuneration and a limited number of guidelines defined by the government, the boards have become more responsible for the way they handle their budget. As a consequence boards now have more freedom to set their own priorities.

Staff Policies

A similar development can be observed with respect to staff policies. Boards of schools have become more responsible for the well-being and the quality of the staff. The government no longer provides centrally organised in-service training programmes. In-service training money is distributed among the schools, which have the obligation to develop their own tailor-made in-service training plan, including purchase of the training programmes they need. In most schools staff committees are being set up to develop such plans.

A second issue in this respect is that the government no longer acts as the unrestricted safety net for teacher unemployment. The money reserved for that purpose in the annual budget of the ministry is now distributed among the schools, enabling them to finance the unemployment benefits of their teachers. As a consequence of this policy, schools with inappropriate staff policies can be confronted with major budget problems.

The third issue in this context is the access to the Disablement Insurance Act. This Act has been the safety net for more than 20 years now for everybody who becomes physically or mentally disabled during their working life, and unable to continue to work. Because of the huge costs for the government caused by the large number of people rescued by this safety net, the government made access less easy between 1995 and 2000. With respect to teacher burnout, schools today which cannot prove that they have done everything in their power to prevent use of this safety net by their teachers and to make it possible for them to continue working can be fined by the government.

Quality Control

At the same time that the government started to govern from a distance, a system for monitoring quality in and of education was set up. A good example of this approach is the school rating system. Schools are rated on the basis of a set of quality indicators and the outcomes of this check are made public (the School Quality Card). Parents can use these cards to select the right/best school for their children. On the other hand, school boards/public authorities can be held responsible if a school does not meet the criteria. Recently, a number of parents sued a city council – the formal public authority responsible for a school that failed to meet the criteria – for reimbursement of the money they had invested in extra support for their children. A school that continues to underachieve after repeated warnings may even lose its grant from the government (OECD, 1992).

The changes mentioned above, and the intensification of quality control in education, affect teachers' professional lives in so far as they can be put under pressure by the local authorities to teach in such a way that the school will meet the criteria. The decentralisation of the responsibilities for budget and staff policies has provided the school boards/local authorities with the necessary power to direct teachers in the 'desired' direction. Teachers are no longer king or queen in their own classroom.

Curriculum Reform in Junior Secondary Education

A second far-reaching change that teachers in junior secondary schools have had to face relates to the content of the profession and the kind of students they teach. In the early 1990s the educational goals for the 12-16-year-old age group were brought into line; that is, the same goals for all students. As a consequence, the curriculum for junior secondary was reformed with respect to both the content and the methodology. In the new curriculum, the acquisition of skills (cognitive skills, social skills, learning skills, basic technical skills and caring skills) and the apprehension of knowledge are of equal importance. Because acquiring skills at all levels has become an important object in the curriculum, teachers teach less, students work more on tasks, and teachers are expected to guide students' learning processes rather than to transfer knowledge.

The new curriculum – basic secondary education for the 12-16 age group– has led to a process of amalgamating the then existing different types of schools for junior secondary education. As a consequence, teachers teach a different curriculum and no longer teach students of a specific level but rather the whole range of junior secondary. This puts new demands on their professional knowledge and skills because they have to teach kinds of students they have never taught before. For example, a teacher with a qualification in an academic subject can/will be assigned to teach students from preparatory vocational education, who have a practical rather than an academic attitude to school learning.

However, this sweeping change is a challenge for teachers and an incentive to further their professional development. The large majority of teachers have taken up this challenge. Nevertheless, changes in education do not take place overnight and so the reform in junior secondary is progressing step by step.

Curriculum Reform in Senior Secondary Education

An even more sweeping change is expected to take place in senior secondary schools in the years ahead. Throughout the 1980s a number of problems regarding the preparation of the new generation for the twenty-first century and keeping the budget within acceptable limits were identified. With respect to senior secondary this resulted in the following requirements:

- to make the system more efficient, that is, to decrease the average number of school attendance years and to make better use of the available teaching time by breaking down the barriers between the traditional school subjects where possible;
- to better attune senior secondary to the input demands of tertiary education (higher vocational and university education);
- to increase student motivation by making them more responsible for their own learning processes, and to emphasise the necessity of self-regulation in learning (learning to learn).

The result is a new curriculum for senior secondary that offers the students four streams; each stream prepares for a limited range of studies in tertiary education: (i) pure sciences, mathematics and technology, (ii) nature and medical professions, (iii) economics and society, (iv) culture and society. In all subjects, acquiring the subject-related cognitive skills (productive knowledge) prevails over the acquisition of reproductive knowledge.

In order to facilitate student responsibility for their own learning, major changes in the teaching methodologies took place as of 1999. The number of teaching hours devoted to the traditional mode of whole class teaching has been reduced considerably and students mainly work either independently or in small groups on the basis of learning tasks (weekly tasks, monthly tasks, yearly tasks). For the first phase in this reform, the central objective is the increase of time spent on active student learning, also within the context of the traditional class setting. In the near future students will increasingly determine what they do and how and when they will do it.

For schools this reform implies adapting the school buildings to the new requirements; that is, creating areas suitable for self-study and extending computer facilities. The new timetable consists of only a limited number of whole class or large audience instruction periods, in addition to self-study periods, small group teaching, and teacher office hours for those who need extra help. For the teacher's role this reform implies a more drastic change. That role is expected to change from mainly being an 'instructor' to becoming the 'coach' of student learning processes. In the new context the teacher being present during all school hours may replace the principle of defining teacher workload on the basis of the number of teaching periods per week. It is obvious that all these changes will affect teacher work life.

Debate on the Professional Status of Teachers

The professional status of teachers is the issue of an equivocal debate between the government, the teacher trade unions, and other interested parties. It is emphasised in this debate that high quality teaching makes a difference in a student's school career. Furthermore, ideas such as career differentiation (from novice teacher, via junior teacher to professional teacher and finally to senior teacher), promotion criteria, merit pay, the development of teaching standards, teacher accreditation and the like are points at issue. What makes this debate so ambiguous is that on the one hand, because of the envisaged growing shortage of qualified teachers, the Minister of Education has recently decided to allow unqualified people, who have a higher education diploma in one subject or another only, to enter the profession on the condition that they are prepared to qualify by following a (part-time) teacher training programme. Related to this, we may expect that in the years ahead, in spite of all the discussions about the professionalisation of the teaching profession, the debate on the entrance requirements to the profession – competent but not qualified – will start again. On the other hand, an important advisory committee to the government on the status of teachers has recently recommended raising all teacher education to university level. In view of the rapid increase of teacher shortages it is highly questionable whether this recommendation will be implemented at all.

METHODOLOGY

So far we have discussed the contextual factors that define teachers' work life in the Netherlands. In the following part of this chapter we will report on the design and the outcomes of our study on Dutch teachers' reactions to all the changes they are confronted with, and on how they perceive the implications of these changes for their work life.

Design

The data in the Dutch study were collected in two phases. The first phase was an interview study in which 30 secondary school teachers were interviewed along the lines of the interview schedule, with internationally agreed upon open-ended questions. These teachers were chosen to cover a broad range of subjects taught, amount of experience, and type of secondary education in which the teachers were working (ranging from lower secondary to pre-university; see earlier section on 'Structure of the System'). Of the teachers that we approached, 85% were willing to participate in the study.

All the interviews were audio-taped and transcribed. The answers were coded according to the internationally developed category system. A second researcher coded 10 interviews and an inter-rater reliability (Cohen's kappa) was calculated for the categories. On average, for all the categories, Cohen's kappa was 0.86 with a lower level of 0.67. This was considered to be an acceptable reliability.

In the second phase, data were collected from 91 teachers with a questionnaire distributed by mail. The questionnaire was developed from the interview schedule. The respondents were asked to answer the questions by ticking one or more of the appropriate pre-coded categories. All the categories that had been chosen by one or more of the respondents in the interview study were included in the answering options of the questionnaire. Categories that had not been chosen were left out. The teachers were chosen randomly from all the teachers of 17 secondary schools known to the researchers because of student teachers' placement and beginning teachers' guidance programmes. The response rate for the questionnaires was 69%.

Sample

The student body of the schools of the teachers surveyed ranged from 300 to 3000. Some were located in rural areas, others in urban and suburban communities. All denominations of schools common in the Netherlands were present in the sample. The schools to our knowledge have no specific characteristics that make them not representative of the population of Dutch schools.

In order to compare the data about the 121 teachers in our sample with those presented on the Dutch teaching force in secondary education in 1998 (see the section on the 'Structure of the System') we must bear in mind that our data were gathered in 1996. Considering the low influx of teachers in the period 1996-98 we may assume that on average, the amount of experience and age of the teachers in 1996 was a little lower than in 1998. From a study conducted on Dutch physics teachers in 1984 and 1993 we estimate that this difference is about one year (see Wubbels & Brekelmans, 1997). The average age of the teachers in our sample is

42.3 and the average number of years of experience 17.0. Following the categories of Table I, the age distribution is 22% between 21 and 35, 62% between 36 and 50 and 16% between 51 and 65 years. The distribution of work experience over the categories in Table II is 7% with 0-5 years' experience and 21% with 6-10 years' experience, 57% with 11-25 years' experience and 16% with 26-40 years' experience. This means that our sample is considerably younger and is a little less experienced than the Dutch teaching force generally. Probably this is an indication that our results hold for a more active group of younger teachers than for the broader Dutch secondary teacher population.

In our sample 84% are male and 16% female. Therefore, in our sample male teachers are over-represented compared to the percentage of males (70%) in the teaching force.

RESULTS

In this section we describe the general trends in the Dutch results, with reference to the international results whenever a striking difference from the international data is noticed. Our analysis is based on frequencies of answers and correlations that are presented in tables, and cross-tabulations of several variables that are available from the authors.

We remind the reader of the fact that teachers in the interview or when answering the questionnaire have chosen a change that had affected their personal work life. All consequent reference to feelings, contexts, effects and other variables is connected to that specific chosen change. These changes therefore differ from teacher to teacher.

Feelings about the Change

Teachers in the Netherlands feel rather positive about the change (4.3 on a six-point scale ranging from 1 = very negative to 6 = very positive). This feeling is related to several characteristics of the change and the role of the teacher that will be discussed in the following sections, but it is not related to age and gender of the teacher. That this feeling is not related to age goes against the stereotype that older teachers are less willing to innovate.

The Change

Table IV presents the frequencies for answers in response to the questions about the domain, origin and objective of the most important change, and the mean score for the feelings of the teachers about the change.

Character of change		n	Feeling
Domain	School management	10	3.50
	Teaching	82	4.50
	Learning outcomes	7	4.43
	Student experiences	18	3.89
Origin	Teachers	23	4.91
	School	22	3.95
	Community	3	4.00
	Government agencies	48	4.10
	Other (unsure)	20	4.67
Objective	Improve education	55	4.58
	Improve accountability and efficiency of education	26	3.81
	Social objectives	25	4.44
	Other	11	3.91
Teacher role	Resister	5	1.60
	No role	1	4.00
	Supporter	20	4.80
	Implementer	66	4.26
	Shared decision-maker	–	–
	Planner	24	4.79
	Initiator	–	–

Table IV. Number of teachers mentioning characteristics of most important change, and their role, and the mean score on a six-point scale representing the feelings about the change (1 = very negative; 6 = very positive).

Domain

The most frequently mentioned domain of change in the Netherlands is teaching, including both changes in the curriculum and in the teaching methods. This is mentioned more frequently in the Netherlands than in any other country, but also in England and Israel this frequency is relatively high. Many teachers felt that these two domains were closely related and that a change in one was necessarily connected to a change in the other. Most teachers referred either to the reform of basic secondary education (see earlier section on 'Curriculum Reform in Junior Secondary Education') or the new curriculum for senior secondary education. Some teachers, however, mentioned older changes, such as the introduction of laboratories in science education examinations that made it necessary for the teachers to include laboratory work in their lessons.

In the category of school management, mergers of schools were mentioned. In the Netherlands there is a continuing trend towards larger schools including many different types of secondary education. These mergers appeared to have an important impact on teachers' work lives because of the emotional aspects of having to teach another type of students, and having to cooperate with new colleagues, for example.

How teachers feel about the change is related to the type of change. They feel much more positive about changes in teaching than in the school organisation.

Origin

Our results show that the origin of the vast majority of changes in Dutch secondary education can be described with three categories: initiated by national government agencies, the teachers, and the schools. Although the government adopted a strategy to govern from a distance, about 50% of the respondents felt that the origin of the most important change was a government agency. Some teachers have, however, more feelings of power and agency about changes. When describing the same changes, they mentioned teachers as the origin. Although the government announced and required the introduction of basic education, some teachers felt that they were the origins of the consequent changes in their teaching. A relatively large group of teachers (20) said they were unsure of the origin of the change. In the interviews, teachers expressed that they were not sure if general trends in society, universities or the government had started the changes. For the changes in school administration, teachers usually referred to school management as the origin of the change.

How teachers feel about the change is related to the origin: they feel much more positive about teacher-initiated than about school- or government-initiated changes.

Objective

The most frequently mentioned objective of the change was improvement of education, primarily student learning, and to a lesser degree general improvement of instruction and updating of content. Improvement of personal and social development of students was also mentioned often. Under the category 'improvement of student learning', both new goals such as modern physics, environmental consequences of technical developments, and skills such as problem-solving were mentioned. Under social development most frequently mentioned was the need for schools to help students become self-regulated learners.

Teachers feel more positive about changes that have as their objective the improvement of student learning, rather than the improvement of accountability.

Pace of Change

The pace of change in the Netherlands is not intended by its originators to be abrupt or discontinuous. In the perception of the teachers, over 80% of the changes are intended to be implemented gradually. Teachers mentioned that in practice, however, a lot of the innovations have to be implemented in a short period, although the period in which they could get acquainted with the innovation was rather long. Apparently this period is not used by the teachers to prepare themselves for implementing the change.

The Role of the Teacher

From Table IV we can see that most of the teachers see themselves as implementers, planners and supporters. The most active teacher role in the Netherlands, planner, is taken by teachers in changes that are mentioned in all categories of origins. In line with the observation that teachers can see themselves as the origin of change even when the government is the official initiator, some teachers in our sample see themselves as planners in these types of changes. In those cases they describe their role as a member of a school committee or coordinator in the subject matter department. The implementers see themselves as faithful and in general rather enthusiastically following lines that have been developed by their colleagues in the same or other schools.

Only very few teachers think of themselves as resisters and this role is observed usually in the case of government-initiated changes. Here it is important to mention that our sample may be biased; teachers who have reacted in a resistant way to educational changes may also be less willing to participate in a research project.

Not surprisingly, resisters feel much more negative about the changes than other groups of teachers, with planners and supporters being the most positive.

Helping and Impeding Forces

The forces mentioned by Dutch teachers that help implementation of change by and large are the same as those observed internationally. It seems, however, that Dutch teachers more than other teachers rely on their own capacities rather than on the support of their colleagues. They mention more often than teachers in other countries their own attitudes and capacities as helpful for successful implementation of change, and less often refer to help from their colleagues (Table V). This may be an indication of a rather individualistic character of teaching in the Netherlands. Dutch teachers often are referred to as 'kings or queens in their own classrooms'. That metaphor also shows that they have to rely on themselves when changing their teaching. Similarly, Dutch teachers mention relatively frequently that they themselves are an impediment to change because of lack of competencies while relatively few teachers mention lack of consultation as an impediment (Table V). In agreement with this result, teachers who see their attitudes and capacities as a helping force are a bit more positive (4.7) about the change than those who do not (4.0).

		Dutch		International
Forces *helping* implementation	Own attitudes regarding change	68	(59%)	39%
	Own competence	40	(35%)	22%
	Colleagues' help	27	(23%)	31%
Forces *impeding* implementation	No consultation	2	(2%)	14%
	Too many changes	47	(41%)	25%
	Self incompetence	35	(31%)	16%

Table V. Number and percentage of teachers mentioning some forces helping or impeding change.

These differences from other countries also could be an indication that teachers in the Netherlands are less ego-defensive than those in other countries. A counter-indication of this interpretation of the data is, however, the fact that Dutch teachers more often than teachers in other countries mention as an impediment that too many changes at the same time are introduced. Finally an explanation for the remarkable position of Dutch teachers could be that in the Netherlands more than in other countries, changes take place in the domain of teaching, the field where the teachers' capacities are most prominent.

Impact of the Change

From Table VI we can see that on average the teachers felt that the change had much impact on their work life but that their feeling about the change was not related to the amount of impact. The impact on students was rated as moderate, and the more teachers see the impact of the change benefiting students the better they feel about the change. No strong relationships were observed for the amount of impact with domain, origin or objective of the change.

An overview of the types of influence is presented in Table VII. Hardly any relations were observed between the type of impact and the feelings of the teachers about the change.

Impact on:	Range	Mean	Correlation with feeling
Work life	1= no; 6 = all of it	3.77	0.09
Students	1 = no; 6 = all of it	3.26	0.20*
Professional development	1 = negative; 3 = positive	2.10	-0.11
Participation in similar future change	1 = negative; 3 = positive	2.56	0.26
Participation in any other future change	1 = negative; 3 = positive	2.10	0.49**

Table VI. Mean scores and range for impact of change on several variables, and correlation with teacher's feelings about change.

Impact on things teachers do	Interactive teaching	96
	Pre–post teaching	75
	Personal coping	60
	No change	6
	Other	11
Impact on relationships	Negative	16
	No change	44
	Positive	65
Impact on use of time	Poorer time use	67
	No change	11
	More prioritising	32
	Better time use	20
Impact on students	Negative	23
	No change	13
	More differences between students	40
	Positive	64

Table VII. Number of teachers mentioning a particular impact on things teachers do, their relationships and use of time, and impact on students.

Teachers' Work Lives

It appears that in the Netherlands most changes affect both teaching in class and the planning of teaching. In fact, teachers complain that they have to spend more time and pay more attention to teaching, planning and students' work. Despite that complaint, the changes in teaching are considered positive because teachers notice that new, more informal and personal teaching methods account for easier relationships with students.

In the personal coping category, teachers refer to improving their own competence by studying and participating in in-service training activities, and to a more rushed life. The changes that they are involved in demand more work. It is important to mention that in the category 'other' we observed that teachers mention that the change has started a process of learning from each other.

From the cross-tabulations it appears that teachers who see themselves as implementers more than other teachers have problems with classroom discipline and feel that they have less control over the use of their time. Apparently, if a teacher is more a follower than an initiator of change, it is more difficult to implement the change in class without having problems with classroom discipline.

Teachers' Relationships

Only a small minority of teachers feel that the change had a negative influence on their relationships with other people (mainly colleagues). Teachers reporting better relationships equally often refer to relations with students (because of more informal, personal approaches to teaching) and to colleagues (because of the need to cooperate with them to implement changes).

Teachers' Use of Time

With regard to the use of time, relatively few Dutch teachers mention a better use of time. Many report poorer use of time; more time is used both for planning of lessons and for meetings. A smaller group of teachers also complains about lack of control over the use of their time.

Teachers' Professional Development

The change on average hardly affected teachers' professional development. This small effect in the group is, however, a consequence of the fact that one rather big group of teachers (60) reports a positive influence on their professional development and another (48), a negative influence. Teachers in the first group report that they have developed better teaching strategies, learned about student learning and individual differences, developed a broader content knowledge, and have rethought their way of teaching in general. The second group refers to time pressure as an impediment for professional development.

Students

By and large, positive effects on students are reported, such as students working harder, being more motivated and working more seriously on their tasks. It is, however, striking that some teachers report positive effects on students, whereas others report negative effects of the same kind of change. More differences between students are reported because of more heterogeneous groupings in lower secondary education.

Future Attitudes

The change on average hardly affected teachers' willingness to participate in other changes in the future. Teachers' answers about their willingness varied. Their willingness very much depends on the nature of the future change. They are in favour of participating in changes to improve classroom teaching but are much more negative about changes which would cost a lot of time or involve school organisation.

Their willingness to participate in a change similar to the one discussed in the study was more often positively than negatively influenced (Table VI). This is understandable because most of the changes in this study were about classroom teaching and, as mentioned before, teachers are willing to participate in changes in classroom teaching.

For all variables we investigated whether they were related to the teacher's disposition towards future change. No strong relationships were found between this attitude and domain, origin, or objective of the change that was the topic in this study. For the role of the teacher we found that the influence of the change process on their willingness to participate in future change was more negative for resisters than for teachers in other categories.

If teachers see time as an impediment to change they are less willing to participate in future change than if they do not see time as an impediment. However, if colleagues are seen as an impediment to change then they are still willing to participate in future change. Apparently opposition of colleagues is seen as an impeding factor different from lack of financial resources. This may be caused by the teachers' perceptions that they have some influence on their colleagues, whereas financial resources are felt to be outside their control.

Finally, three positive relationships were found: teachers' willingness to participate in future change is stronger if the amount of impact of the change on work life is stronger (correlation 0.20, $p < 0.05$); if the impact on student learning is stronger (correlation 0.21, $p < 0.05$), and if the teachers' feelings about the change are better (correlation 0.49, $p < 0.01$). Somewhat surprisingly, the impact of the change on professional development is negatively related to future willingness to participate in change (correlation 0.24, $p < 0.01$).

CONCLUSIONS AND DISCUSSION

From our data we conclude that in the Netherlands, much more than in other countries, educational changes concern classroom practices. These changes have considerable impact on teachers' work lives and teachers by and large feel rather positive about these changes. They feel less positive about changes that are required outside their classrooms. It is remarkable that the more teachers see the impact of the change on students, the better they feel about the change. In general they are willing to participate in changes in the future if these changes apply to classroom practice and help improve student learning.

These results corroborate conclusions from a survey about job satisfaction (Berkhout et al, 1998). In this survey some 10,000 teachers were asked to score their satisfaction on a scale from 1 to 10. The average scores of the various sub-groups in the sample were between 6.2 and 7.2. Female teachers scored higher than male teachers, and teachers with university-based training scored lower than did those with a higher education background. In spite of the continuous flow of changes in education that teachers have had to face during recent decades, and all the discussions on teacher status and teacher remuneration, this survey shows that teachers are still satisfied with their jobs. This means that teacher morale in the Netherlands remains high.

The high morale is illustrated in our study also by the teachers' confidence in their own attitudes, competence and professional development, as forces helping the implementation of reform. That the teachers are not unrealistic, however, can be seen from their awareness of their own lack of competence as an impeding force. These results can be interpreted as a result of the rather individualistic character of Dutch teachers. From Hofstede's study (1994) on cultures in organisations, we know that compared to other cultures, Dutch culture is relatively individualistic. For teaching, this means an emphasis on one's own personal teaching style and personal responsibility for success. Teachers therefore rely on themselves and tend to cooperate informally rather than with strict agreements and shared plans.

According to Hofstede, Dutch culture is relatively feminine and power distance (the degree of inequality between people) is low in the Netherlands. These two characteristics contribute to Dutch society being an egalitarian consensus society. There is emphasis on equality of roles, equivalence, solidarity and solving problems by negotiating instead of fighting. For teaching this implies that teachers are expected to treat individuals as equals and that the government has to negotiate about educational reforms with all parties involved. Similarly, the school administration has to put a lot of energy into ensuring teachers' cooperation in changes. Thus, teachers can have a considerable influence on implementation of reforms.

Because of the length of most negotiation processes in a consensus culture, there is usually a considerable time span between the first announcement and the final introduction of a reform in the Netherlands. This is recognised by the teachers in our sample in their rating of changes as gradually implemented. In the time between announcement and implementation of reform, a number of teachers, groups of teachers or entire schools may, and usually will, take initiatives to experiment with the proposed changes in their schools. In Hofstede's terms, Dutch culture is characterised as not very high in uncertainty avoidance. The voluntary educational experiments during the 'incubation time' illustrate that Dutch teachers are open to risk-taking and experimentation. They do not avoid uncertainty and, as shown in this study, they see themselves as planners and active implementers even if the government, in fact, is the initiator of change.

Acknowledgement

We thank Joanne Hoornweg and Monique Groot Zevert for their help in data gathering and processing, Yvonne Sweers for running SPSS programmes, and Machteld Vonk for translation of the questionnaire into Dutch.

References

Berkhout, P.H.G., Zijl, M. & van Praag, B.M.S. (1998) *De leraar op de drempel van het milennium*. Amsterdam: Stichting voor Economisch Onderzoek van de Universiteit van Amsterdam (SEO).

European Commission (1995) *Key Data on Education in the European Union*. Luxembourg: Office for Official Publications of the European Communities.

Hofstede, G.H. (1994) *Cultures and Organizations*. London: HarperCollins.

Ministry of Education and Sciences (1989) *Richness of the Uncompleted: challenges facing Dutch education*. Zoetermeer: Author.

Organisation for Economic Cooperation and Development (1992) *Reviews of National Policies for Education: the Netherlands*. Paris: OECD.

Organisation for Economic Cooperation and Development (1995) *Education at a Glance: OECD Indicators*. Paris: OECD.

United Nations (1993) *World Population Prospects: the 1992 revision*. New York: UNESCO.

Vonk, J.H.C. (1996) The Changing Social Context of Teaching in Western Europe, in B.J. Biddle, T.L. Good & I.F. Goodson (Eds) *International Handbook of Teachers and Teaching*, pp. 985-1051. Dordrecht: Kluwer Academic Publishers.

Wubbels, T. & Brekelmans, M. (1997) A Comparison of Student Perceptions of Dutch Physics Teachers' Interpersonal Behavior and their Educational Opinions in 1984 and 1993, *Journal of Research in Science Teaching*, 34, pp. 447-467.

The Impact of Educational Change on Teachers of the 'Rainbow Nation'

JOHAN BOOYSE & CASSIE SWANEPOEL

INTRODUCTION

In 1996 the authors took part in an international study on the effects of change on the work lives of teachers. Details of the design of this cross-cultural study are supplied in the Introduction. One aim of the research was to obtain rich, descriptive data about the contexts, activities, beliefs and feelings of teachers in and about their particular educational settings. This implies that the research was primarily concerned with understanding the experiences of teachers regarding educational change from their perspectives, and possibly arriving at context-bound generalisations.

This chapter presents some of the results of the South African section of the study and has two primary objectives. The first is to familiarise the reader with changes in educational policy and practice that have taken place in South African education between 1994 and 1996. This factual account of educational changes that were either planned and/or implemented constitutes the context within which the responses of the teachers interviewed have to be considered. The second objective is to present the major findings of the study as derived from a qualitative analysis of the interviews.

EDUCATION IN SOUTH AFRICA AFTER 1994:
A RAPIDLY CHANGING LANDSCAPE

The inauguration of Nelson Mandela as President on 10 May 1994 marked the end of the apartheid era and the beginning of a period of transition to an egalitarian and democratic society. Regarding education, this was also the beginning of a transition from 'apartheid education' to 'non-racial, non-sexist, non-elitist and democratic education' (Republic of South Africa [RSA], 1994, p. 10).

When the new government came into power its immediate education focus was on expanded access, which, *inter alia*, implied the provision of more schools and a desegregation of existing schools. At that stage there were 11.8 million learners enrolled at schools in South Africa. Plans were in place to introduce free and compulsory education for learners from the beginning of 1995, and the Minister expected between 150,000 and 350,000 extra learners to seek enrolments. At the beginning of 1995 schools were therefore expected to cater for approximately two million learners in the first year of school. At the same time there were 285,400 full-time equivalent teachers employed in schools, of whom 64% were fully qualified, 29% under-qualified and 7% unqualified. This implied a learner–teacher ratio of approximately 32:1 (Sidiropoulos et al, 1995, pp. 241, 247, 251).

The government was also determined to change the basic philosophy and orientation of the education system, from an inclination towards separation/segregation to an emphasis on inclusion/integration. School doors were opened for populations that previously, for various reasons, did not have full access, and programmes were created for those not in school. All such programmes had to be primarily concerned with fostering success, not filtering out those who do not succeed, since failure was understood and addressed as a systemic, not an individual problem. Therefore a process was set in motion to develop new curricula, teaching strategies and assessment mechanisms that would permit, encourage and support successful learning.

The Road to Educational Change

After 1994 almost all education policies evolved through a three-phase process. During the first phase broad discussion documents, often referred to as Green Papers, were published. The compilers usually engaged in special efforts to identify and consult all potential role players. Simultaneously, the government appointed special task groups or committees to investigate particular aspects of the proposed education policy. Consequently, the Green Papers were widely discussed. Then followed the publication of a White Paper. In most instances the publication of White Papers also led to extensive public debate and the formulation of both comments and recommendations regarding aspects of the envisaged policy. Finally, appropriate legislation was promulgated and implemented. Since 1994 South Africans have experienced a proliferation of Green Papers, White Papers and legislation dealing with education.

It is also important to note that South Africa is governed on the basis of a Constitution (Act 108 of 1996, RSA, 1996a). This Constitution contains a Bill of Rights with a particular significance for education. It enshrines the rights of all citizens of the country to:

- basic education, including adult basic education;
- further education, which the state, through reasonable measures, must make progressively available and accessible;
- receive education in the official language(s) of their choice where reasonably practicable;
- establish and maintain at their own expense, independent educational institutions on condition that such actions do not discriminate on the basis of race, are registered with the state and that standards – not inferior to those of comparable public educational institutions – are maintained (RSA, 1996c, chapter 2).

Indications of Fundamental Educational Change Being Considered

One of the first draft policy documents which specifically focused on education and training and which the government released for comment was published on 23 September 1994. This White Paper (RSA, 1994) indicated that the new government was directed at the creation of a single, national department of education and nine new provincial departments of education, working in close liaison with each other. It was committed to the 'significant and visible' unification of all existing education departments. Prior to 1994 the control of education was divided among multiple, racially differentiated departments. This resulted in an excessive fragmentation of education into as many as 19 different education departments that, in turn, prevented the implementation of a single, national policy of education. Until the eve of the election it was generally assumed that South Africa's multiple education authorities would be integrated into a single institution. However, as a result of compromises made during the drafting of the country's Interim Constitution, pre-tertiary education was destined to become the responsibility of nine different provinces.

In addition to providing for the formulation of principles to guide the implementation of affirmative action on appointments and promotions in the various new department(s), the White Paper also envisaged the fundamental restructuring of education through the introduction of a National Qualifications Framework (NQF). This NQF had to be developed by an important body that had to be established through legislation, namely the South African Qualifications Authority (SAQA). The NQF had to be directed at encouraging new and flexible curricula and facilitating the movement of students from one qualification to another. It also had to enable learning to be assessed and certified, regardless of whether the particular type of learning had been achieved in formal programmes, by personal study, or by experience in the workplace. The draft document proposed that the NQF comprise eight qualification levels (RSA, 1994).

The September 1994 White Paper also suggested a feasibility study into the concept of an independent National Institute of Curriculum Development to advise the Minister of Education on the development of school curricula. The development of a completely new curriculum was considered essential for schooling and for other contexts 'in order to rid the education and training system of the legacy of racism, dogmatism and outmoded teaching practices' (African National Congress, 1994, p. 10). This view led to the development and introduction of outcomes-based education.

In the White Paper the government also announced its intention and commitment to provide at least 10 years of free and compulsory education. The implication of this announcement was that all children in the age group 5-14 would be required by law to attend school or, alternatively, be in school until they had completed the equivalent of Grade 9. However, the government also indicated that, due to a lack of sufficient funds, the implementation of this commitment would only be gradually phased in from January 1995 with the enrolment in Grade 1 of all children aged six. In the course of time and as capacity increased, compulsory education would be extended to the other age groups.

An important feature of the September 1994 White Paper was the government's argument that the remuneration of teachers should be linked to ability rather than to the qualifications they held. This point of view corresponded with views expressed in *Restructuring Teacher Supply, Utilisation and Development* (Hofmeyr et al, 1994), a report commissioned by the University of the Witwatersrand's Centre for Education Policy Development, also published in 1994. It identified a number of matters that were regarded as shortcomings in the state's teacher education policy. Amongst these were:

- the inequitable distribution of teachers across the country with oversupply in urban areas and an undersupply in rural areas;
- a shortage of teachers in English, mathematics, science and technical subjects;
- the under-qualification or lack of qualifications of about half of all teachers;
- a perceived lack of quality in teacher training;
- a (financially) unsustainable upward trend in the teacher salary structure;
- an under-representation of female teachers in education management (Hofmeyr et al, 1994).

In December 1994 some of these views were reiterated when yet another, similar type of report, *A Policy Study of Teacher Supply, Utilisation and Development in Gauteng* (1994), was published by Jaff et al. They came to the conclusion that teacher training in South Africa was inefficient, costly, unequal and poor in quality. According to the report a quarter of the province's teachers were studying to improve their qualifications with a view to promotion or higher salaries, but were not necessarily becoming better teachers. It was also stated that the Province of Gauteng had a surplus of white (mainly Afrikaans-speaking) teachers and a shortage of teachers in English, mathematics, science and technical subjects.

It appears as though the reports mentioned above encouraged the government to commission a national teacher education audit to be conducted during 1995. The results of this audit will be discussed briefly at a later stage.

To a large extent 1994 was characterised by intense debate on the nature of the changes required to transform the education system into one that would accurately reflect the new philosophical outlook the government was attempting to establish and promote. One can only concur with Van Schalkwyk's (1998, p. 118) view that if education represented the Nationalist government's greatest failure, it represented the greatest challenge for the African National Congress (ANC) government.

First Concrete Steps toward the Redesign of the Educational System

The White Paper on Education and Training (RSA, 1995b) that was published in March 1995 did not differ substantially from the draft paper published in September 1994; it merely clarified minor issues. As a consequence the envisaged nine provincial departments of education were formally established in April 1995 and all formerly segregated state schools were opened to learners of all races. This represented the first step in the National Department of Education's commitment to provide 10 years of free and compulsory education. Whereas substantial powers were vested in provincial legislature and governments to organise and manage educational affairs, the National Department of Education was assigned the task of determining national policy regarding norms and standards for syllabi, examinations and the certification of qualifications.

In the course of 1995 several other important education documents, including legislation, were drafted by both the national and provincial education departments, discussed in various forums, and sometimes even heavily disputed. Towards the middle of 1995 the Gauteng Education Department, for example, completed legislation regarding the management of schools and tabled a School Education Bill in the Provincial Legislature. As a result of serious complaints by more than one political party to the effect that it granted 'excessive powers' to the provincial Member of the Executive Council (MEC) for Education, the

Bill was eventually (in September) referred to the Constitutional Court. The Bill, excluding the disputed clauses, was approved by the Premier in December 1995 (Gauteng Department of Education, 1995).

New Promotion Criteria

In July 1995 the Gauteng Education Department announced the introduction of new promotion criteria for learners at school. From the end of 1995 learners in this province could be promoted to the next grade without having achieved a pass mark. A particular learner's teacher would be required to consider that learner's 'development and emotional strength' before taking a final decision on whether or not the learner should be promoted. Learners would only be held back if it was 'apparent that they do not have the ability necessary to master the learning demands of the next grade'. According to a spokesperson of the Gauteng Education Ministry, teachers should in this regard not consider learners' marks only, but also take into account 'skills the child has acquired, like reading and writing, which are the key in a child's promotion to the next grade' (Nkoana Maloka, in Van Schalkwyk, 1998, p. 119).

On a national level the *Report of the Committee to Review the Organisation, Governance and Funding of Schools* (better known as the Hunter Report) (Department of Education, 1995a) was released in August 1995 and two enabling education bills were gazetted shortly thereafter, namely, the National Qualifications Framework Bill and the National Education Policy Bill.

The Management of Education

The National Education Policy Bill was tabled in Parliament in September 1995. It gave far-reaching powers to the Minister of Education who could determine national policy on the coordination, evaluation, financing, governance, management, monitoring, planning, programmes, provision, staffing and well-being of the education system. He could also, for example, decide on learner–teacher ratios, compulsory school education, admission and determination of the age of admission, length of the school day, curriculum framework, and language in education. Corporal punishment was outlawed. The Bill guaranteed the right of every person to basic education and equal access, the right to be instructed in a language of choice if reasonably practicable, the right to freedoms of conscience, belief, expression and association, and the right to establish education institutions based on a common language, culture or religion and gender (RSA, 1996b).

However, this Bill gave rise to widespread discontent. The African Christian Democratic Party, Democratic Party, Freedom Front, Inkatha

Freedom Party, National Party and the Pan-Africanist Party, for example, presented a petition to the Speaker of Parliament, which stated that the Bill was regarded to be unconstitutional because it allocated too much power to the Minister of Education and undermined that of the provinces. The various political parties insisted that it be referred to the Constitutional Court. Consequently the Bill was passed in both houses of Parliament but could only be promulgated by the President after the Constitutional Court had ruled on it (Sidiropoulous et al, 1996, p. 137).

In October 1995 the President approved the SA Qualifications Authority Act (Act 58 of 1995) that provided for the establishment of the envisaged NQF that was mentioned earlier. A later regulation under this Act set out the requirements for the registration of national standards and qualifications. In particular the regulation provided for the establishment of National Standards Bodies and Standards Generating Bodies.

In November 1995 the Department of Education published a White Paper that dealt with the proposals contained in the Hunter Report. It recommended the introduction of a compulsory school fee and the prohibition of all types of schools other than independent (private) and public. This effectively abolished the 'model C schools', introduced by the previous government, which had had total control over admissions and met all their own maintenance and running costs, with the state paying only teachers' salaries. Amongst other things this particular White Paper noted that a national school bill would not reach Parliament before the middle of 1996. Since it assumed that provincial legislation would follow in the second half of 1996, January 1997 was regarded as the earliest date for the implementation of a new school finance policy (RSA, 1995c).

Towards a New Language Policy

The publication of the above-mentioned White Paper was followed by the publication of a discussion document that detailed a new language policy. This document recommended that:

- at least two languages of instruction should be offered in primary schools, one of which should be the home language of a 'significant' number of learners;
- one language only (where possible, the particular learner's vernacular) should be taken into account for promotion in Grades 1, 2 and 3;
- a second language should become compulsory in Grade 3;
- two languages should be passed in Grades 7 to 12 – one being an official language, of which there are 11 in South Africa) and one the learner's home language – however, the language of instruction need not necessarily have been the learner's vernacular;
- learners be encouraged to take a third language from Grade 4 (Department of Education, 1995b).

Referring to this document, the Minister of Education commented that this envisaged policy would be directed at promoting multilingualism and removing all forms of linguistic discrimination (S.M.E. Bengu, in Sidiropoulous et al, 1996).

Also in November 1995 the report of the *National Teacher Education Audit*, referred to earlier, was published. This research was done by a consortium of education institutions which, amongst other things, concluded that:

- South Africa had an oversupply of teachers;
- teacher education was inefficient;
- institutions providing teacher education were cost-ineffective;
- some students entered teacher education programmes merely to obtain a higher education qualification but had no intention of ever taking up teaching after graduation (Department of Education, 1995c).

As in the case of the September 1994 White Paper and other related reports on teacher education, this report recommended that the salary scale of teachers be restructured and divorced from being qualifications-driven.

A Legal Base for 'Right-sizing'

An important Act promulgated in 1995, which cannot be regarded as educational legislation but which had a distinct bearing on educators, was the Labour Relations Act (No. 66 of 1995). For the first time in the history of the country, teachers were officially included in the labour movement. This Act paved the way for the establishment of an Education Labour Relations Council in 1996. Henceforth, all registered teacher organisations had to be consulted on all matters related to the welfare of teachers. Teacher unions on the one hand and the Minister of Education on the other became the key players in education labour relations (RSA, 1995a).

However, a more important event intimately related to the implementation of the Labour Relations Act was the Department of Education's decision in 1995 to undertake a programme known as 'right-sizing'. It was perceived that the education departments in the Western Cape and Gauteng had a learner–teacher ratio more favourable than that of the other provinces. Consequently, a large number of teachers in these two provinces were given a choice, either to relocate to an area where their skills were desperately required, or to accept a severance package. Since the size of the packages was determined by the number of years the teachers had been employed by their respective departments, the option to accept a voluntary severance package appealed most to those with the greatest experience, and this resulted in many school principals and deputy principals, as well as a large percentage of well-qualified, highly effective teachers, opting to leave. In addition, because the 'right-sizing' exercise did not take account of possible future demographic trends, it led to education in some schools practically grinding to a halt. In Gauteng, for example, 80,000 new learners moved into the province's schools at the beginning of 1997, just as the teachers were moving out, and in the Western Cape 3000 teachers had to be rehired after 6000 had been retrenched during 1996 (Van Schalkwyk, 1998, p. 121).

New Directions in South African Education Mapped Out

In February 1996 a sequel to the White Paper gazetted in November 1995, entitled *Education White Paper 2: the organisation, governance and funding of schools*, was published. The proposals made in this White Paper, together with some amendments, were later incorporated in the South African Schools Act (Act 84 of 1996), which received Presidential assent on 6 November 1996.

Funding of Education

The main aim of the South African Schools Act (RSA, 1996c) was to establish a unified national school system. It focused on proposals related to the funding of school education and the powers of governing bodies which had not been finalised in the February White Paper. The Act provided for the equitable funding of public schools by the state. The Minister of Education was required to set norms and standards for the funding of public schools, whilst governing bodies had to attempt to supplement the resources provided by the state. Governing bodies were also allowed to charge school fees provided that a resolution to do so had been adopted by a majority of parents attending a meeting convened for the purpose of approving the school's annual budget. The Act stipulated that all parents would be liable to pay school fees and could be prosecuted for failure to do so. However, it was made clear that learners could not be refused admission to a public school due to their parents' possible inability to pay the fees. Therefore, governing bodies were also assigned the task of determining procedures for the exemption of parents who were unable to pay.

The Role of Governing Bodies and a Clear
Demarcation between Two Types of Schools

The Act compelled each public school to appoint a governing body comprising parents, teachers, the principal, members of the non-teaching staff, and learners (in Grade 8 or higher). Parents had to constitute the majority of voting members. The Act set out extensive powers and functions for school governing bodies. Governing bodies could also apply for additional powers to, for example, maintain school property, determine an extramural curriculum, purchase textbooks, or pay for services to the school. Provincial education departments had to provide training for all governing bodies to enable them to perform their functions well.

In addition, the South African Schools Act recognised only two categories of schools as recommended in the Hunter Report, namely, public and independent schools. All schools previously declared state-aided schools would devolve upon the state and their immovable property would revert to the state. As regards public schools situated on private property, an agreement had to be reached between the owner and the provincial authorities within six months of the commencement of the Act.

All schools that were previously registered as private schools would be deemed to be independent schools after the enactment of the South African Schools Act. This Act guaranteed every person the right to establish an independent school provided that it was registered with the provincial department and did not discriminate on the grounds of race. It also allowed for subsidies to be granted to independent schools and for a parent to apply for the registration of a learner to receive education at home.

Examples of Other Important Changes

Other important provisions that were included in the Act are the following:

- school attendance was made compulsory for all learners from the year in which a learner turned 7 to age 15 or Grade 9 whichever occurs first;
- public schools were compelled to admit learners without 'unfairly discriminating in any way' or administering any form of admission test;
- learners were given the assurance that they would not be refused admission on the grounds that their parents were unable to pay school fees;
- corporal punishment was outlawed in no uncertain terms;
- in future, learners with special educational needs had to be educated at 'ordinary' public schools where this was 'reasonably practicable' – the so-called 'mainstreaming' of learners (RSA, 1996c).

Many other changes were introduced in the South African sphere of education after 1996. However, for the purposes of this chapter, the above overview should be sufficient to indicate the huge dimensions of educational change that took place in South Africa during the period in which the international study on change was conducted. In summary, it appears as though, at the time of the investigation, educational policy and practice were located in a human rights model, which required the nature of the education and training system and its style of operation to reflect the democratic values and principles that are rooted in the country's Constitution.

THE STUDY ON CHANGE

If the objectives of the international study on change and of this chapter are taken into account, the question arises as to how the above-mentioned educational changes impacted on the work lives of teachers. Therefore, with awareness of the danger of excessive generalisation and over-simplification, in the following section the results of the South African leg of the study are presented. Prior to this, a number of explanatory and substantiating remarks appear to be essential.

References to Black and White Teachers

From the 1994 White Paper on Education and Training (RSA, 1994) it can be concluded that, for many years, a large proportion of black teachers (and for the purposes of this discussion, brown and Asian teachers should possibly be included in this group) have been teaching in an environment characterised by a lack of proper facilities, overcrowded classrooms, insufficient personal training, a lack of professional support, the complete absence of a culture of teaching and learning, a lack of discipline, and a pursuit of political rather than educational goals by both learners and teachers.

In contrast, white teachers were generally well trained and used to a teaching environment characterised by relatively strict discipline, smaller classes than in schools for blacks, sufficient facilities and support, an emphasis on teaching and learning (despite criticisms related to the particular curricula and methods that were used), parent involvement, and a climate mostly conducive to teaching and learning.

Consequently, when the results (transcriptions) of the study on change were analysed, the researchers were alerted to the possibility that, at the time when the research was conducted, the attitude of black teachers towards particular aspects of change may have been radically different from that of white teachers. Eventually this possibility proved to be reality: a significant distinction between the responses of black and white teachers was found. The following discussion of research results will therefore inevitably include indications of the sometimes divergent perspectives on educational change that black and white respondents respectively held. In addition, to avoid both unwieldy, lengthy sentences and unnecessary repetition, schools that during the apartheid era were reserved for black and white learners respectively, will be referred to as 'black schools' or 'white schools'.

Timing of the Research Project

In order to be in step with the international research project, the fieldwork was done during April/May 1996. When the following remark by an interviewee (pertaining to the enrolment of black learners in a white school and the respondent's school being compelled to convert to a dual-medium school) was noted, the researchers realised that the timing of the research project may have had a significant impact on the findings:

> *We did not really know what to expect. Had we known what we know now, we would have reacted much more negatively.*

It should be kept in mind that, although the new government officially came to power in May 1994, in practice it was only towards the beginning of 1996 that the nine provinces of South Africa reached the stage at which they could begin to implement national legislation and introduce their own provincial legislation. Although major educational changes were planned, only a few (such as the opening of previously segregated schools to all learners irrespective of colour and creed) had already been introduced at a grass-roots level when the interviews were conducted. In practice, teachers were not yet under the legal obligation to implement all plans. However, teachers should at least have been aware of some of the government's plans and envisaged policies for the country's education system. One can therefore assume that teachers, at the stage when the interviews were conducted, may to a greater or lesser degree have been familiar with the new government's way of thinking about education, but had not yet in practice been subject to all of the proposed changes.

If one keeps in mind that people's experiences of change always seem to pass through at least two major phases – one of expectations regarding the change, followed by a phase of dealing with sobering realities and realising the actual implications of change – it can be concluded that in April/May 1996 South African teachers were to a large extent still anticipating change. If one studies the transcriptions of the interviews against this background, there is sufficient reason to believe that teachers were most willing to engage in what can be called a discourse of good intentions, but that they did not yet realise the full implications and (often unexpected) effects of the changes the government envisaged.

Composition of the Sample

Similarly to the other country research teams, in regard to the composition of the research sample, it should be noted that the South African research team also used a combination of stratified purposeful and operational construct sampling to select a sample of 40 secondary school teachers in the Pretoria metropolitan area. In order to make this sample as representative as possible, the size of the school (based on the number of learners enrolled), its geographical location, the population group to which the majority of learners attending the particular school belonged, and the language of instruction used in particular schools were considered. Principals of each of 10 selected schools each identified four teachers to be interviewed. The criteria for selection were that potential respondents had to have been employed at the school for at least three years, and as a group the four teachers had to be representative of the school's staff composition in regard to gender, age, post-level and number of years' teaching experience. This resulted in two schools being selected from each of the Mamelodi and Atteridgeville areas (schools providing education primarily to black learners, one to the east of Pretoria and one to the west); one from Eersterust (a school primarily catering for the education of brown learners, sometimes also referred to as 'coloureds'); one from Laudium (a school attended primarily by Asian learners); and four schools from Pretoria (previously providing education primarily to white learners, one school in the north, south, west and east of the city respectively). There were between 800 and 1500 learners enrolled at all of these schools. The final sample of staff members selected consisted of 15 black, 4 brown, 4 Asian, and 14 white teachers (three interviews did not satisfy scientific requirements and had to be rejected). This sample was fully representative of Afrikaans- and English-speaking teachers, males and females, junior and senior teachers in terms of post-level, and of teachers with more and less teaching experience.

Attempts to Focus on Educational rather than Political Change

When the fieldwork was conducted, almost all interviewers reported that respondents spontaneously reverted to a discussion of political issues. In one of the interviews, a black teacher accurately summarised the situation:

> *Everything is seen in terms of politics. Even the type of cool drinks which you drink shows what you are. Politics is everywhere and has caused deep scars. Children are abused for political misdeeds.*

The interviewers reported that they found it difficult to steer the respondents into a discussion of changes directly related to educational matters. In addition, although interviewers were repeatedly reminded to

185

make sure that the type of change the respondent selected for further exploration and elaboration fell in the category of evolutionary change, not imposed change, the transcriptions of interviews indicate that the respondents were inclined to divert into discussions of change forced upon them by means of either actual or expected legislation.

Qualitative Nature of the Study

The fact that qualitative research methods were employed in this study on change must be emphasised. The intention was to select 'information-rich cases for study in-depth' (Patton, 1990, p. 169) in order to understand something about these cases without necessarily having to generalise to all such cases. However, to escape some of the dangers of a study such as this in relation to reliability and validity, the researchers decided to include in this chapter only matters referred to by at least 20% of all those interviewed (views expressed by at least eight respondents representing at least two different schools).

Keeping these introductory remarks in mind, attention can now be paid to the results of the South African study on change. Unless specifically indicated to the contrary, all quotations are from the transcriptions of interviews.

ASPECTS THAT IMPACTED ON
THE WORK LIVES OF TEACHERS

Almost all the aspects of educational change which were identified by teachers as having had the greatest effect on their work lives can be linked to the government's main objective with the transformation of education, namely, to extend access into the system. In this regard the Constitution of the Republic of South Africa guarantees its citizens the full and equal enjoyment of all rights and freedoms available in the country. It explicitly states that the state may not unfairly discriminate against anyone on the basis of, for example, race, gender, sex, ethnic or social origin, age, religion, culture or language (RSA, 1996a, p. 9). These and other related provisions of the Constitution required the Minister of Education to create and apply uniform and equitable admission practices in all public and independent schools, which he did. During 1995 and 1996 legislation was promulgated which opened all formerly segregated state schools to learners of all races, guaranteed the right of every person to be instructed in the language of his/her choice, made school attendance compulsory, and ensured that access to a school could not be refused on the basis of the learner's parents not being able to pay school fees. However, as can be deduced from the following exposition, it was precisely the implementation of these ideals that impacted most on teachers' work lives.

Changing Demographic Composition of Many Schools

When all previously segregated state schools were opened to learners of all colours and creeds, the demographic composition of many schools, in particular white schools, changed significantly. Relatively large numbers of black learners moved into white, brown and Asian schools. The opposite did not happen though. Relative few white, brown and Asian learners enrolled at black schools. To the researchers it therefore did not come as a surprise to find that the largest percentage of respondents attributed the types of change that had the largest impact on their work lives, to the 'opening (of) access to learners of different colour and language'. Most interviewees did not shy away from explicitly stating: 'The integration of black learners into schools has affected my work most'.

Increased Learner–Teacher Ratios

One of the first effects of this migration to white, brown and Asian schools was a drastic increase in the size of classes at the targeted schools. Most of the teacher-respondents who took part in the study and were employed at such schools complained about large classes and the fact that 'we have become used to classes consisting of 30-35 pupils, but these days classes consisting of 35-45 are not uncommon'. One of the teachers indicated that he had 70 learners in his Northern Sotho (a local language) class, another that there were 48 learners in his mathematics class, and yet another that she had to teach 38 learners in her English class.

Although in the apartheid era, large classes used to be a characteristic of black schools, the latter also experienced an increase in number of learners per class: in a particular interview the researcher was told that 'we try to make it [the number of learners per class] 40, but this year it is about 49 people. In some classes we find ourselves with 60 kids'. However, it appears as though the reason for the increase in learner numbers was different from that which was applicable to white schools. According to one of the respondents, most black schools experienced a sudden influx of older learners; 'the lost generation that came back to school'. When requested to explain the reference to a 'lost generation', he indicated that civic organisations had embarked upon a campaign to promote a culture of teaching and learning and that they had forced some of the learners who dropped out of school during the apartheid era to return to school. Unfortunately, in most instances these learners revealed a reluctance to comply with these demands. Apparently:

> they [attended school] just for the first term ... and then they
> vanish[ed] only to surface again the next year. There was a

*general fever to attend school, but after three months some of
them just never came back.*

The increase in learner–teacher ratio at all schools, irrespective of their
demographic composition, can of course also be ascribed to the 'normal'
annual growth in enrolment and the extraordinary, once-off growth due
to the introduction of compulsory education for learners from the
beginning of 1995. However, another very important reason was the
government's attempts to balance its budget by means of teacher
rationalisation. During 1996 and 1997 literally thousands of teachers
were retrenched. By April 1997 more than 19,000 teachers had applied
for voluntary severance packages, and approximately 24,000
redeployment opportunities had been gazetted. It is noteworthy that a
person such as the political analyst and journalist, Alistar Sparks, who
has in the past been very sympathetic to the ANC, could in January 1997
no longer conceal his dismay over the government's handling of teacher
rationalisation:

> *The Education Department's policy of encouraging the
> retrenchment of school teachers is one of the most bizarre acts
> of self-immolation that is possible to imagine. Here is a
> country which desperately needs teachers, perhaps more
> urgently than anything else, yet it has just retrenched 12 000 of
> the best of them – and is set to lay off thousands more in the
> course of this year. This is sheer madness. It is rather like a
> man in the desert dumping his water bottles to lighten his
> load. (Sparks, quoted in Van Schalkwyk, 1998, p. 121)*

Whatever the case may be, these tendencies did not leave practising
teachers untouched. An Asian teacher, for example, expressed the view
that it leaves teachers feeling disconcerted if children are being harmed
by a lack of understanding on the side of policy makers:

> *The great guns ... say that they are out to give our kids the best
> education. But are they doing this by retrenching teachers and
> loading the classes? Aren't they doing them a greater
> disservice?*

Another teacher, employed by a prominent white school, showed
unmistakable signs of anxiety, fear and uncertainty when he complained
about the fact that 'schools are constantly threatened by the idea of staff
rationalisation, [in particular because] nobody knows exactly how it will
be implemented'. He indicated that many schools have been 'caught
unaware by an unexpected reduction in staff'.

Sentiments similar to these were also detected in a relatively large
percentage of the other interviews that were conducted. A teacher in a
brown school, for example, reflected a degree of desperateness when
questioned about the number of learners in her class: 'My Grade 10 class

averages 47 pupils. Frankly, sometimes I just sit back and don't know where to start'. In doing so, she actually reiterated what one of her colleagues had said in an earlier interview, namely, that she doesn't even bother to know the learners as individuals. 'They are just like blobs in the benches in front of you. It all sounds pretty dreary, but unfortunately it is true!'

Apparently the problem of increasing learner–teacher ratios was aggravated further by the fact that even relatively large schools with an enrolment of 1500 learners or more found it impossible to group together learners with varying abilities into homogeneous classes. One of the teachers, for example, mentioned that he had:

> *a class of 40 pupils which includes those only able to obtain 10% as well as those with a 98% ability. In addition I have to offer five different levels of Mathematics, including Additional Maths. I have to compile an examination paper and by means of exactly the same paper evaluate both pupils with an IQ of 84 and those with an IQ of 145.*

The migration of black learners to white, brown and Asian schools also resulted in heterogeneous school populations and classes in regard to language and culture, which also confronted teachers with new challenges.

Heterogeneous Classes in Regard to Language

During and after 1996 much public discourse has taken place on the issue of language in schools. This included debates on the medium of instruction in schools as well as the promotion of particular languages as fields of study. In this regard it has to be kept in mind that before 1994 the country had only two official languages, namely, English and Afrikaans. However, the country's new Constitution provides for 11 official languages which currently all enjoy equal status and respect. In addition, sign language also enjoys the status of an official language for purposes of learning. The Constitution states that every learner enrolled in a public school has the right to receive education in the official language of his/her choice where such education is 'reasonably practicable'. In determining what is reasonably practicable, factors such as the need to redress the results of past racially discriminatory laws and practices, equity, and practicability have to be taken into account.

The research confirmed a tendency, reported in the media, that a large number of single-medium schools were converted into either dual- or parallel-medium schools. At least two of the schools included in the survey changed to become dual-medium schools towards the end of 1994. One teacher described this as a 'phenomenal achievement' and indicated that for the first time teachers really came into contact with and realised the problems inherent in language and cultural differences. What troubled him the most was the fact that:

> *everything had to be done twice; everything had to be*
> *repeated: first it had to be presented in Afrikaans and then the*
> *same subject matter had to be explained to learners who*
> *preferred English as their medium of instruction.*

However, at the beginning of 1996 both these schools were converted to parallel-medium schools which the staff generally regarded as fortunate because, since then, 'teachers can speak either Afrikaans or English in class. They are not compelled to use both languages'. For most Afrikaans-speaking teachers, the obligation to use English as a medium of instruction nevertheless remained 'an emotional shock'. Some of the Afrikaans-speaking teachers also recorded difficulties regarding their evaluation of the work of black learners, 'in particular because one can so easily discriminate against black pupils as a result of their amusing [*sic*] accent ... I constantly have to guard against being misled by poor pronunciation'.

Another interesting aspect of the study is the finding that most white teachers experienced a large degree of frustration as a consequence of their inability to communicate in one or more African languages. The researchers were told that, since black learners preferred to speak to each other in their own language and the teacher did not know what they were saying, teachers felt disconcerted 'because sometimes you get the feeling that what they are saying [amounts to] ... criticism about you'. According to a particular teacher, she 'can read their facial expressions or their body language and [she] actually feel[s] uneasy'. She felt excluded from the conversation on the basis of a language inadequacy which gave rise to a type of polarisation that could eventually become detrimental to the learner–teacher relationship: 'it has become very much "them" and "me". The children aren't intentionally hostile but it is terrible if they are speaking and you feel that they are not saying anything good about you'.

However, it was not only teachers who experienced difficulties and frustrations regarding the use of English as a medium of instruction. Black learners in white, brown and Asian schools experienced difficulties in communicating and learning via the medium of English as their second, and quite often only their third language. A teacher from a white, English-medium school managed to summarise this dilemma in a very competent way:

> *[the fact that English is not the black learner's vernacular] is a*
> *double hurdle, because we are not only crossing the threshold*
> *of mother tongue to English. We are crossing from everyday*
> *English to exotic English which includes the Greek terms*

where English itself has borrowed from. It is awkward enough
for the English child!

He regarded the teaching of the natural sciences as being particularly
problematic due to their relatively complicated terminology.

Another respondent put the dilemma she experienced into
perspective:

We talk science in four different concepts: energy, force, power
and momentum, whereas in the black languages there is only
a single word to describe all those concepts. So when you are
[trying to distinguish between these concepts] ... they are
treating it as a merged conglomerate. We talk about power in
terms of a motor whereas they think of a figurative powerful,
like a powerful tribal leader.

In general, teachers seemed to hold the opinion that '... the [English]
language is very difficult [for black learners] to understand. It is just
basic stuff that they don't know, like basic English terms'. In an
interview with a teacher at a brown school, the respondent attempted to
illustrate the extent of the problem by indicating that, in one of her
classes (on a secondary school level), she cannot say: 'Please close the
door', because some black pupils will keep staring at her until she says:
'Tshwalela lebate' (the same request in Sotho) merely because they don't
understand basic English.

In an effort to correct this situation, teachers apparently have no
other option than to try first to improve the learner's language abilities
and then to pay attention to the required subject content. A relatively
large number of teachers echoed one respondent's explanation of how
she tries to cope with the language dilemma, namely, that she has 'to go
back to very basic explanations, teaching [Grade 12 students] things that
I would have taught for my Grade 8 students ... it is like how you would
explain to a Grade 1 that is doing Shakespeare'.

As could have been expected, teachers also expressed their concern
about the effect of these and other language problems on those learners
who were sufficiently conversant in the English language. Almost
without exception it was indicated that English mother-tongue learners
became 'very frustrated because of [teachers'] manner of delivery which
are very deliberate ...'.

When one of the interviewees from a brown school was encouraged
to elaborate on the particular language problems she had experienced,
she noted in passing: 'Strangely enough, [black learners] understand
Afrikaans better than English'. This gives rise to the question why black
learners prefer not to use either their own language or Afrikaans in cases
where the latter was understood better than English. Apparently, English
is regarded as a vehicle for socio-economic access and mobility. Some
regard English as the common linguistic instrument required for national

integration, but there also appears to be a common fear amongst black people in South Africa of polarisation and restricted access to the perceived economic benefits attached to English.

Heterogeneous Classes in Regard to Culture

After the education authorities had removed all legal barriers prohibiting access to schools, previously white, brown and Asian public schools generally allowed black learners into their classrooms and taught them without any reference to cultural differences. On the surface it appeared as though schools were made accessible to all learners without any ado. However, the interviews constituting part of the study on change suggest that conflicting views in regard to how newcomers to a particular school should be treated were often expressed.

Apparently some role players preferred the language, culture, traditions and ethos of the receiving schools to remain unchanged. This was exemplified by the turmoil at a primary school in Potgietersrust, a town in the Northern Province, where the vow of parents of white learners to bar black learners from attending 'their' school resulted in the parents of prospective black learners applying for, and eventually obtaining, a Supreme Court interdict against the school governing body's refusal to admit their children. An Asian respondent commented as follows:

> [Potgietersrust Primary is] an Afrikaans school with an Afrikaans culture who [sic] is having black kids going in there, making the school change its whole ethos; its whole culture. I think if black kids going to Potgietersrust are prepared to speak Afrikaans and to take on the norms of the Afrikaans culture, it is fine. But to come in and want to shake the barrel and to force them to become a dual medium school ... I have a problem with this. You cannot have pupils come in and want to change the whole school to accommodate the pupils.

During the interviews some teachers gave detailed accounts of difficulties they experienced in their teaching practice. One of the respondents, for example, explained how he conducted an experiment in class to illustrate that 'charges can jump'. Thereafter he attempted to apply what learners should have learnt by asking them to explain the phenomenon of lightning. To his disappointment black learners completely ignored what they were taught in class about the movement of electrons. Instead they talked 'about gods punishing and striking down'. To his mind 'they are living in another world'. Another respondent recalled a similar incident and then commented as follows: 'We explain natural phenomena in terms of scientific principles whereas we are dealing here with people with a totally unscientific basis. It is based on ancestors and calling up of spirits and all this sort of thing'.

These teachers' appraisal of the situation can be summarised in the following explanation provided by one of the interviewees:

> *Cultural differences are enormous: [black children] are so tumultuous when they are together ... even if they stand next to each other, they would still shout at each other ... whereas Afrikaans-speaking [white] children would enter the class, sit down and commence working. The two cultures also experience humour in different ways: black children often laugh when I am discussing something very serious. Ideally they should have a teacher of their own who understands their language ... because even if I were to study and master their language, I would not be able to master their culture.*

On the other hand, a small number of respondents also advocated a complete integration of schools and a total reconstruction of society via education. Although they also experienced problems in bringing together learners 'that come from different worlds, different cultures, different languages, different moral and ethical values', they were convinced that a full assimilation of cultural traits was possible:

> *Answering [the] questions [of white and black learners respectively] is like dealing with two different things: answers for white kids are different from answers to black kids ... unfortunately, in South Africa, there is this white/black thing ... the biggest problem we face in our schools at the moment, is to get pupils from different cultures together.*

In some schools these divergent points of view resulted in rather serious racial conflict that took the form of derogatory and racial name-calling, racial harassment, and physical confrontations, such as an incident at the Vryburg Secondary School during which a black learner allegedly stabbed a white learner in the neck with a pair of scissors. In others, the bringing together of different cultural groups appears to have had positive effects: according to a white teacher at an English-medium school, 'the whites have developed more tolerance and the blacks more discipline ... in the sense of mental discipline and organising their thoughts'.

Lack of a Culture of Learning Including a Lack of Discipline

For the past four decades many South Africans (especially black South Africans) have consistently objected to and resisted the principle of segregated education which was placed on the statute book in 1953. During this period the various strategies of resistance displayed a noticeable progression from fairly peaceful protest to violent confrontation. Towards the middle of 1970 black schools were transformed into ideological battlefields when black students involved themselves in general political struggles that were primarily directed at the creation of a non-racial, democratic state. In 1996, when the international study on change was conducted, many geographical areas of the country were still characterised by a breakdown in teaching and learning, particularly the secondary schools in Gauteng. It was also to be expected that the lack of a culture of learning would be one of the aspects that impacted considerably on the work lives of teachers.

In this regard black teachers despondently complained about their learners' total lack of interest in whatever is happening in the classroom, not giving any indication of a desire to rectify this situation. One respondent, for example, claimed that learners:

> *just walk to school and back. You can give a test in one class and tomorrow give the same test in another class. They won't even know it. They are not interested in education. They are also a bit more unruly.*

Another alleged that 'they are so aggressive ... they don't do their homework ... they don't care ... because there is no corporal punishment. So you are helpless'. Yet another interviewee indicated that she stays relatively far from school and finds it extremely upsetting 'when I get to school [only to find] it abandoned and I have travelled 64 kilometres for nothing'.

Although white, brown and Asian teachers expressed similar sentiments, they spontaneously and without exception mentioned not only attempts they have already made but also additional plans they devised to change the learners' attitudes. According to a particular respondent, 'it was a major adjustment for [black learners] to be given homework. This is something that did not exist in their milieu ...'. Therefore, according to another, their 'main task [was] to teach pupils how to organise and manage themselves'. In a similar vein, a brown teacher explained how she 'tried to pretty [her] room by putting up charts' but later found 'the walls covered with graffiti, [her] charts ripped off [and the] overhead projector's mirror missing'. Her intention was, nevertheless, to persist with efforts to make her learners aware of (her) aesthetic values.

A matter intimately related to the lack of a culture of learning, and which also significantly influenced the work lives of teachers, was the government's decision to outlaw corporal punishment. During the interviews a black teacher criticised the government for its actions:

> *It is a very big mistake that our people up there [the government] is allowing corporal punishment to be forbidden in our schools. We have radical, disobedient pupils at school*

*who do not care about any other punishment. They will
become dropouts in life ...*

A white teacher was also critical:

*We have witnessed the decay of discipline ... The Afrikaner
community believes that as the twig is bent so the tree grows.
Policy makers on a national level have interfered with
teachers' exercising of discipline and ... thereby left them
without any authority.*

A brown teacher expressed the opinion that 'children don't want to work
any more. They have to be coached and now that corporal punishment
has been abolished, it just makes things worse ... and there is no
alternative for it.'

It is interesting to note that in quite a number of instances, the
matter of corporal punishment was linked to perceptions concerning
ethnic orientation, as in the following quotation from a black teacher's
interview:

*The lack of corporal punishment is a huge problem. The
[black] children are living in a violent community. They don't
understand anything that is not violent. They backchat and
are blatantly rude. They will quickly point out that you cannot
do anything to them.*

A white teacher even went so far as to attribute the abolition of corporal
punishment to 'an attempt [by government] to reconcile the Afrikaner
culture with that of black culture'.

However, probably the most balanced opinion in this regard was
expressed by a white, English-speaking teacher who maintained that:

*in the old political system I was led to believe that ... black
kids were crying for education and like little sponges were
ready to mop it up ... [because they perceived education to be
the vehicle that would] get them out of their social strata. The
reality is that they are not really that different from the white
kids [in regard to] disciplinary problems.*

Fear of a Drop in Standards

Because formerly white schools (and to some extent brown and Asian
schools) were assumed to have maintained high standards compared
with schools formerly reserved for black learners, widespread fears of a
drop in academic standards at public schools arose, particularly amongst
members of the white population of South Africa. The interviews
conducted in 1996 also attested to this. Most of the respondents regarded

the maintenance of 'academic standards [as] a major issue'. According to them, 'standards will undoubtedly be compromised'.

Whereas some respondents regarded a drop in standards as an inevitable result of increased learner–teacher ratios and the associated lack of individual attention, others expected the language problems they experienced eventually to result in talented learners losing interest in learning and not performing to the best of their ability. Simultaneously some respondents voiced the fear that certain learners' inability to adequately express themselves in their second or third language may prevent them from fully mastering the learning content, and that teachers would be pressurised by education authorities to allocate a pass mark to learners who had not complied with the required standards.

These fears intensified when, for example, new promotion criteria were announced in July 1995, and when it became clear that the government was serious about the introduction of a new school curriculum modelled on outcomes-based education. Since attendance at independent schools was regarded by many as a means of upholding standards and simultaneously protecting oneself against the absorption of one's (minority) culture, language or religion, the fears concerning an expected drop in standards led to a significant increase in the number of independent schools in the country: between 1995 and 1997 the number of schools registered with the Independent Schools Council increased by 99% to 290 and in 1998 there were 836 independent schools in eight of the provinces (no data were available for the Northern Province at the time) (Hansard, 29 June 1998). Simultaneously, more and more long-established schools opted to write the examinations set by the Independent Examinations Board. Another area of independent provision that grew significantly was that of home schooling.

Quite a number of other aspects which apparently affected the work lives of teachers, such as the rise and growing influence of teacher unions, difficulties experienced with assessment, a lack of facilities and a lack of sufficient and timely support for teachers to introduce the required changes, were also mentioned during the interviews. However, keeping the objectives of this chapter in mind, the necessity to further elaborate on these matters is eclipsed by the requirement to pay attention to the practical consequences of these changes and the emotional effects on the teachers involved.

PRACTICAL AND EMOTIONAL EFFECTS
OF EDUCATIONAL CHANGE IN SOUTH AFRICA

An Increase in Workload and Changed Teaching Methods

In order to cope with the increase in the number of learners who entered a particular school and the simultaneous rationalisation of teaching staff, schools were compelled to increase the number of learners per class and to reduce the number of free periods staff members used to have. Almost all the teachers interviewed indicated that they did not enjoy the 'luxury' of 'a single free period at school any more' and that in the final analysis, it was their families that had 'to make the sacrifices' as far as the use of their personal time after school was concerned. According to a particular respondent, '... it probably sounds outrageous, but I now have to start making appointments with my own family. And this is becoming an irritation for most teachers'.

At the same time, teachers' duties have also 'increased dramatically'. Interviewees often alluded to the fact that they could not find 'time any more for interaction with colleagues', which they experienced to be 'very negative'. In order to be informed of changes required by government and to plan the implementation of these changes on a local level, they were required to attend an increasing number of meetings. However, the most important reasons cited for 'the teacher's task [having] become more difficult and time consuming' were the demands of lesson preparation, catering for heterogeneous classes, and the requirements of a new system of assessment.

The respondents, almost without exception, indicated that the task of lesson preparation had become more demanding and time-consuming. Whereas English-speaking teachers maintained that 'there is a much bigger burden on the teacher to ensure respect and be innovative, be more on the ball and to have a much wider cross-section of knowledge', (especially white and brown) Afrikaans-speaking teachers indicated that they had 'to spend more time on the compilation of examination papers and preparation for classes' mainly because 'everything had to be translated [which] created a great deal of tension and stress'. According to them, education authorities tend to forget that it is not only the learners who are required to study through the medium of a second or third language; this often applies to the task of teachers as well.

Concerning the circumstances in classrooms, almost all white, brown and Asian respondents referred to the fact that they previously 'dealt with homogeneous groups. Now we have to cater for heterogeneous groups, the members of which cannot all maintain the same tempo'. The respondents frequently found that they 'had to spend more time on matters that [they] usually assumed pupils to have mastered already – matters such as terminology'. Prompted by a remark by one respondent that 'black kids have an attitude towards meticulousness. They want to write neatly and thus slow, whereas the white kids want to get through the work', the researchers made a thorough study of the transcriptions, focusing on indications of cultural differences. It then became clear that one reason why the teaching task of teachers has become more complex, demanding and time-consuming than ever before was that teachers had to try to deal with cultural differences between learners, for example, with this perceived attitude of

197

black learners towards meticulousness versus the perceived task orientation of white learners, without the necessary background and training. A brown respondent effectively summarised this dilemma:

> *We are forced to change our teaching methods. This has been a sore point because we don't know how to. We haven't been taught how to deal with multi-culturalism or multi-lingualism in the classroom. Most of the experienced teachers were retrenched and due to affirmative action appointments, you have people in top positions who aren't able to help you because they don't know what to do either.*

In an effort to cope with the changed and changing demands of teaching in heterogeneous classes, a relatively large number of the teachers apparently:

> *had to revert to very elementary teaching methods ... [mainly because] the black kids did not have the background knowledge required. Neither did they have the skills of discovery and thus you had to resort back to the old sort of a teacher standing in front, lecturing. You were basically forced into a particular teaching method.*

In general, the teachers regarded it to be a pity that this forced change in teaching methods 'reduced pupils' activities [and rendered] the teacher the only active one'. This situation also had the potential to defeat the purposes of the envisaged system of outcomes-based education because, according to a certain respondent:

> *you basically have to spoon feed pupils ... half of the class don't have the [required] skills. This must first be developed ... they can't take responsibility for their own learning. It puts more stress on my time and it takes longer to get through the work. It's like telling pupils who don't understand the alphabet, to write. They must first be taught the alphabet.*

It is interesting to note that some black teachers appeared to have had reservations with regard to the use of certain teaching methods:

> *... new methods do not work so well within our cultural context, especially where it has been inherited from the white culture ... the other teachers think one is crazy to want to work according to the method of the whites, which does not fit in with their own culture.*

However, from the transcriptions accumulated during the fieldwork, it isn't clear to which methods this interviewee referred.

The change involving larger classes characterised by a heterogeneous demographic composition also necessitated a changed system of assessment. White, brown and Asian teachers especially seem to have been overwhelmed by the divergent demands of learners in their classes, to such an extent that they felt incapable of 'pay[ing] individual attention to all the pupils in a class' and thoroughly and objectively assessing each learner's performances and abilities. Whilst some respondents argued that 'assessment requires detailed record keeping which involves immense amounts of paper work ... we have actually grown into a paper industry' and that assessment has become too time-consuming for them to manage, others referred to a culturally and/or ethnically determined sensitivity that surrounded the whole issue: 'One has to be very much more careful in monitoring black learners' work. They are very, very critical and very keen to compare your standard of assessing one pupil against another'. Whatever the case may be, it seems as though the new system of assessment that invariably had to be adopted has increased the workload of teachers beyond comprehension.

Judging from an Asian teacher's response to a question on the effect of the above-mentioned and similar additions to her workload on her career as a teacher, these circumstances must have profoundly changed the attitude of all South African teachers towards their profession: 'I am just going to the class, delivering my lesson and not knowing if the pupils understood what I said, and not having the time to find out whether they understood'. Therefore, at this stage, the question arises as to the emotional effect on teachers of the educational changes that were discussed earlier.

Emotional Effects of Educational
Change on South African Teachers

As previously indicated, the findings of this study have led the researchers to conclude that the experiences of black teachers regarding the educational changes introduced after 1994 were completely different from those of white teachers. Only one of the black respondents appeared to have been negatively affected in general. As she felt that she 'could not tolerate [the effects of change] any longer', she was quite determined to find another occupation 'as soon as possible and leave the teaching profession'. All the others indicated that they regarded the changes as major improvements in the South African education system and that they could recall only positive experiences of change. It is also interesting to note that, contrary to what the researchers expected, all the Asian respondents revealed positive to very positive attitudes toward the educational changes under discussion. Only one of them indicated that he had lost interest in teaching as a result of certain changes, but was quick to point out that he was not 'totally negative about this change'; that he was in fact 'somewhat positive'. According to him, 'if you had been in the teaching profession for 28 years, you know that in the end you are still going to win ...'.

However, most of the white and brown teachers interviewed held fairly negative views regarding the effects of these changes on their work lives. Some white respondents did not hesitate to indicate that their 'levels of stress have increased dramatically' and that ever since these changes were introduced, their 'whole life started revolving around the school'. As a result they 'occasionally [felt] as though the demands of teaching are too enormous to handle. At times [they] became totally disheartened because of the sheer extent of all the changes'. Others were more cautious, but eventually also revealed feelings to the following effect: 'If I have to be quite frank ... to change in this manner, is a heartbreaking experience'. Pent-up emotions can also be discerned in remarks such as the following:

> One becomes furious when these [black] kids are afforded an opportunity to be taught by well-qualified teachers, provided with stationery and good textbooks, and still they do not show the slightest appreciation for any of these privileges. Some teachers have become so frustrated that they are no more concerned about whether a pupil pays attention or not.

and, 'We are much more tolerant than before ... much more flexible ... but they really stretch your levels of patience'. Even one of the white respondents who throughout his particular interview impressed the interviewer with an exceptional professional attitude towards teaching, could not at the end of the interview resist articulating feelings of despair:

> I am a born teacher. My grandfather was a teacher and I have always aspired to become a teacher. I regard it as the most rewarding occupation there is. But even I have become disheartened. I view myself as one of the most positive staff members of this school, but even I have started seriously considering alternatives.

There is little doubt that for most of the white respondents, educational change since 1994 has been accompanied by emotional experiences that can possibly be described as traumatic.

Brown teachers' responses also included rather negative points of view. One brown teacher became very depressed when questioned about her impressions of the change that has taken place. She actually confessed that 'I just get through the day and go home, looking for a pocket of sanity, because it is like a madhouse in school'. A colleague of hers indicated that he felt 'alienated' in the school where he had been teaching for many years. He continued: 'You wake up in the morning and you don't want to come to school – your motivation is gone. You can't even crack a joke in class, because it is not understood'.

GENERAL CONCLUSIONS REGARDING TEACHERS' EXPERIENCES OF CHANGE

In general the findings of the study seemed to indicate that teachers were subjected to too many changes in too short a span of time. Most respondents complained that:

> *in theory, it was something that was going to be developed over time, but in practice it was faster than expected or anticipated ... the pace at which changes came, surprised most people.*

In addition, in spite of government attempts to consult all potential role players and to engage them in extensive public debate by means of Green and White Papers, teachers expressed the opinion that they have:

> *not really been given the opportunity to get out there and be part of the entire situation. Too often people not involved in the teaching situation ... are making decisions on our behalf and having the final say.*

The teachers who formed part of the research sample also felt that they had been deceived by the education authorities because the latter did not provide them with the necessary assistance to implement the relevant changes: 'We have been inundated with circulars ... but nobody has been here to spell out things to us. Nobody has ever come to our school to assist us'. More than one respondent aired the view that 'there should have been a more creative involvement on the part of the Department [of Education]'.

Simultaneously the teachers interviewed displayed an amazing degree of professionalism and dedication to their teaching task. Even though they claim to have experienced many difficulties related to the implementation of change, few regarded surrendering their passion for teaching as a viable option 'because all occupations are subject to change'. Instead they maintained that they were 'born to be teachers and [therefore had to] ... accommodate change and make things as easy as possible for themselves'. After all, according to the respondents, 'a teacher does not kick against the pricks'.

A FINAL OBSERVATION

The motto of South Africa's new coat of arms, written in the Khoisan language of the /Xam people and which most citizens of the country cannot even pronounce yet, is *!ke e: /xarra //ke*. This literally means *diverse people unite.* On a collective scale it calls for the nation, which is often referred to as the 'rainbow nation' because of its extraordinary heterogeneous demographic composition, to unite in a common sense of belonging and national pride; it calls for *unity in diversity* (Government Communication and Information Service, 2000).

In more than one way this motto bears particular significance. For example, it represents a notable diversion from and extension of the ideal embodied in the previous motto, *unity is strength.* In addition the two nouns contained in the new motto give an indication of the tension that exists between two broad and divergent philosophical points of view which constitute the basis of almost all political, cultural and socio-economic theories, policies and practices in South Africa: one point of view characterised by an emphasis on unity at all costs, and one characterised by an emphasis on the undisputed existence of diversity. Simultaneously, the specified relationship between these two nouns (unity *in* diversity) has the effect that the motto sets a goal for the citizens of the country while giving expression to an immense dilemma facing the country, namely, how to effectively accommodate diversity within a unitary state; how to ensure the peaceful co-existence of heterogeneous population groups that are very much divergent (in some instances, even the direct opposites of each other) in respect of, for example, language, religion, culture, and socio-economic circumstances.

This study has confirmed both the existence of the above-mentioned, divergent points of view, not only on a macro- but also on a micro-level (in the individual teacher's classroom), and the tension that has arisen from these points of view. Whether all role players in South African education have the courage and wisdom to transcend political ideology and, in the interest of sound education practice, give effect to *!ke e: /xarra //ke* as a goal, not as a dilemma, remains to be seen.

References

African National Congress (1994) *A Policy Framework for Education and Training.* Braamfontein: ANC Education Department.

Department of Education (1995a) *Report of the Committee to Review the Organisation, Governance and Funding of Schools.* Pretoria: Department of Education.

Department of Education (1995b) *Towards a Language Policy in Education: discussion document.* Pretoria: Department of Education.

Department of Education (1995c) *The National Teacher Education Audit.* Pretoria: Department of Education.

Gauteng Department of Education (1995) School Education Bill, *Provincial Gazette Extraordinary No. 30.* Pretoria: Government Printer.

Government Communication and Information Service (2000) http://www.gov.za/symbols/coatofarms.htm 10 July.

Hofmeyr, J., Simkins, C., Perry, H. & Jaff, R. (1994) *Restructuring Teacher Supply, Utilisation and Development (TSUD): report for IPET task teams.* Johannesburg: Edupol, The Urban Foundation.

Jaff, R., Rice, M. & Hofmeyr, J. (1994) *A Policy Study of Teacher Supply, Utilisation and Development in Gauteng.* Johannesburg: Edupol, The Urban Foundation.

Patton, M.Q. (1990) *Qualitative Evaluation and Research Methods.* Newbury Park, CA: Sage.

Republic of South Africa (1994) Draft White Paper on Education and Training (Education and Training in a Democratic South Africa. First Steps to Develop a New System), *Government Gazette* 351(15974), 23 September. Pretoria: Government Printer.

Republic of South Africa (1995a) Labour Relations Act, Act 66 of 1995, *Government Gazette* 366(16861). Pretoria: Government Printer.

Republic of South Africa (1995b) White Paper on Education and Training, *Government Gazette* 357(16312), 15 March. Pretoria: Government Printer.

Republic of South Africa (1995c) White Paper 2: The Organisation, Governance and Funding of Schools, *Government Gazette* 365(16839), 24 November. Pretoria: Government Printer.

Republic of South Africa (1996a) Constitution of the Republic of South Africa, Act 108 of 1996, *Government Gazette* 378 (17678), 18 December. Pretoria: Government Printer.

Republic of South Africa (1996b) National Education Policy Act, Act 27 of 1996, *Government Gazette* 370(17118), 24 April. Pretoria: Government Printer.

Republic of South Africa (1996c) South African Schools Act, Act 84 of 1996, *Government Gazette* 377(17579), 15 November. Pretoria: Government Printer.

Sidiropoulos, E., Mashabela, H., Mackay, S., Gordon-Brown, C., Frielinghaus, J., Musiker, C., Swanepoel, H., Gallocher, R. & Forgey, H. (1995) *Race Relations Survey, 1994/95.* Johannesburg: South African Institute of Race Relations.

Sidiropoulos, E., Jeffery, A., Mackay, S., Gallocher, R., Forgey, H. & Chipps, C. (1996) *Race Relations Survey, 1995/96.* Johannesburg: South African Institute of Race Relations.

Van Schalkwyk, R. (1998) *One Miracle is not Enough.* Sandown: Bellwether.

What Has Change Got to Do with It? Teachers' Work Lives: US perspectives

TSILA EVERS & NÓRA ARATÓ

CHARACTERISTICS OF THE US EDUCATIONAL SYSTEM

Where Are We From? The Origin of Our Troubles

'If an unfriendly foreign power had attempted to impose on America the mediocre educational performance that exists today, we might well have viewed it as an act of war', declared the publication that was recognised as the 'trigger' for change in April 1983 (National Committee on Excellence in Education [NCEE], 1983). *A Nation at Risk: the imperative for educational reform* (NCEE, 1983) listed the following indicators of the 'risk': the USA lagging behind in international comparisons of student achievement; the high proportion of functional illiteracy; low achievement on standardised tests; decline in science achievement scores; and the increased number of remedial math courses at a time when there is an accelerated demand for highly skilled workers.

> *Secondary school curricula have been homogenized, diluted, and diffused to the point that they no longer have a central purpose. In effect, we have a cafeteria-style curriculum in which the appetizers and desserts can easily be mistaken for the main courses. Students have migrated from vocational and college preparatory programs to 'general track' courses in large numbers. The proportion of students taking a general program of study has increased from 12 percent in 1964 to 42 percent in 1979.*

> *This curricular smorgasbord, combined with extensive student choice, explains a great deal about where we find ourselves*

> *today. We offer intermediate Algebra, but only 31 percent of*
> *our recent high school graduates complete it; we offer French*
> *I, but only 13 percent complete it; and we offer Geography, but*
> *only 16 percent complete it. Calculus is available in schools*
> *enrolling about 60 percent of all students, but only 6 percent*
> *of all students complete it. (NCEE, 1983)*

The period between 1985 and the present has been a time of change for the USA (initiated by this stern message) – and for many other countries – marked by intense education reform. It is well documented by an Organisation for Economic Cooperation and Development (OECD) 26-country survey that studies the trends in policy (OECD, 1996).

There were three waves of reform in the USA, according to Finn & Rebarber (1992). The first, starting in the 1980s, hoped to fix the existing system. As a result, performance standards were reintroduced, better teaching/instructional models were implemented, and better textbooks were published. But after a while it seemed to have accomplished too little. Although the gap between minorities and mainstream white students became less marked, and 'back to basics' installed accountability in the educational system, Scholastic Aptitude Test (SAT) scores and information on achievement and attitude reported by the National Assessment Educational Progress (NEAP) surveys seemed to have reflected a low plateau (Finn & Rebarber, 1992).

The second wave in the 1990s was more drastic. The reformers did not merely wish to fix but, rather, to restructure the educational system. The reformers changed school government, demanded even more accountability from teachers, and enabled parents to participate more widely.

The third wave gives more choice in the form of charter schools, home schooling, more parent enabling, and increased teacher empowerment to some extent. A more detailed analysis of this educational reform follows.

In the USA the mid-1980s was an exceptional period for state activity to improve public education. The widespread sentiment was that the educational system could not repair itself without external leadership. This leadership emerged from the states. According to Finn & Rebarber (1992) this was a radical change, since historically, local controls and federal controls seemed to be the most influential in policy-making. The rhetoric of educational reform was widespread and pervasive. State legislatures passed numerous education-related bills, increased state aid, and examined findings of hundreds of task forces and commissions. Governors vied to be the first with reform programmes. In 1989, the nation's governors established six National Education Goals (Firestone et al, 1992), which highlighted improvements that should be made by the year 2000. These goals related to education outcomes such as the importance of completing high school education, and of attaining better results in all subjects, and that the USA be the first in the world in mathematics and science. In other words, the two challenges for future state reform efforts were to develop policies that promote higher-order thinking for all students and to increase the coherence in state educational reform (Firestone et al, 1992).

For the first time, the mandate to teach complex skills and oversee their implementation was taken out of the hands of universities, which used to be regarded as the pinnacle of expertise. Power shifted to the states and local government; this is truly a paradigm shift. One of the most dramatic changes to education, after completion of this research, has been the 'No Child Left Behind' Act of 2001. The intent of this law was to close the perceived achievement gap by minority students. The Act has expanded the role of the federal government in education into every public school in the USA.

Efforts to teach complex skills and content more effectively to a wider range of students are complicated by the governance of American education, which is much more fragmented and decentralised than in many other developed countries. The American educational system consists of overlapping and often conflicting formal and informal policy components on the one hand and, on the other, myriad contending pressures for immediate results that serve only to further disperse and drain the already fragmented energies of dedicated and well-meaning school personnel (Finn & Rebarber, 1992). School personnel are daily confronted with mandates, guidelines, incentives, sanctions, and programmes constructed by a half dozen different federal congressional committees, state administrators, legislative committees, boards, commissions, and courts. This overview might suggest that the problem is not just a matter of centralisation versus decentralisation, but also of government overload and contradiction. Teachers are asked to work in a very contradictory environment (Hargreaves, 1995). This is very well reflected in the survey results of the Consortium for Cross-Cultural Research in Education completed in nine countries (Menlo & Poppleton, 1999).

A Bird's Eye View of the US Educational System

Schooling in the USA is compulsory between the ages of six and 16 in most states. Public schools are free and, in 1997, 10% of all US elementary and secondary school students attended private school. Most of the US secondary schools are neither specialised nor selective. Rather, the secondary school system allows students to choose from a set of required and elective courses. Competency tests, if any, assess students' skills at comparatively low levels and are not comparable to other countries' exit examinations. However, access to post-secondary education often requires that students take a standardised national test which is only one criterion of several (e.g. grade-point average, essay, recommendation, and involvement in extra-curricular activities) used in making admission decisions.

As highly decentralised as the US education system is, states and local school districts set most policies, guidelines, and priorities for public elementary and secondary schools. There is no national curriculum or student assessment system in use. However, in recent years, states and educational organisations have been working to develop common and comprehensive content standards and curriculum frameworks in all subject areas. There are general patterns in the subjects taught, although the curriculum implemented in schools varies widely.

According to Diane Ravitch, formerly the Assistant Secretary of the Office of Educational Research and Improvement, the movement for more accountability and national standards is at times in conflict with the very core idea of individualism in the American system. However, she documents the fact that the application of standards is not new to the American educational system. Standards have been presented, historically, in a cyclic manner (Ravitch, 1995).

Where Are We Now?

While being committed to ensure that all students achieve to their full potential in the twenty-first century, the US Secretary of Education (Riley, 2000) addressed the following concerns: the standards movement, high-stakes testing, expansion of pre-K programmes and after-school opportunities, effective discipline codes in schools, class sizes, teacher quality, and affordability of higher education.

Accordingly, at the present, the following facets of educational waves can be detected as reflecting major movements: (1) accountability – with developing standards for student performance, state departments of education assessment tests, and comparative studies between the USA and foreign countries; (2) curriculum – assessment tests reflecting shifts, parental involvement in subject matter, more dynamic teacher training, and different structures and forms of schooling; (3) school district boundaries revised – exposure to wider social contacts, sharing resources, and bussing for integration; (4) charter schools – specialised with regard to cultural and ethnic backgrounds, academic level, and subject matter; (5) alternative educational methods and approaches – home schooling, open schools, team teaching, and inter-disciplinary teaching; (6) high attention given to mathematics and sciences – as a result of technological changes at large, while humanities and social sciences have received less attention.

THE CHANGE STUDY

Reform movements in education have a substantial impact on teachers' lives. This impact is the focus of the study done by the Consortium for Cross-Cultural Research in Education (CCCRE).

We have taken one segment of the educational process under our magnifying glass to investigate how teachers respond to educational change under various circumstances. Our premise was that a high-quality and satisfied teaching staff is the cornerstone of a successful educational change. Job satisfaction is one of the factors involved in understanding teaching quality and retention and, indirectly, has an impact on the outcome of the implemented change, whether the end-result is success or failure. Hence the question regarding how satisfied teachers are with the changes becomes very relevant.

Groups other than those in the teaching profession have designed most educational changes. Typically, the changes implemented are followed by assessments of their impact on students. However, there has been little research on the impact that change has had on teachers. This is an oversight since teachers are the key agents in the implementation of change. As Lambert (1998) says, 'Teachers represent the largest group of adults in the school and the most politically powerful'. In this study it is the voice of the teacher we are listening to. Part 1 examines: how teachers perceived change; what coping strategies teachers used; how the perceived origin of change influenced the acceptance of, or resistance to the change; what hindered or helped the implementation; and what role teachers played in the change, that is, whether they have been initiators or implementers. The study was conceived as an in-depth, small-scale questionnaire–interview survey with uni-cultural and cross-cultural references, utilising both quantitative and qualitative procedures.

Methodology

The US sample, as well as those of the other countries, was deliberately small – altogether 50 interviews were conducted – to allow for a qualitative and in-depth study of Michigan teachers' reactions to change. The participating teachers were those who expressed a willingness to be interviewed. Collectively, they represent men and women from both suburban and inner-city schools located in the metropolitan Detroit area. In several pilot rounds the Consortium teams developed the interview schedule, and it was eventually modified twice in order to incorporate the knowledge gathered through the initial results. The interviews were conducted individually and lasted for one-and-a-half to two hours, were taped, and eventually transcribed for coding and analysis. After an initial reduction of categories, the analyses were based on cross-tabulation, correlation, ANOVAs, and the Newman–Keuls procedure.

RESULTS

Change Characteristics and Antecedents

The Nature of the Most Important Change

Teachers were asked to identify the three educational changes which had the greatest impact on their working lives. Then they were asked to narrow it down further and to choose the one they perceived as the most important. The rest of the interview focused on the most important change. Overall, 40% indicated that 'new teaching methods' was the most important change. The second highest ranking change was 'student experience', indicated by 24% of the teachers. 'School management change' ranked third. Consequently, teachers perceived changes that impacted on them and their classrooms directly as the most important outcome. Interestingly, comparison with other countries shows that the US teachers mirrored their international counterparts.

The Perceived Origin of Change

In the case of the US teachers, about one-third perceived the change as originated by the government. As one teacher said, 'This was mandated from Washington'. Other teachers (16%) noted that the change agent was the state or the local community. In other words, almost half of the teachers perceived the changes as coming from some form of government. However, over half of the teachers thought that the change was either school or peer initiated. This is a positive sign, since not all the changes in question were perceived as being imposed from above. Therefore, they could be viewed more favourably (Sikes, 1985; Hargreaves, 1994). Some teachers were active participants. Several of them substantiated their active participation by emphasising the details of their cooperation: 'Saturday mornings we would get together ...' or, 'I was invited to share in everything'.

The Perceived Objective of Change

Around 40% of the US teachers believed – along with their international counterparts surveyed – that the objective of the change was to improve education. Frequently change was perceived as an attempt '... to keep up with changes in the society, such as technology'. Some teachers attributed an even higher purpose to the change, like one teacher who believed that the main objective was '... that students will become better participants in a democratic society as a result of the engagement in the curriculum'. Only 30% believed that the objective of change was to promote social changes. In a country where social changes are often imposed on the educational system (Finn & Rebarber, 1992), the perception of a less socially driven agenda is positive. An additional 25% of the teachers believed that the change came to increase accountability and efficiency. Some representative comments follow: 'To learn how to learn effectively and to learn how to communicate'. In a variation on that theme one teacher said, 'Accountability ... We aren't getting the results we need, so the pressure comes down to teachers to produce'. Another teacher seemed to have combined the objectives, stating, 'It was threefold – money, retention of students and retention of teachers'. No doubt the teachers perceived many of the changes as coming under the umbrella of accountability, which was a key to the three waves of reform.

The Teachers' Role in Change (Sense of Ownership)

Our implicit theory was that teachers who feel more involved in the process would have a more positive approach to changes (Sarason, 1996). However, less than a quarter of the sample saw themselves as initiators of the change. They were the ones who were satisfied, and not surprisingly: one teacher said, 'I was invited to share in everything'. Another, who was highly involved, stated, 'We were the initiators. We consulted each other'.

However, not all were pleased. More than one-third (36%) of the sample perceived themselves as implementers and the rest thought of themselves as 'having roles', 'involved in sharing in decisions', or saw themselves as 'planners' and 'supporters'. One teacher bitterly noted that 'I was required to implement it, but was not consulted'. Those who felt 'left out' sensed that the change was 'all encompassing and everybody was affected' and 'adjustment and new guidelines were the possible alternatives'. However, unless the person is directly involved in initiating a change, he/she may perceive it as an imposition. Therefore, even peer-initiated changes might be met with the same resistance as a totally externally driven change (Fullan, 1993). A higher sense of ownership requires an initiator and not a mere implementer or participant in the process of decision-making.

Herein lies the problem. In the total cross-national sample, more than 40% of the teachers saw themselves as implementers. It suggests that both the US teachers and their counterparts in other countries may harbor negative feelings toward change.

The Timetable for Change

Our belief was that a rushed change, especially if imposed, would influence teachers more negatively than a more gradual process. The majority (over 58%) of the US teachers believed that they had the luxury of implementing the change gradually, which induced them to be more favorably disposed towards change. However, the rest of the teachers perceived the changes as abrupt and their reaction became less positive. One person commented, 'It was like a bomb: immediate and mandated. It was ready to go off and we had to keep changes in mind. More now than at the beginning'. One said rather wisely, 'I don't know if such a change can be implemented wholeheartedly, because ... it is a day-by-day, lesson-by-lesson process'. This last comment is very realistic. It connotes that implementation may take much longer than scheduled.

Factors that Helped Implement the Change

In answering which factors helped to implement the change, the majority (75%) of the US teachers said that it was the support provided to them, whether it was from the school, district, colleagues, or students. Many cited supportive leadership that 'allows for freedom and flexibility'. Substantial numbers of teachers indicated that it was a sense of professionalism that induced them to proceed, as in: 'Own personal decision'. One teacher put it very succinctly: 'My own philosophy; a passion I have for learning, my hard work. A lot of hard work'. Thus, help is a combination of extrinsic and intrinsic factors. Support emerges as extremely important. Collegial help was high on the list of positive factors both in the USA and in the cross-cultural sample. The following examples illustrate this: 'Talk with others of the same mindset and get over frustration', 'A willingness on the part of my colleagues to share'. The sharing seems like an experience that not only facilitates change, but also may drive it. Collegial support is the key to the endurance of many teachers in the trenches (Yee, 1990; Evers, 1992).

Factors Hindering Change

In answering which factors hindered the implementation of change, 60% quoted a lack of system resources, whether it was human or physical. One teacher said, 'The powers that be didn't take into consideration the reality of the kids – where they were coming from'. However, over one-third claimed that it was a lack of personal resources, that is, time and personal stamina. For example, one teacher stated, 'Time ... grappling with the content ... making the actual transformation'. Another was more sarcastic: 'The attitude of the in-service people. That, this [the change] is just a minor little extra thing that you are going to have to do'. In a few instances, extremely bitter teachers questioned the validity of the change, as happened in the case of an eminent teacher of a secondary school: 'It is my personal conviction to be against these changes. I belong to the old school and am a conservative person'. Ideological differences often are a source of friction in schools (Hargreaves, 1994). In this case, the resentment to change was a psychological hindrance. Implementing too many changes without proper training, preparation and time was regarded as a hindering factor by teachers in the USA – and by several other counterparts worldwide.

Teachers felt that, overall, the changes were imposed without due consideration to the enormity of the task. It required time, stamina, a change of attitudes, and a 'reality check'. These were not givens.

IMPACT OF CHANGE

Impact on Teachers' Work Lives

The majority (66%) of the US teachers, similarly to their counterparts in other countries, believed that changes have greatly affected them on many fronts and in many ways. Only a few (25%) believed that changes did not have a significant impact on their work lives. The former finding corresponds to teachers' responses in the interviews where they indicated that changes had a significant impact on them. However, the latter is quite puzzling in light of the cumulative evidence to the contrary; it ought to be analysed in more depth. One possible explanation could be that those teachers who claimed change did not impact on them had not implemented the changes once their classroom doors had closed.

Impact on Relationships with Others

Asked how the change affected their relationship with others, teachers felt that they had more positive relationships both with colleagues and students (36% and 44% respectively). One teacher stated, 'Students relate to teachers better. It is a special feeling'. Another commented, 'It made me less of an instructor and more of a facilitator'. However, 22% claimed that their relationships had become more negative. As one commented, 'I became short-tempered even with friends. Stopped talking with colleagues because I am tired of convincing people and tired of stereotype arguments'. About 16% lamented that they had less time with family. Only very few (8%) said that there was no change. It seems that changes do impact on teachers both positively and negatively. They do not leave them neutral.

Impact on Teachers' Time Management

The question of how change affected teachers' use of time at work again induced a yin–yang dichotomy. It should be interpreted in the context of the answers to the impact on relationships with others. Many teachers claimed a poorer use of time – '30% of the time is devoted to personal problems and it is a rate that increases by the year' – and 16% claimed that they had less time with family. This finding indicates that time management may be a problem. However, over half (52%) claimed to have developed a more efficient time management structure: 'Cut down on the amount of grading'. One-third of the interviewees said that they prioritised time more efficiently. Very few respondents indicated that the change had not altered their use of time.

When teachers were asked to be 'off the record', they complained about the time it took to plan the changes, carry them out, and evaluate their usefulness. The time factor merits more in-depth study.

Impact of Change on Teachers' Professional Development/ Practices

Remarkably, teachers do not report changes in their practices, though they do report other changes. Don't they change them? 'They do,' says Richardson (1990) but they do not necessarily report on a change in practices per se. On the other hand, they do report on overall changes. For example, the majority of teachers' professional development was, reportedly, very positively affected by the change. Since the importance of professional development is usually mentioned by teachers as one of the most satisfying aspects of their life, it can be inferred that change had a positive impact on their self-efficacy (Bandura, 1997). Self-efficacy is a strong contributor to both satisfaction and student achievement (Goddard et al, 2000) and as such is a very important change. In one instance, a teacher stated, 'Any time I hear the term "professional development" I am more interested. I am more open to things I have control over'. Or speaking about technological changes impacting on teaching: 'It has been a rebirth'. Or commenting on team-teaching: 'I like the fact that we are decision makers in the programme, we developed it, so it is easier to take ownership of it'.

Compared to other responses, this was a very robust impact which seems fitting, since professional development is usually linked to change. Few – almost 20% of the teachers – reported the change as having a negative impact on their professional development. Some were even bitterly negative: 'Since graduation I have taken classes every other year. Now I think it is a waste of time'. This sentiment is understandable, but does not represent a large segment. Very few thought that there was no impact at all on their professional development. It is interesting to note that the impact seems to be very positive cross-culturally as well. That is fitting, as a big portion of the changes was aimed at greater professionalism.

Amount of Student Learning Affected

About 60% of the teachers thought that student learning was positively affected to a great extent. Here, we see again a relationship between teacher engagement and achievement (Fredericks et al, 2004). Combined with the fact that most teachers perceived the change as designed to affect education and teaching, this proportion seems fitting. Consequently, it adds to the positive light in which teachers saw the overall change. For example, speaking about the introduction of mastery learning one interviewee remarked, 'Some kids helped pull other kids up. They help one another'.

Mastery learning is repackaging an old concept. It is an old idea – students and teachers do not move on to new material until everybody has mastered the old material. It does represent a return to 'accountability' in a most profound sense. It posits that everybody needs to pass the mastery requirements. However, one must note that 40% of the teachers perceived these changes as having a negative impact on students' learning. On the whole, 'copying and random learning' were quoted as negative consequences of mastery learning. Any implementation of change must take into account this opinion.

Teachers' Feelings about the Change

More than 58% of the teachers felt either 'very positive' or 'positive' about the change. As a result, 40% of the teachers would favour participation in future changes. This affective response might be the most revealing finding of the US study. Our study was conceptually based on a quest to understand whether a positive experience with change will help teachers become more accepting of it, and whether they might engage more eagerly in change implementation in the future as a result of their positive feelings. Unfortunately, we found out that the positive experience, in and by itself, may not have a significant impact on teachers' willingness to engage in change-related activities in the future. A more detailed explanation follows in the next section.

Willingness to Participate in Any Similar Future Change

When we asked whether teachers would be more willing to participate in future changes, about half of the teachers in the US sample reported no impact of the participation in change implementation on their future participation in other changes. Consequently, in spite of their positive feelings towards change, teachers are not very enthusiastic about participating in similar endeavours. However, it is also important to note that 40% of the teacher body reported positive impacts on their willingness to engage in future changes, as was explained earlier. Therefore, the positive feelings were somewhat conducive to future participation but they were not very strong. This lack of enthusiasm can be explained in a couple of ways. First, the lack of ownership that teachers claimed might offer a partial explanation. After all, only 25% of the teachers saw themselves as initiators. We know that teachers feel that change is external to them even if initiated by colleagues (Fullan & Stiegelbauer, 1991), but it can be assumed that a small proportion felt real ownership while the rest may have felt forced into the implementation procedure. The latter may have decreased their willingness to participate in future changes. A second explanation may be found in the amount of difficulty that any change triggers and in the amount of extra work it generates. Teachers are weary of change because it introduces new challenges and requires new efforts.

It is also interesting to note that the willingness to participate in a future change is related to how the origin of change is perceived. This holds true cross-culturally: wherever the change was perceived as government-imposed, the impact was perceived as more negative; in countries where it was perceived as coming from a local origin, it had a more positive impact.

DISCUSSION AND IMPLICATIONS

Changes perceived as having the greatest impact are the ones closest to the classroom sphere: teaching methods and students' experiences. This was, not surprisingly, reflected in the responses of all teachers cross-culturally. The significance of teaching methods and students' responsiveness to teachers have been found in many studies over the years (Lortie, 1975; Kottkamp et al, 1986; Hargreaves, 1995). The implication of this finding is that changes in areas deemed most important by teachers are going to grab their attention and are the most likely to be developed.

Teachers' sense of ownership proved to be a critical factor. It could be related to their overall uneasy attitude towards participation in future changes. Most of them did not have a sense of ownership. We suspect that their perception of being imposed upon, even when the changes were perceived as positive, created negative emotions. That sentiment is echoed elsewhere (Hargreaves & Bascia, 2000). The rich body of knowledge culled from the literature of organisational psychology indicates that participative decision-making has a positive effect on work attitudes (Lock & Latham, 1984). A great deal of research on effective schools confirms that their teachers fully participate in making decisions (Ashton & Webb, 1986; Rosenholtz, 1989). However, teachers are not satisfied with just any participation. They want a *real voice* from the initial brainstorming phase all the way to the implementation stage. Perhaps this is a further clue as to why teachers are reluctant to engage in change. The implication of this finding is that a sense of ownership must be given to teachers, if one wants to engage them in change.

Another factor, which emerged as crucial, was the support teachers received or failed to receive for the implementation of change. Support from colleagues was very prominent for the US teachers. This finding has been consistent with what is described in the literature (Rosenholtz, 1989; Yee, 1990; Evers, 1992; Good & Brophy, 2000). Having this support was crucial since it allowed teachers to have a sounding board and to interact, and provided a source of teaching strategies critical to learning new ways. The implication of this finding is that support networks should be developed at both the individual school and at school district levels.

Another crucial factor was the teacher's own sense of professionalism and self-efficacy. This is a crucial yet tenuous factor. Teachers who feel competent are more open to change and are more satisfied. It is interesting to note that a crucial aspect of feeling competent is the availability of feedback from colleagues (Ashton & Webb, 1986; Good & Brophy, 2000). The implication of this finding is that collegiality should be encouraged, as should a sense of competence. Teachers need to visit each other's classes and give peer feedback.

Teachers who enjoy collegial support and a sense of competence are more open to change. Responsiveness to future participation in change is rather elusive. Even those who felt positive about the change were rather reluctant to engage in future endeavours. It may be an inherent problem related to anxiety about leaving a zone of comfort. In this respect teachers share a lot in common with people in many professions. The implication is that change implementation will always be problematic. One should view it as part and parcel of the process.

CONCLUSIONS

This chapter sought to answer the following questions:

- What are the perceptions of teachers about the innumerable changes they experienced in their work lives?
- Given these perceptions, would teachers be willing to engage in future changes?
- Have teachers been aware of the political battles in education?

As we noted in the introduction to this chapter, in the USA there were three successive waves of reforms closely following one another. The reform initiatives, standards of accountability for teachers, school restructuring, changes in the governance and financing of public schools, and conflicting power distributions were introduced and implemented both individually and in combination. Given that context, have teachers given us 'savvy' answers?

Teachers saw the changes through the lenses of their classrooms, as it ought to be. When we asked them about the origins of the changes, they correctly indicated that changes originated in definite sources and came from either the state or national governments, or from the local school board, or from peers. This reflects the trend in the reform movement that indicates a circulation between the national and local sources, while initiatives are gained from different levels of the educational process.

When teachers were asked about the most important changes, they reported on what mattered to them the most in their classrooms and in their schools. They mentioned many changes that were 'objectively' correct. But what really mattered to them most was how that change impacted on them and their students.

When asked about the main objectives of these changes, teachers took the high road. None said that it was the result of politicians and interest groups latching onto an issue and exerting pressures. They thought it came to improve education (40%) and to promote social change (30%). Some said that it came to increase accountability (25%). All declared that the various reform waves had certain objectives and that they were all anchored in reality.

When asked if they had been given enough time to process and implement the changes, teachers often complained. After all, it is a known fact that changes came fast and were contradictory in nature. However, the US teachers were quite forgiving. A majority (58%) responded that they were given enough time. Only 40% thought that the pace was too quick. Therefore, we conclude that teachers tend to perceive the real value of the situation, try to adjust to changed circumstances, and cope with changed requirements.

When it came to the final analysis and teachers were questioned about the nature of changes, the majority responded positively. This attitude demonstrates a commitment to the improvement of education in the USA. This commitment prevails despite all the difficulties.

In the big picture of the US educational reforms, teachers are a decisive factor. In our interviews, they analysed the reality intelligently. On the whole, they espoused changes, albeit with some resentment about the pace and complexity of those changes. Most teachers have been working hard toward their realisation. They deserve not only a voice but also a very sincere thank you.

References

Ashton, P. & Webb, R. (1986) *Making a Difference: teachers' sense of efficacy and student achievement.* New York: Longman.

Bandura, A. (1997) *Self-efficacy; the exercise of control.* New York: W.H. Freeman.

Evers, T. (1992) Factors Affecting Job Satisfaction in Secondary School Teachers in Michigan, unpublished dissertation, University of Michigan.

Finn, C. & Rebarber, T. (1992) The Changing Politics of Education Reform, in C. Finn & T. Rebarber (Eds) *Education Reform in the 90's*, pp. 175-193. New York: Macmillan.

Firestone, W., Rosenblum, S. & Bader, B. (1992) Recent Trends in State Educational Reform: assessment and prospects, *Teachers College Record*, 94(2), pp. 254-277.

Fredericks, J.A., Blumenfeld, P.C. & Paris, A. (2004) School Engagement: potential of the concept, state of the evidence, *Review of Educational Research*, 14, pp. 59-109.

Fullan, M. (1993) *Change Forces: probing the depths of educational reform*. London: Falmer Press.

Fullan, M. & Stiegelbauer, S. (1991) *The New Meaning of Educational Change*. Toronto: OISE Press.

Goddard, R.D., Hoy, W.K. & Woolfolk, A. (2000) Collective Teacher Efficacy: its meaning, measure and impact on student achievement, *American Educational Research Journal*, 37, pp. 479-507.

Good, T. & Brophy, J. (2000) *Looking in Classrooms*, 8th edn. New York: Harper & Row.

Hargreaves, A. (1994) *Changing Teachers, Changing Times: teachers' work and culture in the postmodern world*. London: Cassell.

Hargreaves, A. (1995) School Renewal in an Age of Paradox, *Educational Leadership*, 52(7), pp. 1-19.

Hargreaves, A. & Bascia, N. (Eds) (2000) *The Sharp Edge of Change: teaching, leading and the realities of reform*. London: Falmer Press.

Heave, G. (1992) *The Teaching Nation*. Paris: Organisation for Economic Cooperation and Development.

Kottkamp, P.R., Provenzo, E. & Cohn, M. (1986) Stability and Change in a Profession: two decades of teacher attitudes, 1964-1984, *Phi Delta Kappan*, 64, pp. 559-567.

Lambert, L. (1998) *Building Leadership Capacity in Schools*. Alexandria, VA: Association for Supervision and Development.

Lock, E. & Latham, G.T. (1984) *Goal Setting: a motivational technique that works*. Englewood Cliffs, NJ: Prentice-Hall.

Lortie, D. (1975) *Schoolteacher: a sociological study*. Chicago, IL: University of Chicago.

Menlo, A. & Poppleton, P. (Eds) (1999) *The Meanings of Teaching: an international study of secondary teachers' work lives*. Westport, CN: Bergin & Garvey.

National Committee on Excellence in Education (NCEE) (1983) *A Nation at Risk: the imperative for educational reform*. Report no 065-000-001772. Washington, DC: US Government Printing Office.

Organisation for Economic Cooperation and Development (1996) *International Educational Education Indicators: a time series perspective*. Paris: OECD.

Ravitch, D. (1995) The Search for Order and the Rejection of Conformity: standards in American education, in D. Ravitch & M. Vinovskis (Eds)

Learning from the Past, pp. 167-190. Baltimore: Johns Hopkins University Press.

Richardson, V. (1990) Significant and Worthwhile Change in Teaching Practice, *Educational Researcher*, 19(7), pp. 10-18.

Riley, R.W. (US Secretary of Education) (2000) Seventh Annual State of American Education Address. Washington DC: US Department of Education.

Rosenholtz, S. (1989) *Teachers' Workplace: the social organization of schools.* New York: Longman.

Sarason, S. (1996) *Revisiting the Culture of the School and the Problem of Change.* New York: Teachers College Press.

Sikes, P.J. (1985) Teachers' Careers in the Comprehensive School, in S.J. Ball (Ed.) *Comprehensive Schooling: a reader.* Lewes: Falmer Press.

Yee, S. (1990) *Careers in the Classroom.* New York: Teachers College Press.

The Teachers' Voice.
Examining Connections: context,
teaching and teachers' work lives

JOHN WILLIAMSON & PAM POPPLETON

INTRODUCTION

The nine country accounts in Part One of this book clearly indicate that teachers perceive there has been a significant impact on their work lives in the last decade. The teachers' views are of systems that have experienced either massive shifts in socio-political and economic aspects, or major upheavals in curricula, expectations about pedagogy and accountability, and they, as teachers, have had both to respond to, and lead these changes. The changes reported have all shown schools to be perceived at government and system level as instruments of nation building and economic development. Changes have been described at three levels and, not surprisingly for such dynamic contexts, the countries often fit more than one category. For the purpose of presentation here, however, countries can be described as relating to one major category rather than to them all.

Reform. In the case of some countries, for example, South Africa and Hungary, there has been nothing less than the goal of creating a new state, or in the case of the People's Republic of China (PRC), to develop a more market-oriented economy from the present basis of a planned, command economy. In the chapters in Part One the details of how broad political shifts have created challenges involving the state are presented from the teachers' perspectives.

Restructuring. At the second level, there have been changes to the system and/or structure of education. In Australia, England, Canada, and the USA, for example, there have been significant changes to both the

221

content and context of education. Governments in these countries – of both the Left and the Right – have tried to ensure that all youth complete a full secondary education, while societal expectations about what will be learned have moved to accommodate demands for more general education at the same time as addressing the calls for more vocationally focused curricula. Teachers as the mediators of these system-level changes have unique insights into these matters.

Innovation. The final category is at the school and classroom level. At this level some countries, for example, the Netherlands and Israel, have focused on the implementation of particular curricula or on the integration of more information and communications technology into existing school curricula. Individual teachers have also been considered as a source of innovative pedagogies.

This chapter provides a comparative analysis of the major issues that emerge across the separate country reports, relating change to teachers' work lives. The issues described relate to the following nine areas that were explored in the interviews: the context of the change; the governance of teachers in the particular context; the origin of the change reported; the professional independence or empowerment of teachers in relation to the change; the focus of the change; the teachers' role in the change development and implementation; the nature of support for teachers as they begin to work in the changed environment; the impact of the change upon the teachers' work lives; and finally, the teachers' reported attitude to participation in future change. The authors describe a variety of contexts, from the most macro socio-economic-political level to the more micro-classroom-teacher level. In doing so they present the perceptions of the teachers in the study in ways that speak of the 'insider' rather than some more external or objective voice. As such, while these are unique views on the context described, they are no more or no less than the views of the teachers in the study.

THE CONTEXT OF THE CHANGE

In terms of contextual change, South Africa provided the most dramatic and turbulent example from the country case reports. Booyse in his chapter noted that the election of Nelson Mandela as President on 10 May 1994 marked the end of the apartheid era and the beginning of a period of transition to an egalitarian and democratic society. This in itself was a signal moment in the country's history, and for education represented a move from apartheid education to 'non-racist, non-sexist, non-elitist and democratic education'. As part of this political and social change the government also determined to change the basic philosophy and orientation of the education system, from one based on separation and segregation, to one with an emphasis on inclusion and integration. In practice, this meant that schools were to cater for a range of students who previously did not have full access, and new programmes were created for those who were not in school. For the teachers, this meant the development of new curricula, the use of new pedagogical approaches, and new assessment mechanisms aimed at facilitating, encouraging, and supporting successful learning. This important suite of actions followed from a statement at the time of the 1994 election, in which it was claimed these actions were needed 'in order to rid the education and training ... system of the legacy of racism, dogmatism and outmoded teaching practices' (African National Congress, 1994, p. 10). The South African report describes how education has been and continues to be a major contested area of policy and practice. This is, as the author asserts, because the origins and trends of education in South Africa have been political in nature, with opposing points of view in constant conflict. Contrary to what was expected in the general euphoria brought about by the radical political changes in 1994, this dichotomy still is evident and education in South Africa still experiences major crisis.

The country report from Hungary describes significant change in the wake of an economic recession. The shake-up in the political process and institutions was also reflected in education. In keeping with the notion of a more involved and devolved system, the authors trace how the Public Education Act in 1985 both simultaneously removed centralised bureaucratic control over the curriculum and devolved more independence to schools. This meant schools were now responsible for curricular and pedagogical innovation within broad legislated frameworks, and that the parents and wider community were centrally involved in decision-making about their schools. Subsequent legislative changes in 1993 and 1996 to the Law of Public Education mandated more change. In what was now arguably a more transparent system, for example, it was decided that the data relating to the attainment levels of secondary school students would be made public, along with the particular admission rates to the competitive university system. The financial crisis in Hungary in the 1990s has had major consequences for education. For example, the amount contributed by the central government was decreased as a proportion of its budget, and the state and local contributions were to supplement this sum. With the financial crisis, teachers suddenly found that their salaries (on 1998 data) fell dramatically and are still in the region of less than three-quarters of the per capita annual income. It is little surprise that the teachers report that teaching is not a prestigious occupation. However, the country report concludes on a positive note and suggests that the phases of crisis and adjustment might now have reached some stasis and might, in fact, be now allowing for positive change.

The report from the PRC shows a dynamic nation with its over 1.2 billion people, largely agriculture-based, moving quickly to a more market-oriented economy. In this environment teachers (approximately 3.8 million in secondary schools alone) are seen as important contributors to the nation's development. However, the magnitude of the population, the competition for resources for all social development, and the infrastructure needed to provide for the people has meant that there are major challenges in the area of funding for education. Of all of the countries described, the PRC is identified as the most centralised and politically controlled. The State Education Ministry (SEM) clearly determines policy and has the authority to ensure it is implemented. This means that all aspects of education, such as school policy, education goals, curricula and assessment, are prescribed. The ideology and political presence of both Marxist–Leninist thought and Mao Zedong is still central to many educational debates. When coupled to the traditional Asian Confucian values, it is not surprising to see the education system putting primacy on the development of the individual as a member of a social group rather than, as in non-Asian countries, as an individual somewhat independent of others. In this context, therefore, where the PRC leadership has moved recently to free the economy from a tight command chain to a more market focus, it is not surprising to see attention on the education system to provide the people who will carry the country into the twenty-first century. Nor is it surprising to note the conundrum that the various government agencies now face as they begin to reform elements of the education system, so as to provide for more 'individual development' within the PRC political framework. It is the teachers who are asked to mediate this major philosophical shift. As the authors note, 'Economic competition in the twenty-first century will, in some way, be the competition of the quality of human resources'. They go on to say that the resources to achieve the aspirations are not likely to be found in the short or even medium term, but that teachers are confidently facing the challenge of changes, particularly in the pedagogical and assessment areas.

The Israel country account reports on the heavy immigration to the country in the last couple of decades, particularly the recent immigration from the former USSR and Ethiopia. It also alludes to the recent serious outbreaks of physical fighting between Israel and some of its neighbours. The educational system is characterised by two aspects, the first of which is the heterogeneity of the students. For example, they attend schools divided along national, religious and ideological lines. It was noted that each of these groups has its own school sub-system and they strive to maintain their unique cultural distinctions. Consequently, there are diverse emphases and foci which are reinforced at the political level as each group strives to maintain its 'separateness'. This can result in those involved in the political process assigning more importance to political partisan interests than to educational considerations. The authors note that 'This pluralistic framework poses serious educational challenges to Israeli democratic society', and highlight that the 'deep-rooted ethnic gaps between Jews and Arabs, uncompromising disagreements between orthodox and secular groups, and social distance between new immigrants and Israeli students still prevail'. The second major aspect is the centralised control of the educational system. The country account describes a historically tightly coupled system where issues such as educational policy, the regulations relating to employment of teachers, and decisions regarding curricula and materials are centrally decided. These centralised policies have been supported in the past as a way of ensuring both overall academic excellence and the provision of equality of opportunity. Recently, the government has allowed more innovation in school management and some relaxation in regulations regarding school registration. The Israeli teachers, therefore, were seen as constantly adjusting to factors as diverse as demography, ideology, pedagogy, and technology.

The remaining five country accounts, namely, Australia, Canada, England, the Netherlands and the USA, all differ from the other four countries in the study. These five countries, by and large, did not face the same external change environments as the other four countries. In Hungary, Israel, South Africa and the PRC, it was seen that there were, at the macro-level, major socio-economic and political changes. In the five countries to be discussed here, there were turbulent contexts but they were at the meso-level and, in large part, generated internally to the country. Also, in broad terms, these are countries where a hitherto decentralised system has recently tried to define and implement a common core curriculum for all schools. The five countries will be described in alphabetical order.

Australia is a federation of six states and two territories with a central Commonwealth government with major taxing powers. Education is constitutionally the responsibility of the states and territories but they have had very limited revenue-raising taxes. Accordingly, the Commonwealth provides the vast majority of the money for the higher education sector, and a significant amount for the compulsory years sector, mainly through direct grants to the states and territories for government schools and non-government schools (both Roman Catholic systemic and other independent). They also provide financial support through targeted programmes, such as information and communications technology (ICT) provision or 'school-to-work' transition. More recently, the Commonwealth has expressed displeasure at the perceived levels of students' literacy and numeracy, and they have worked with the second level of government to provide extra resources for these areas. In return for the additional financial support, the Commonwealth has required that minimum targets be met. It is, of course, not compulsory for the states and territories to participate in these schemes; however, the Commonwealth has financial leverage and all states and territories are involved. In the mid 1990s a conservative Commonwealth government was elected and, as indicated in the country account, 'the social, economic and political organisation of Australian society was embroiled in a continuing process of profound restructuring'. Also in the two decades from 1980, Australia's macro-economic situation vis-à-vis the rest of the world was seen as characterised by a lack of international competitiveness. As a consequence, there was a flurry of reports, policies and programmes *inter alia* to improve learning programmes in the compulsory years, encourage students' participation in education beyond the compulsory years, and new measures to provide educational and social justice for all students. In the present context, as indicated in the country account, teachers report confusion as they note resources being cut, at the same time as they are asked to teach inclusion students and implement across-the-board testing of specified student learning outcomes, in the form of 'back to the basics' and, at the secondary level, focus on school-to-work education.

Canada is a federation with a political system comprised of a central and several provincial governments. Education is the responsibility of the provincial governments. The country account describes Ontario as the most populated of the provinces and with the exception of one other it is the most ethnically diverse, with many students who have differing linguistic and cultural backgrounds. The central government was characterised as following policies that resulted in government cutbacks in the 1990s and this was reflected in cuts in the finances to the provinces. At the provincial level, the Ontario government was seen also as pursuing a 'right wing' ideological approach which culminated in 'verbal attacks [on the public sector] ... accompanied by wage freezes, amalgamations, job reductions, and a demand for more work for the same or less pay'. In relation to teachers, the government has stated that 'Ontario students are not receiving the level or type of education they need to cope and prosper in modern society'. In this context the author reports on the lack of a single voice for teachers because of the multiplicity of teacher unions, in that they are divided on the basis of gender, language and religion. As a consequence of the financial cutbacks and the ethnic diversity of students coupled with different and higher societal expectations, it is not surprising that the author reports that Ontario teachers appear to be similar to those in many other countries in feeling that they are constantly under negative scrutiny.

The country account from England describes a situation where, until the mid-1960s, there was general agreement about the nature and purpose of education. This changed, however, with the move to what was termed a comprehensive education system, to replace the tripartite system of grammar, secondary modern and technical schools. During the 1970s there was a growing chorus of discontent with the content of education and a perceived decline in standards. In a series of publications called the 'Black Papers', 'progressive' schools and teachers were singled out as responsible for this condition, and this has shaped the education debate until the present day. In 1976 during the so-called Great Debate about education, the Labour Prime Minister James Callaghan declared that former policies had failed and that schools were now not sufficiently preparing students to 'do a job of work'. This direct linking of the goal of education to the labour market, rather than to the all-round development of the individual, was to be a defining characteristic of the debate over the last two decades. In the almost 20 years of Conservative government from 1980, the consensus about education was totally fractured and education as a public service was replaced by one based on technical efficiency in the market place. As the author asserts, 'Under the influence of the market model, equality of opportunity was replaced by freedom of choice, teacher autonomy by accountability, and the needs of the child by the needs of industry and commerce'. The instrument for this shift was the 1988 Education Reform Act (England and Wales) that introduced a National Curriculum, a complex multi-age student assessment programme, delegated budgets to schools, and significantly increased the role of parents on school governing boards. The magnitude of the changes led to dissatisfaction and anxieties from all sectors in the education system and so, in 1993, teachers boycotted tests that were scheduled to be introduced for primary-age children. This led the Conservative government to set up a review committee chaired by Sir Ron Dearing to review the curriculum and the tests. The Dearing Committee recommended changes to both areas and returned teachers to their more historical role as central to curriculum development. By 1994, therefore, teachers were speaking of 'pre- and post-Dearing' education decisions. At the next general election, the Conservatives were defeated by 'New' Labour under the leadership of Tony Blair, who became the new Prime Minister.

The Netherlands's Constitution allows for full freedom to found schools and also to decide their religious affiliation, or pedagogical focus. This freedom is exercised within a number of educational laws that define the structure of the educational system, the outline of the curriculum, the minimum number of students for the school, and so on. As a result, the country account describes how the majority of schools are private (60%) and the minority (40%) are public. The schools are financed on an equal basis, but the central government determines the regulations regarding examinations, qualifications of teachers, expenditure of public monies, and so on. The authors report that the teaching force is ageing and that this will create a number of challenges as, concurrently, the number of children is increasing. The main challenge is that, with typical retirement rates, it is likely that there will be a significant overall teacher shortage, and already there are shortages in the curricula areas of mathematics, sciences and foreign languages. In addition, the authors stated that when compared with other European countries, Dutch teachers are paid, on average, less than their counterparts elsewhere. A major response to these issues has been a government decision to allow those people formerly decreed unqualified to teach now to be able to teach. The authors also report that the Government has pursued a policy in education for the last two decades that is characterised by a belief that market forces will guarantee both effectiveness and efficiency, and this has resulted in 'a "withdrawal" of the central government from having first responsibility for all affairs in public life that can be dealt with by the private sector'. As part of the political philosophy of the government, an evaluation system of schools based on a number of criteria – the so-called 'School Quality Card' – was introduced. The authors reported that this system is now used by parents to select the 'right/best' school for their children. Schools that consistently do not meet the criteria may have their government grant removed. The second major shift has been in the secondary school curriculum, where now there is an equal focus on cognitive skills, social skills, learning skills, basic technical skills, and caring skills. As a consequence, teachers now teach a much wider range of curricula and students.

The USA country account commenced with the frequently cited quotation from the *A Nation at Risk* (National Committee on Excellence in Education, 1983) report: 'If an unfriendly foreign power had attempted to impose on America the mediocre educational performance that exists today, we might well have viewed it as an act of war'. *A Nation at Risk* and the new federalism espoused by the Reagan administration mobilised previously latent opinion about the economy, jobs and education. Among the specific indicators mentioned in *A Nation at Risk* were that the USA was falling behind other countries on international comparisons, there was a high proportion of functional illiterates in the society, there was low achievement on standardised tests, there was a decline in science achievement scores, and the number of students in remedial mathematics classes had increased, all at a time when competition for highly skilled workers had increased. The authors report how the USA had responded to this perception with a plethora of policy changes that had increased teacher accountability, provided paradoxically for both a 'back to the basics' curriculum for the primary (elementary) school at the same time as arguing for a more cognitively oriented curriculum, and promoted more choice through such initiatives as charter schools and home schooling. It is interesting to note that much of the initiative for change has come from state governors, who have established numerous task forces and commissions, rather than from the universities. The authors call this shift of power to the states and the local government away from the universities a 'paradigm shift'. The authors report good coming from the increased role of the states, as it replaces much of the decentralised and diffuse local policies with more comprehensive content standards and curriculum frameworks in all subject areas. As in many countries the authors note that the authorities in the USA have focused on the curriculum particularly as it relates to science and mathematics and the integration of ICT with other curriculum content.

THE GOVERNANCE AND CONTROL
OF TEACHERS AND TEACHING

The country accounts showed very different patterns and degrees of control by the state over teachers and teaching. The PRC represented the most direct control over teachers in terms of how they were selected, trained and employed, and what curricula they could teach. It was described as a 'top–down' system and places teachers in the category of civil servants as distinct from ordinary employees. It is a status that carries certain benefits, such as lifetime employment with career progression over known salary scales, but also certain disadvantages, such as the requirement of unquestioning conformity to government policies and legislation (Neave, 1992). From a professional viewpoint, the servant of the state is less able to adapt to the diverse needs of those being served or to adopt creative solutions to problems. At the other end of the continuum, the USA demonstrated the lowest level of centralised control as each state had established its own criteria for teacher accreditation and, at present, there are no central mandates regarding curricula. Perhaps Australia and Canada represent the middle position in as much as the central government can influence teachers through its control of finances, specific targeted and cooperative programmes, and broad curricula frameworks, but it is the various states, territories and provinces that have constitutional authority for education, that directly employ the majority of teachers, and that determine the specifics of the curriculum. The system of government in England and the Netherlands has a central government and local employing authorities without a state or provincial layer of government in between. In this they have some similarities with Australia and Canada, but significant differences also. It is likely that even with the English Core Curriculum, the 'post-Dearing' reforms mean that teachers have regained some of their autonomy. In the Netherlands, because the government provides the finance for teachers' salaries and sets the criteria for registration as a teacher, it is likely that there is some reasonably direct control. In Hungary the teachers have moved from a system where there was a high level of control to one where there is less control in most areas of the teachers' work lives. In

South Africa teachers are toward the higher-control end of the continuum, as the state begins those actions it considers necessary to redress the years of apartheid. Prior to this, during the 1990s, black teachers particularly reported uncertainty and fear about their employment. Israel presents the case of a centralised system but balances it with strong union protection for individual teachers. Accordingly, there is a high level of individual initiation and involvement by the teachers.

From the above it is obvious that the degree of central control of teachers, pedagogy and curricula is a very complex issue to analyse, for it involves a number of aspects including finance, certification, employment, and state centre–periphery relationships. As was seen, these elements operate at both implicit and explicit levels. The relatively informal nature of authoritative relationships may, in fact, cover a strong degree of central or local government influence through the control of finances, certification requirements, appointments, and so on. Conversely, a system such as that in the PRC, which displays a high degree of central control, may have individuals and regions operating as a fairly loosely controlled system because of the sheer size of the system, the growth of the market economy, and the pressures on educational institutions to find supplementary sources of income.

In the main, however, it is possible to see that those systems that were very tightly controlled have embraced some degree of relaxation, and those that were initially very lightly controlled have moved to more control. In the latter cases, if it is coupled with a move from direct control of institutions, it is replaced by a shift toward a control of the curriculum or by means of specification of criteria for employment as a teacher. The reason for the shift to what is essentially the middle ground is reported as the same for all countries, namely, to ensure a creative, well-educated workforce that can compete economically and internationally.

THE ORIGIN OF THE CHANGE

The various country accounts show two patterns of response to the question of where the genesis for the reported change originated. For some countries it was external to the school, and perhaps even external to the educational system, coming, in fact, from the central or state/provincial/local government (e.g. Australia, Canada, England, the PRC, South Africa, the Netherlands and the USA). For example, one of the Michigan (USA) teachers spoke for many: 'This was mandated from Washington'. A Canadian teacher reported that while the government had the idea for the change, they had no suggestions regarding the implementation: 'The Ministry of Education ... have a dictum, but no plan of action'. In Australia one teacher spoke for many by stating, 'It was very much pushed on you. It was almost, "Well too bloody bad – it's coming in and you've just got to put up with it". And although it was sugar-coated a lot – they weren't that rude – you couldn't get away from the fact that the changes were being forced on you'. This disconnection between policy decisions and instructional and curricular tasks at the classroom level was evident in many country accounts.

For the teachers in the other countries, for example, Hungary and Israel, the origin of the change was perceived as internal to the school. In Hungary a number of teachers spoke about the broad collapse of the previous regime, but attributed the specific changes in education to initiation by the school or teachers. For example, 'Pedagogues of the school initiated the change. The Marxist curriculum has [sic] collapsed and since there was not a national trend, a local change was initiated'.

In light of the various country reports of the origin of change, it is interesting to see how, in broad terms, they reflect two major foci: first, a concern to ensure that the educational system, as an instrument of the state, provides better skilled employees so as to allow the country to compete economically globally and at the same time unify the people as a nation; and second, to address a specific internal educational issue such as a more appropriate local curriculum. The majority of country accounts, however, clearly show the change as originating from outside the school and the teachers. In light of research concerning implementation of externally imposed change (e.g. Fullan, 1985, 1993), the importance of teacher efficacy in the utilisation of materials (Ashton & Webb, 1986), and the work relating to Levels of Use (LoU) of new curricula and so on (Hall & Loucks, 1977), it appears that the majority of the countries were initiating change in a model (top–down) that has been shown to be less successful than more collaborative approaches.

THE PROFESSIONAL AUTONOMY OF TEACHERS IN RELATION TO THE CHANGE

The country accounts in the main show the teachers paradoxically to have both little professional autonomy in relation to the nature of the change to be implemented and, on the other hand, a high degree of independence over how the change will be actually implemented in their classroom. This paradox is particularly evident in relation to curriculum, testing of students, and pedagogy. For example, the authors report that employing authorities expected all curricula and testing changes to be implemented, but the decisions about the actual pedagogy to be used in the classroom were still left to the teacher. In no country account, for example, did teachers report that they – as classroom practitioners – have the major responsibility for the change. Anecdotal information suggests, for example, that the recent discussions about curriculum, governance and assessment reform have come from interest groups, their leaders, politicians and academics, rather than from the occupation itself.

The broad question of professional autonomy is one that is touched upon by several of the authors. In the Netherlands, for example, in a context that acknowledges high quality teachers make a difference to students' school careers, there is reported an ongoing discussion over teacher professionalism involving a career structure from novice through to expert or 'professional', merit pay, the development of teaching standards, and so on. At the same time the authors report that the government had just decreed that people formerly deemed unqualified will be allowed to enter the profession under the condition that they are prepared to undertake a teacher preparation programme on a part-time basis. This account clearly picks up several of the major issues in this complex area and will be part of any long-term thinking about teaching as a 'profession' rather than simply as a craft or occupation. The South African account indicates that while teachers were receptive to the various changes that have been proposed over the recent past, by and large they have not been professionally equipped to achieve successful implementation. The account also points to the significant rise in teacher unionism as a feature of the 1990s. Although many of the country reports speak about the upgrading of the status of teaching and adding to the profession's knowledge base, few accounts provide detailed information about this area or membership of unions and/or professional associations.

The country account from England reports on the teachers' perceptions of their professional autonomy in what was termed 'pre- and post-Dearing'. The notion of a 'profession', where there is weak occupational control over selection, entrance and training of those coming into the occupation, does not fit with the commonly held view of what makes a profession (see, for example, Abbott, 1988).

In Australia and the USA the authors allude to the fact that the overall perception of teachers as professionals was being eroded by the increase in such matters as accountability, less involvement in curriculum development, and more implementation of centrally designed material. Overall, the data from the country accounts would tend to indicate that the occupation of teaching has not organised itself, nor argued for more of a leadership role in discussions about curriculum, assessment, quality, and so on. As such, teachers have become employees of the state who, on the information presented here, become vulnerable to central and local politicians when members of the community argue that certain tax-funded activities are not being performed properly.

THE FOCUS OF THE CHANGE

The focus of the changes in the country reports may be categorised into five or six main groups. The categories, of course, are dynamic and often interwoven or linked; however, they are analysed separately here for ease of discussion. In addition, the country accounts often refer explicitly and implicitly to several of the categories as the focus of the change. The broad categories of change discussed were: the curriculum, pedagogy, teacher–student relationships, student learning, social change, school organisation and structure, student experiences and a more general category of improvement of education. Five broad categories will be presented here.

The Curriculum

In the curriculum area the countries reporting a focus included Australia, England, Hungary, the Netherlands, and South Africa. In the Netherlands there were extensive changes in three areas. The first was to ensure a more integrated curriculum by 'breaking down' the traditional school subjects where possible; the second, to better link the secondary school curriculum to the articulation requirements for higher education; and finally, to increase student independence by highlighting student-centred and lifelong learning approaches. The England account reports how, in the first round of data collection, the National Curriculum was the major issue for teachers. In this phase the teachers' concerns were to deal with the practical problems of implementing the new curriculum and its associated schemes of assessment. It was interesting to have teachers describe their anxieties at this time as 'working in the dark', and the government as 'moving the goalposts'. On the other hand, the headteachers were not so concerned, and stressed the positive potential in terms of standardisation, consistency and balance in the curriculum. In the later data collection round (1995) the teachers reported that more time was devoted to curriculum and whole-school planning than before, and the headteachers reported that they were still mainly concerned with financial management and governance of schools. In the case of Hungary the teachers reported that the curriculum changes involved the complete reworking of the social science and humanities curricula to remove the political propaganda that had been included under the former regimes.

Pedagogy

The second category related to change in pedagogy. The countries where this was reported as a major focus included Australia, England, Hungary, Israel, the Netherlands, the PRC and the USA. In the USA account, change in teaching methods was the largest response, and as in other country reports it was linked to new technologies, for example, 'to keep up with changes in society, such as technology'. In Israel computerisation of teaching methods and materials were mentioned. In the Australian account changes in this category related to both the integration of ICT into ongoing classroom curricula activities and to the new pedagogical approaches needed in response to the implementation of the Inclusion Policy, whereby children who previously were in 'special' schools (e.g. children with physical and psychological disabilities) were integrated into standard classrooms. In the PRC account the authors report that more student-centred learning approaches, such as discussion, are being trialled in the context of the changes required by the government to improve student competencies.

Teacher–Student Relationships

The third category relates to teacher–student relationships. In this domain the Canadian and South African accounts give special mention to different aspects. In the Canadian example it was the more narrow transition from elementary (primary) to secondary school. As students move from the first of the compulsory school sectors to the next it has often been observed that some students appear to 'lose' motivation and seem to not operate at the same intellectual level as they had previously. To assist in the transition from one school level to another, in Canada it was decided that a scheme that was used in other provinces would be implemented in Ontario, the main feature of which introduced a role for teachers that was more supportive of their students. On the other hand, in South Africa it related to the much larger task of essentially rebuilding positive relationships between teachers and students following the 'breakdown of the culture of learning' in many of the formerly segregated black schools. It was described in the account how the former apartheid system had resulted in many of the black youth being involved in political activity rather than educational activity, and this meant they were alienated from the traditional focus of schools, that is, teaching and learning.

Student Learning

The fourth category was the improvement of student learning. In the country reports from the Netherlands, PRC and the USA this is seen as a particular focus. In the Netherlands, for example, the curricular changes meant change at both the lower and senior secondary school level. At the senior level not only were there four identified 'streams' now for tertiary study (i.e. pure science, technology and mathematics; nature and medicine; economics and society; and culture and society) but the emphasis was on the facilitation of student responsibility for their own learning. This has meant that the number of hours allowed for whole-class teaching has been cut and the students are expected to work either independently or in small syndicate or task groups. The teacher in this new context is expected to be a 'coach of student learning processes'. In the PRC the decision to change the economic system to a more market-oriented focus led to calls for more independent learners. Teachers therefore have the somewhat complex and conflicting goals of facilitating the students' personal and social development to ensure the successful implementation of the economic changes deemed necessary, while preserving the present tightly controlled political system. The authors report that the teaching strategy to bring about a more independent, student-focused approach is based on a discussion and problem-based method. In the USA the teachers' comments reflect both the need to produce more independent learners ('To learn how to learn effectively and to learn how to communicate') and to be able to work together ('They help one another').

Social Change

The goal of broad social change was the fifth category. In this domain the countries of Hungary, Israel, South Africa and the USA were the most strongly represented. In Israel, for example, the teachers reported that a more positive relationship between students (including values related to human relations, friendship, integrity and loyalty) was a major goal. In the USA about one in three teachers saw the building of positive social change as a major focus of the initiative. In the context of these two countries where the assimilation of large numbers of immigrants is a major social feature, this goal is understandable. In the case of South Africa it is the change necessary to bring together the peoples already in the country. In Hungary the country account places this goal in the context of moving from a Communist regime to a more democratic one, and the need to encourage a more inclusive social system.

The categories described here fit with broad foci in the literature (Organisation for Economic Cooperation and Development [OECD], 1994, 1996). The country differences, in terms of emphases, need to be seen as part of each country's unique aspirations and requirements at the time of the study. This aspect of the 'snapshot' being bounded by a particular historical context must be emphasised. For South Africa, for example, the challenges coming from the cessation of the apartheid regime are reflected in their particular foci. Similarly, in Canada the issue of transition reflected the concerns that faced the particular province of Ontario at the time of the study. The teachers' voices tell us eloquently of the range and significance of the changes that they were asked to address.

THE TEACHERS' ROLE IN THE CHANGE

The study, as outlined in the Introduction to this book, asked all researchers to follow as closely as possible a structured format in data gathering. This was to ensure data were gathered on a number of key topics and to facilitate cross-cultural comparisons. One of the key questions, therefore, was to ascertain from teachers their role in the change. The country accounts vary in the reported role of the teachers; for example, in Hungary, Israel and the Netherlands the authors state that the teachers' role was, in the main, initiator of the change. In the Hungary account it was reported that as the Marxist school curricula collapsed, 'pedagogues of the school initiated the change', and 'small working groups of teachers headed by the principal could claim the ownership of designing the change'. In Israel the authors report that the largest group of teachers saw themselves as having initiated change. This was seen as proposing the need and the ideas for change and, as reported by one teacher, 'I started to feel that I can influence and lead to value change in students and some teachers'. In the Netherlands the teachers saw themselves as 'planners' and as having a high degree of control even in those situations where the government proposed the change. The teachers reported they were members of school-wide committees or within-subject departments to plan the implementation of the change.

The teachers from Australia, Canada, England, the PRC and the USA, on the other hand, reported that essentially they were 'implementers' of change decisions made outside the school. In Australia, for example, while teachers saw themselves as being involved in 'a considerable degree of locally based innovation efforts' they reported that the changes being considered in this study were developed outside the school. A typical comment was, 'The stuff came out of the blue really. Here it was – and then we had to implement it all by a set date'. In Canada the majority of teachers saw themselves as having little influence on the planning and initiating of the change. A typical response was, 'We had groups coming in and telling us about it, not much input from us was requested' and 'it was dropped on us'. Likewise in England, the majority of teachers saw their role as implementers. One teacher typically reported both disenchantment and non-involvement:

> *personally, I wasted hours and hours of work doing one thing to be told about two years later that the goalposts were going to be changed and we could do it some other way. The net result is that I've lost interest and don't care a fig about it.*

In the PRC it was stated that 'the upper administrations or government always initiates educational change and teachers are only required to be involved passively'. In the USA the largest group of respondents reported they were implementers. One teacher noted that 'I was required to implement it, but was not consulted'.

It is interesting to note that in a couple of countries there emerged a group of teachers who reported they were more likely to see themselves as 'resisters' to the change discussed. In Australia and perhaps England this is particularly the case and, as the authors reported, there has been a period of significant and sustained change at all levels in the educational system. It appears from the limited data available from the country reports that where teachers see themselves primarily as the agents to implement externally developed and planned changes aimed at improving what they see as organisational effectiveness (rather than students' learning), they are likely to close their doors and continue to teach as they did previously. For example, in Australia, teachers who reported the changes were 'to save money' or to 'manage the system better' reported less benefit and use from the cited changes.

The role of teachers in change initiation and implementation has been an area of study for many years (see, for example, Fullan, 1985; Darling-Hammond, 1990; OECD, 1990). It is possible to see in the literature a number of studies that have looked at the individual teacher (e.g. Hall & Loucks, 1977) and those that have looked at more collegial or group approaches to change. In all of the studies there are a number of key features that relate to successful change implementation and these include, *inter alia*, an active involvement by the teachers, since they are the agents who mediate between the change agenda and the actual change in the school or the classroom. This gives rise to a paradox: on the one hand the research studies show how central teacher involvement is to successful implementation. On the other hand, as governments see education as an instrument for national economic growth, for example, they begin to intervene directly in school curricula, administrative structures, assessment practices and so on and deliberately not listen to the teachers. The teachers' perceptions reported here show this paradox clearly.

FACTORS THAT SUPPORT OR INHIBIT CHANGE

The implementation of change, especially at system or whole-school level, requires a great deal of support for it to succeed. All of the country accounts reported some assistance – of varying kinds and levels – to all teachers in the study. For some teachers, such as those in Hungary, there was almost universal comment that they were provided assistance by the employing system or school. For other teachers, the picture was more varied. In the USA the role of colleagues was highlighted in two capacities, first as a knowledgeable professional and second as a psychological support, as exemplified by the following statement, 'A willingness on the part of my colleagues to share'. Similarly, in Australia and England the role of collaboration and collegiality was central. A teacher in Australia stated, 'You become more dependent on your colleagues. If you want help, you turn to them, rather than to whoever the consultants used to be', while a teacher in England said, 'There are much closer relationships with colleagues, more understanding of teaching methods, a spread of new ideas'. Notwithstanding the role of collegiality in successful change, there were several reports of teachers saying that the change was essentially individual and intrinsic to them. The Netherlands teachers, for example, report that their own attitudes and capacities feature in the successful implementation more often than the support of colleagues. In the Canadian report, the role and value of professional development activity was seen: 'Workshops on cooperative teaching and evaluation [were helpful in implementing change]'.

All authors noted the lack of resources to implement the change. The resources deemed lacking varied from physical resources (e.g. computers, classrooms) through to teacher time to fully understand and implement the change as designed. One teacher in the USA, for example, said the biggest obstacle was, 'Time ... grappling with the content ... making the actual transformation'. In the PRC the physical material supplied to support the change was seen as inadequate and, often, so was the trained personnel to implement the change. In Australia and England the lack of time, physical resources and the simultaneous multiple changes were described as the main impeding factors.

The teachers' reports reinforce what we know about the successful implementation of change: the proposed change must be seen as important by the teachers; the requisite physical materials must be provided; where the change involves a new skill or knowledge there must be an opportunity for the teachers to obtain these either from colleagues or from external professional development agencies; a realistic amount of time must be given for the acquisition and implementation of the new knowledge and skills, and teachers must be allowed to implement the initiative with the understanding that they will sometimes not achieve total mastery of the new change on first attempt (Fullan, 1993; Williamson & Cowley, 1995; Black & Atkin, 1996).

TEACHERS' WORK LIVES

A major interest of the study was to consider, from the teachers' viewpoint, the impact of change upon their work lives. Accordingly, all research teams asked their respondent teachers to describe the impact the change had upon their work life. The teachers' comments and the questionnaire data show a pattern of significant impact in all countries; however, not all teachers were affected equally nor were all countries, as a whole, equal in level of impact. This is not surprising, as teachers will have different individual responses to the changes, depending on both personal and contextual factors. On the other hand, it does indicate that the common system- or school-level approach of assuming 'one size fits all' will not connect to the majority of teachers.

Hungary and the USA differ from the other countries in reporting a sizeable proportion of teachers who experienced little or no impact on their work lives. In both countries there appear to be two distinct clusters of responses with a majority reporting a significant impact and a large proportion (around 25%) reporting no impact. In Hungary, the majority of teachers said that the changes had resulted in their work being 'all consuming' and now preparation needed more time and energy. In the USA there was a similar picture, with teachers reporting less time for non-school activities.

The country accounts for Australia, Canada, England, Israel, the PRC, South Africa, and the Netherlands all reported that teachers experienced significant impact on their work lives. In Australia the majority reported an increased workload and a rise in the level of stress associated with teaching. A typical comment was, 'There wasn't time to come to grips with the issues involved; there was a lack of time to work collaboratively, a lack of time to implement and a lack of professional development'. The teachers' responses pointed to an intensification and a shift in the focus of the core activities of their work. For example, a teacher stated, 'You have a lot more one-to-one contact with people which is non-educational – it's education-related, but it's actually talking about problems students bring with them from outside [the school]'. In England, the changes similarly have had a significant impact for the majority of teachers. The country report placed these overall in a positive light, particularly in relation to fostering curricula-centred collaboration. The concern, however, about becoming too inward looking was noted by a teacher who stated:

> the national curricula have made the school a lot more
> insular. It's stopped me having opportunities to work with
> other schools and stopped me calling upon the experience of a
> lot of people within the school because they haven't got the
> time or energy.

The issue of lack of time for proper planning and implementation was reported also by teachers in the PRC. They mentioned particularly the new pedagogical approaches and assessment as areas where more time was required. In South Africa, the majority of teachers were seen as experiencing a profound effect on their teaching following the election of President Mandela. In the country account it is possible to see how the teachers may have responded to the changes along racial lines; that is, the black and coloured teachers perceived that things couldn't get worse and so overall were quite positive about the changes. On the other hand, the white teachers may have considered any change to have a negative impact on their present conditions and been predisposed to consider it in a negative manner.

Overall the teachers reported significant change in their work lives. This broad conclusion fits with other reports (Fullan, 1993; Hargreaves, 1994) and, as in these earlier reports, the changes have mainly affected the time available for teaching activities, the imposition of more accountability measures, the collaboration with colleagues, and expansion of the teachers' role to include more student advice. The teachers also report that while they feel their workload has increased significantly as a consequence of the changes, they are keen to adopt those changes they perceive as relating to teaching and learning, the core activities of the school, but less willing to do so if the changes are perceived to be aimed solely at administrative effectiveness. This differentiation by teachers about the main focus of the change is an important consideration for school- and system-level administrators. From the teachers' reports it appeared that, before the change was implemented, they needed to have their beliefs about its goal clearly outlined, which means more professional involvement in change decisions, which was often reported.

TEACHERS' ATTITUDE TO FUTURE CHANGE

The question of teachers' likely response to future change was also investigated. Again the country accounts show two broad response clusters, with three countries (Hungary, Israel and South Africa) reporting a positive attitude to participation in future change, the countries of Australia, England, the Netherlands, the PRC and the USA reporting an essentially ambivalent response, and one country, Canada, reporting a negative attitude. In the three countries where there had been significant socio-economic-political change it is perhaps not surprising to see that teachers indicated a positive attitude to change. Here the changes were likely to be perceived as part of a long-term strategy for the country's development within the twenty-first century. In other countries, where the same significant set of contextual factors does not exist, teachers expressed more ambivalence or direct hostility to future changes. No teachers presented as opponents of change per se; as one typical comment was, 'Change is always with us'. In the Australian and the Netherlands country accounts it is possible to discern differing responses to the professional domain of teaching and learning and the other domain of administrative or organisational effectiveness. Teachers reported that they were willing to support the former, as expressed by one Australia teacher: 'while it's probably doubled the time I would normally spend on programming and assessment details, it's improved the way I assess things and made it more positive'.

However, the feeling of cynicism about change was evident in many accounts, with a typical comment being, 'Okay, this was the flavour of the month last year, how long is it going to last?' In the Netherlands data it was found that if the change is linked with the professional domain and core activities of teaching and learning, and the teachers can see how it will benefit their students, they are willing to participate. In the Canadian account, teachers perceived that the Ministry of Education was unclear about the change and had not provided evidence of careful planning for its implementation. As one teacher typically reported, 'not getting the information right away, we had to seek out what we needed to know rather than having it given to us'. For many Canadian teachers the multiple changes also contributed to the negative feeling about future change, for example, 'Change upon change makes one less willing to accept more'.

From these data one can see the importance of the linkage between the focus of the change (i.e. its goal), teacher beliefs about the change and its fit with their students, and teacher behaviour in achieving successful implementation. This linkage is one that fits with emerging thinking about successful implementation in schools but, as yet, has not been drawn within a framework that accords with good theory. In Part Two we turn to the statistical analysis of the coded responses to shed further light on cross-cultural similarities and differences.

References

Abbott, A. (1988) *The System of Professions*. Chicago: University of Chicago Press.

African National Congress (ANC) (1994) *A Policy Framework for Education and Training*. Braamfontein: ANC Education Department.

Ashton, P.T. & Webb, R.B. (1986) *Making A Difference: teachers' sense of efficacy and student achievement*. Research on Teaching Monograph Series. New York: Longman.

Black, P. & Atkin, M. (1996) *Changing the Subject*. London: Routledge.

Darling-Hammond, L. (1990) Teacher Professionalism: why and how?, in A. Lieberman (Ed.) *Schools as Collaborative Cultures: creating the future now*. New York: Teachers College Press.

Fullan, M. (1993) *Change Forces: probing the depths of educational reform*. London: Falmer Press.

Fullan, M. (1985) Change Processes and Strategies at the Local Level, *The Elementary School Journal*, 3.

Hall, G. & Loucks, S. (1977) A Developmental Model for Determining Whether the Treatment is Actually Implemented, *American Educational Research Journal*, 14(3), pp. 263-276.

Hargreaves, A. (1994) *Changing Teachers, Changing Times: teachers' work and culture in the postmodern age*. London: Cassell.

John Williamson & Pam Poppleton

National Committee on Excellence in Education (1983) *A Nation at Risk: the imperative for educational reform* (Report no. 065-000-001772). Washington, DC: US Government Printing Service.

Neave, G. (1992) *The Teaching Nation.* Paris: Organisation for Economic Cooperation and Development.

Organisation for Economic Cooperation and Development (1990) *The Teacher Today: tasks, conditions, policies.* Paris: OECD.

Organisation for Economic Cooperation and Development (1994) *Quality in Teaching.* Paris: OECD.

Organisation for Economic Cooperation and Development (1996) *Lifelong Learning for All.* Paris: OECD.

Williamson, J. & Cowley, T. (1995) Case Studies about Implementing Profiles, *Curriculum Perspectives*, 15(3), pp. 69-71.

PART TWO

Cross-Cultural Analysis of the Effects of Educational Change on Secondary Teachers in Nine Countries

How Educational Change Affects Secondary School Teachers

LEVERNE COLLET, ALLEN MENLO & ZEHAVA ROSENBLATT

INTRODUCTION

Part Two of this book presents a comprehensive cross-cultural analysis of the effects of educational change on teachers. It begins with a quantitative comparison of the characteristics of changes that occurred in the nine participating countries during the mid-1990s. Next, it analyses the effect of these change characteristics on teachers' work lives, on the teachers' affective response to the changes, and on their attitude toward participation in future change. Finally, it presents a comprehensive analysis of the way all these variables interact with one another. Figure 1 provides a brief conceptual framework for the cross-cultural analysis.

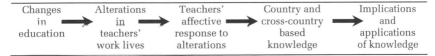

Changes in education	Alterations in teachers' work lives	Teachers' affective response to alterations	Country and cross-country based knowledge	Implications and applications of knowledge

Figure 1. Conceptual framework for cross-cultural analysis.

From 1995 to 1999, the nine country-based research teams collaborated in the analysis and interpretation of the teacher interviews reported in the individual country accounts given in the chapters in Part One of this book. An initial step in the analysis involved the consensual development of international codes for the teacher interview responses. The responses of teachers in each country were coded and quantified, then comparatively analysed using a variety of techniques to test relationships within and between the nine countries.

The *scientific* importance of this work rests in its contribution toward more fully understanding how the different kinds, levels, and sizes of educational/school change enter and positively or negatively modify teachers' work lives – particularly in the context of country variation. The *educational* importance of this work would seem to be contained in the implications that suggest what efforts may be most helpful to facilitate teacher leadership, responsibility-taking, and involvement in school change.

METHOD: VARIABLES ANALYSED

An important objective of this study was to discover which change characteristics influenced how teachers subsequently felt about the change they had nominated. Teacher feelings (the dependent variable) were presumed to be dependent upon the source, type and objective of the change selected (the independent variables).

Since its purpose is a quantitative comparison, this chapter (Part Two) deals only with variables derived from teacher responses that occurred in all nine countries in sufficient numbers to support meaningful statistical analysis. Fourteen variables met this selection criterion. These consisted of four background variables describing relevant characteristics of the teacher sample, four independent moderating variables measuring characteristics of the targeted change, and six dependent variables measuring various effects of the change. Before describing the analytic procedures and their results, it is important to provide a specific description of each of these variables with particular emphasis on the meaning of the possible scale values.

Context or Background Variables

A number of informational items were recorded at the beginning of each teacher interview. Four of these – their country, age, gender, and teaching seniority – were considered as teacher-sample characteristics that were relevant to the cross-cultural comparison. Marital status, which also might have been relevant, is not included here because it was not available in all countries. The following variables define the context or background within which the effect of change was studied.

Country. The numerical values for the country variable were assigned alphabetically: 1 = Australia, 2 = Canada, 3 = China, 4 = England, 5 = Hungary, 6 = Israel, 7 = the Netherlands, 8 = South Africa, and 9 = the USA. Country was a primary independent variable in all subsequent analyses.

Age. The teacher's numerical age in years was collected in all countries. However, for convenient use as an independent variable in subsequent analyses, age was also represented as a three-level categorical variable labelled 'tchr_age' with the following values: 1 = low (youngest to age 34), 2 = medium (age 35 to 44), and 3 = high (age 45 and up). Age might be expected to influence both participation levels and response to change. In general, the three-category version is used in most analyses because it produced higher correlations with dependent variables than actual chronological age.

Gender. Teacher gender is represented as a two-category variable with values assigned alphabetically: 1 = female, and 2 = male.

Seniority. The number of years of teaching experience was also available from the interview. Notice, however, that seniority was highly correlated with teacher age. Consequently it is unlikely to be useful to analyse both age and seniority. Intuitively, seniority seemed more likely to influence a teacher's response to change than age. However, there was a good deal more missing data for seniority than for age. For that reason, only age was used for inferential analyses.

Independent Variables

Four change characteristics were derived from responses to the first four items in the interview schedule: domain of change, initiator of change, objective of change, and teacher involvement in change. These four change variables were the main independent variables in this study (see the first column of Table II in Section 1 following). To simplify analysis, responses to each of these items were grouped into three or four broad categories as defined below.

Domain of Change (Q1)

The international coding manual assigned the domain or type of change described by each teacher to one of the following four mutually exclusive categories. In this presentation some of the codebook category names have been modified so that each category of a given variable began with a different letter. Single-letter representation is necessary in some tables.

1. Management Practices. Changes in policy regarding finances, management practices, and relationships between the school and parents or community organisations.

2. Teaching Practices. Changes in policy or practice regarding subject content or teaching method.

3. Learning Outcomes. Changes in policy or practice regarding student assessment or evaluation.

4. Student Experience. Changes in policy or practice that impact a student's affective experience (enjoyment, interest, or motivation) with school. Although these changes do not directly affect students' learning activities or academic performance, they may ultimately either promote or retard learning. Examples might include changes in the physical plant, class size, student grouping (by ethnicity, gender, etc.), school hours, or subject timetable.

Initiator (Origin) of Change (Q2)

The international coding manual assigned the teacher's perception of the origin, source, or initiator of the change to one of the following four mutually exclusive categories.

1. *Teacher Initiated.* The change was initiated by a teacher or teachers – usually within the respondent's school.

2. *School Initiated.* The change was initiated by the respondent's school, subject matter department, or the school district.

3. *Community Initiated.* The change was initiated by parents, community organisations, or subject matter associations.

4. *Government Initiated.* The change was initiated by local, state, or national government agencies.

Objective of Change (Q3)

The international coding manual assigned the teacher's perception of the underlying objective of the change to one of the following four mutually exclusive categories.

1. *Education Improvement.* The change was intended to improve teaching, subject content, students' academic development, or the validity of the student evaluation process.

2. *Accountability/Efficiency.* The change was intended to improve either the efficiency of school operations or the accountability of the school for student performance, or both.

3. *Social Objectives.* The change was intended to achieve a social objective such as improving students' personal-social growth or a political/cultural goal (e.g. racial parity), or to improve the security or rights of students, faculty, or staff.

Teacher Involvement (Role) in Change (Q4)

The international coding manual originally assigned the role of the teacher in the targeted change to one of seven categories arranged in ascending order according to the assumed degree of involvement. The original seven categories were: 1 = resister, 2 = no involvement, 3 = supporter or advisor, 4 = implementer, 5 = shared in decisions, 6 = planner, 7 = initiator. However, preliminary analysis cast doubt on the assumed linear increase in involvement at each stage of the scale, and suggested that better scale properties would be achieved by combining categories to obtain a three-point scale. It generally achieved higher correlations with dependent variables than the original scale and had the additional advantage that it could be used as a grouping variable in an analysis of variance. The three-point scale defined below is used throughout this chapter.

1. *Low Involvement.* This category included original categories 1 and 2: resisters of the change (which rarely occurred) and persons who had no direct involvement in the change.

2. *Medium Involvement.* This category included original categories 3 and 4: supporters/advisors or implementers of the change.

3. *High Involvement.* This category included original categories 5, 6, and 7: teachers who shared in decision-making, or helped plan or initiate the change.

Dependent Variables

There were eight dependent variables measuring the effects of change in this study. The first five variables measured alterations in teacher work, and the last three dealt with the strength and valence of the impact of change on teacher work life, and three with the strength and valence of teachers' affective response to change. For all the valenced dependent variables, score values had both negative and positive meanings with a theoretical zero (neutral) point at the centre of the scale.

Items Dealing with Alterations in Teacher Work

Amount of Work Life Affected (Q8A-amt). The teacher was asked to rate the amount (how much) of his or her work life that has been affected by the targeted change using a scale running from 1 = none of it to 6 = all of it. Obviously, work life could be affected either positively (e.g. making it more interesting) or negatively (e.g. making it more stressful). An additional valenced version of Q8A was needed.

249

Valenced Impact on Work Life (Q8A-val). A valence (Q8aNeg) was provided by computing the algebraic sum of positive and negative effects listed in subsequent questions and dividing the sum by the maximum number of mentions. The resulting 'impact on work life' variable was labelled Q8A, and had a scale running from −5 (strong negative impact on all work) to +5 (strong positive impact on all work). This valenced version had much stronger relationships with both the independent and dependent variables than the original six-point scale or any other weighted scale.

Impact on Professional Development (Q8F). The teacher was asked to rate the effect of the change on his or her professional development using the following three-point scale: 1 = negatively affected, 2 = no effect, 3 = positively affected.

Amount of Student Learning Affected (Q9A-amt). The teacher was asked to rate the amount (how much) of his or her students' learning that had been affected by the targeted change, using a scale running from 1 = none of it to 6 = all of it. Again, it is obvious that an additional valenced version of Q9A is needed.

Valenced Impact on Student Learning (Q9A-val). The method described for work life (Q8A) was again used to compute an 'impact on student learning' scale running from −5 (strong negative impact on all student learning) to +5 (strong positive impact on all student learning). Once again, the valenced version had stronger relationships with both the independent and dependent variables than the original six-point scale.

To demonstrate the need for valenced versions of Q8A and Q9A, results from both the original (old) and valenced versions of each variable are compared in Section 2 of this chapter (Part Two).

Items Dealing with Teachers' Affective Response

Feeling about This Change (Q10). Each teacher rated his or her general feeling about the targeted change using a six-point scale running from 1 = very negative to 6 = very positive. Note that a positive or negative valence is forced by omitting a neutral central position.

Participation in Similar Change (Q11A). Each teacher rated his or her disposition towards serving in each of 10 different roles in similar change using a three-point scale in which 1 = negative, 2 = neutral, and 3 = positive. The score for this item is the sum of these 10 ratings. Thus the scale value for this item runs from 10 (negative for all roles) to 30 (positive for all roles). Only the total (10 to 30) scale was analysed.

Participation in Any Future Change (Q11B). Each teacher rated his or her willingness to participate in any future change using a three-point scale: 1 = unwilling, 2 = neutral or undecided, and 3 = willing.

ANALYTIC STRATEGY

The major interest of the cross-cultural analyses was to determine the relationships between the characteristics of a change and its impact on teachers, and whether these relationships were similar or different from country to country. In addition to country, a teacher's age and gender may also influence the impact of a change. The approach selected was to begin with simple descriptive analyses and proceed to more complex analyses in three steps. The intent here is to use the information gathered at each step to interpret and explain the results of the subsequent step.

The remainder of this chapter is organised into the following four sections:

Section 1. This section presents percentage distributions of the major categorical variables and descriptive statistics for each of the continuous metric variables. The presentation is followed by a discussion of the meaning of the pattern(s) of results and their implications for subsequent analyses.

Section 2. This section attacks the major question of the study: How do the characteristics of a change influence its impact on teachers, and is the influence the same in every country? At the simplest level, this involves a cross-cultural assessment of the effect of a change characteristic on dependent variables one pair at a time. Since there are four change-characteristic variables and six dependent variables, the results of 24 two-way analyses are presented. The section concludes with a summary that emphasises trends across countries, change-characteristic and dependent variables. A more detailed analysis of the interactions between country and change variables is to be found in the Appendix.

Section 3. This section uses the results from the previous sections and published research to develop a theoretical 'flow of influence' model, and then tests that model using multiple regression equations containing background variables, change variables, work life dependent variables, and teacher-affect dependent variables.

Section 4. The final section provides an integrated summary of findings from all analyses presented in Part Two, and a discussion of their theoretical and practical implications.

SECTION 1: DESCRIPTIVE ANALYSIS

PERSONAL BACKGROUND VARIABLES

Personal background variables (age, gender, marital status, seniority, and school size) for the teachers participating in the study are presented in Table I grouped by country.

Country (n)	Au (50)	Ca (66)	Ch (50)	En (27)	Hu (34)	Is (59)	Ne (121)	SA (37)	US (50)	All (494)
Background variables										
Age										
Mean	41.8	44.7	34.4	43.2	41.3	41.6	42.2	42.1	47.7	42.4
SD	7.7	7.5	9.2	9.0	9.0	7.1	9.0	10.4	7.8	11.7
Gender										
% female	56.0	43.9	72.0	55.6	61.8	37.3	16.0	51.4	56.0	45.0
Marital status										
% married	n.a.	81.8	76.0	81.5	88.2	n.a.	90.9	70.3	74.0	79.8
Seniority										
Mean	17.5	19.1	11.7	16.9	17.6	17.7	16.9	16.9	21.9	17.4
SD	7.7	8.0	9.0	8.9	9.2	3.3	8.3	9.4	8.8	8.4
School size										
Mean	n.a.	1090	1760	1084	n.a.	743	1166	1066	1213	1151
SD		745	763	364		214	620	209	423	607

Au = Australia, Ca = Canada, Ch = China (PRC), En = England, Hu = Hungary,
Is = Israel, Ne = the Netherlands, SA = South Africa, US = the USA,
All = All 9 countries.
n.a. = Not available.

Table I. Descriptive statistics for five background variables.

Looking across variables, means and frequency distributions had large variations. The mean age for the whole sample was 42.4 years (SD 11.7), ranging between 34.4 years (China) and 47.7 years (USA). Canadian teachers were the second oldest (44.7), and the mean age of teachers in the other six countries was quite similar. The mean seniority in the profession for the whole sample was 17.4 years (SD 8.4), ranging between 11.7 years (China) and 21.9 years (USA). Again, Canadian teachers were the second most senior (19.1 years), and the other six countries were quite similar in seniority. In regard to gender distribution, the percentage of female teachers varied greatly among countries. For the whole sample this percentage was 45, ranging between 16% (the Netherlands) and 72% (China). Most of the teachers in the study were married (79.8%). Marital status ranged from 90.9% (the Netherlands) to 70.3% (South Africa). Hungary also had a relatively high marital status (88.2%), while all other countries were quite similar in this regard. Finally, the mean school size in number of students was 1151, ranging from 743 (Israel) to 1760 (China). Other countries (except for the USA, the second highest with 1213 students) were quite similar in this regard.

Looking across individual countries, country profiles varied considerably. Chinese teachers were the most dissimilar from teachers in other countries. They were youngest, least senior, and they tended to work in larger schools. The US teachers were oldest and most senior in the profession, their percentage of females was relatively high, and their marital status was relatively low. American teachers tended to work for relatively large schools. In Hungary the female proportion and marital rate were relatively high. In the Netherlands the percentage of female teachers was the lowest, but the marital rate was high. In Israel the proportion of female teachers was also low. The proportion of females teaching in Australia and England, though, was relatively high.

In sum, gender distribution was the most varied background variable. A high proportion of female teachers was observed in Australia, China, England, Hungary and the USA, while the proportion was low in Israel and the Netherlands. Age, seniority and school size were relatively unvaried, except for two outstanding countries: the USA (high in all three variables) and China (low in age and seniority, high in school size). Marital status was relatively high in Hungary and the Netherlands, and low in South Africa and the USA.

INDEPENDENT VARIABLES

Frequency distribution (percentages) of the independent variables is presented in Table II and discussed in the following sections.

Domain (Type) of Change (Q1)

For the whole sample, the most frequent domain of change was teaching practice [1] (46%). The next most frequent domain was student experience (28%), then learning outcomes (17%), and the least frequent domain was school management (14%). Thus, teachers experienced changes that mainly revolved around teaching issues related to subject matter and teaching methods. They experienced relatively few changes revolving around school management issues, such as financial allocations, administrative management of the school, and relationships with parents and community groups.

A country analysis shows that this pattern, in particular the prevalence of teaching practice, was extremely strong in England (67%) and even more so in the Netherlands (70%). Two countries where the most common domain was other than teaching outcomes were Australia (learning outcomes, 42%) and Canada (student experience, 68%). Student experience was also high in South Africa (38%, almost as high as teaching outcomes). In China, the school management domain was relatively more common than in other countries (29%), and almost as high as the rate of teaching. In Hungary, school management was also relatively high (27%) and equal to the Hungarian rate of student experience (27%).

Country	Au	Ca	Ch	En	Hu	Is	Ne	SA	US	All
n	50	66	50	27	34	59	121	37	50	494
CHANGE VARIABLES										
Domain of change (Q1)										
1 School management	18	12	29	7	27	11	9	8	18	14
2 Teaching	20	18	31	67	46	56	70	41	40	46
3 Learning outcomes	42	2	22	—	—	5	6	14	18	17
4 Student experience	20	68	18	26	27	28	15	38	24	28
Initiator of change (Q2)										
1 Teacher initiated	2	2	26	4	19	26	24	14	26	17
2 School initiated	12	18	26	7	44	50	23	19	28	26
3 Community initiated	2	23	4	4	16	5	3	14	16	9
4 Government initiated	84	58	44	85	22	19	50	54	30	48
Objective of change (Q3)										
1 Improve education	36	36	42	39	62	54	52	27	44	44
2 Improve accountability	34	19	17	42	15	20	25	8	26	23
3 Social objectives	30	45	41	19	23	26	24	65	30	33
Teachers' role involvement (Q4)										
Low	32	23	14	11	18	3	5	41	14	16
Medium	56	52	68	48	32	30	74	35	44	53
High	12	25	18	41	50	67	21	24	42	31

Au = Australia, Ca = Canada, Ch = China (PRC), En = England, Hu = Hungary, Is = Israel, Ne = the Netherlands, SA = South Africa, US = the USA, All = All 9 countries.

Table II. Percentage distribution of independent (change) variables by countries.

To summarise, the domain of change that had the strongest effect on teachers in their work was teaching practice, except for Australia and Canada, where the strongest domains were learning outcomes and student experience, respectively. The domain of change that affected teachers least in all countries except China and Hungary was school management. In China and Hungary school management was not the least dominant, but was second dominant.

Initiator (Origin) of Change (Q2)

For the whole sample, the most frequent initiator of change was government (48%). The next most frequent initiator was school (26%), then teachers (17%), and the least frequent initiator of change was community (9%). Thus, teachers experienced local, state (when applicable) or national governments as the bodies initiating most of the changes, while community (parents, civic groups, educational organisations) was perceived as initiating the least changes.

A country analysis shows that this pattern, in particular government initiation, was extremely frequent in the cases of Australia (84%), England (85%), and quite frequent in Canada (56%). In Hungary and Israel the main initiators were schools (44% and 50%, respectively), not governments. Teacher-initiated change was relatively high in China (26%), Israel (26%), the Netherlands (24%) and the USA (26%). Relatively small differences between teacher initiation and school initiation were observed in China and the Netherlands. In the USA initiation of changes divided almost equally among teachers, school and government. Community initiation was relatively higher in Canada than community initiation in other countries.

In summary, for most teachers the most frequent initiator of change was government (particularly in Australia and England) and the least frequent was community. Only in Hungary and Israel was school the main initiator of change. Teacher initiation was higher in China, Israel, the Netherlands, and the USA than in other countries.

Objective of Change (Q3)

For the whole sample, the most frequent objective of change was improving educational practice (44%), the next was improving students' social development (33%), and the least frequent one was improving accountability and efficiency (23%). Thus, teachers perceived the major objective of changes they experienced to be education-related, in terms of students' academic performance, quality of teaching, updating the content of what is taught and improving student evaluation and assessment systems.

A country analysis shows that this exact pattern was only shared by Hungary, Israel and the USA. In Canada, and particularly in South Africa, the major change objective was social development (45% and 65% respectively). Only in England was the major change objective accountability and efficiency (but its frequency was close to the educational objective, 42% and 39% respectively), and in Australia accountability and efficiency was slightly higher than the social objective (34% and 30% respectively). The social objective category was the lowest (19%) among other objectives in England. In Australia all three objectives shared a similar rating (36%, 34%, 30%), and in South Africa, the accountability objective was the lowest (8%) of all countries.

Generally, teachers seemed to be more interested in educational and social objectives than in administrative (efficiency and accountability) ones, except for England, and to some degree Australia. The social objective was particularly frequent in South Africa.

Teachers' Involvement (Role) in Change (Q4)

For the whole sample, 53% of teachers perceived their involvement in change as medium (supporter, advisor or implementer). Higher roles, such as initiator, planner or shared decision-maker, were reported by 31%. Only 16% perceived their role as low: resisting, or no role at all (see detailed description of variables in the Method section earlier).

This pattern was shared by China, England, the Netherlands, the USA, and to some degree, Australia. Israeli teachers perceived their role as mostly high (67%), as did Hungarian teachers (50%). South African teachers reported a lower involvement in change (41%) than all other countries. The positive power of Israeli teachers' involvement in change is noted in the 97% score from a combined high and medium involvement. Teachers from the Netherlands also had a high combined score of medium and high (95%).

In summary, the majority of the teachers perceived their involvement as medium, and 84% saw their involvement as medium or high. The highest perception of involvement (high and medium) was recorded in Israel and the Netherlands, and the lowest in South Africa.

DEPENDENT VARIABLES

The distributions and descriptive statistics for dependent variables are not discussed here because that information is included as part of the results of the two-way analyses of variance presented in Section 2 following.

SECTION 2: THE INFLUENCE OF CHANGE CHARACTERISTICS ON DEPENDENT VARIABLES

This section attempts to answer the general question of major interest to the study: What is the influence of each change-characteristic variable on the dependent variables, and does that influence change from country to country? Although we recognise that teacher age and gender may somewhat alter results, these variables are ignored here because of small within-country sample sizes and a considerable amount of missing data. Consequently, this section contains an isolated assessment of the effect each change-characteristic variable has on each dependent variable, followed by a summary attempting to integrate the results and derive general principles that may be of use to educators and researchers.

Since each change-characteristic variable has three or four categories, an obvious way to assess their influence on each dependent is to translate the question into sub-questions about differences among three sets of dependent-variable means. Are there differences among: (1) country means, (2) category means for the change variable, (3) the rank order of category means from country to country? These questions can be answered by computing a two-way (country by change variable) analysis of variance for each combination of four change variables and eight dependent variables; that is, the computation of 32 separate two-way analyses of variance. Interpreting and reporting so many analyses in a coherent manner requires an interpretive framework that permits a simplified grouping of change characteristics, countries, and dependent variables. Preliminary analyses of the original response codes (i.e. the versions in effect before the codes were reduced to three or four categories) for the domain, initiator, and objective of change were compared for countries with the lowest means and highest proportions of negative responses on all six dependent variables, versus countries with the highest positive means and lowest proportions of negative responses. This examination suggested that something like a generic 'locus of control' variable explained the differences in the pattern of change characteristics for the low and high groups of countries. A new variable was therefore created to represent these ideas from ratings of 'degree of involvement' in change processes.

THE LOCUS OF CONTROL HYPOTHESIS

The power of personal control derives from locus of control theory. Rotter (1966) studied the generalised expectancies that resulted from internal, personally controlled reinforcement versus externally controlled reinforcement. Based on his work and much subsequent research, it has been demonstrated that persons who are given greater personal control over their life situations developed greater happiness, activity, involvement, and health.

The concept of locus of control can be considered as a dimension of everyone's personality. Each of us can be located somewhere along a continuum of internality to externality (Bavelas, 1978). Persons who view themselves as determiners of outcomes would have a more internal locus of control, and those who view themselves as being subjected to forces in the world around them and not determiners of their own fate would have a more external locus of control. How each person perceives their locus of control can determine the degree of power or control over the events in their lives. It seems reasonable for us to view groups of persons as having a make-up or syntality of character that, overall, rests somewhere on the internality–externality continuum. Thus, persons may exercise more or less agency or power. The sense of power or lack of it has a direct bearing on the degree to which people are willing to participate in activities related to an educational change.

Change Characteristics Grouped by Locus Expectation

An examination of the categories of the domain, initiator, and objective change variables suggested that each set of categories could be assigned to positions on the internal–external control continuum. It was hypothesised that categories assigned to the internal end of that continuum would produce a stronger, more positive effect on dependent variables than categories assigned to the external end. On this basis, it is reasonable to assume that teachers feel more in control when changes are in the teaching or school management domains, are initiated by the school or teacher, and are aimed at educational improvement. These categories in the domain, initiator, and objective variables were defined as 'internal' and the remaining categories for each variable were defined as 'external'.

Country Rankings by Locus Expectation

When the Table II percentages of teachers in these three 'internal' categories are averaged, countries can be ranked in ascending order of teacher control as follows: (1) Canada (28.2%), (2) Australia (28.3%), (3) South Africa (35.7%), (4) England (38.0%), (5) China (51.3%), (6) the USA (52.0%), (7) the Netherlands (59.0%), (8) Hungary (65.7%), and (9) Israel (68.7%). It is hypothesised that the pattern of means for valenced variables will be consistent with this order. Note, however, that the Canada versus Australia percentages are virtually identical and several other pairs of percentages are quite close: for these pairs, a reversed outcome would not contradict the hypothesis.

ANALYSIS OF VARIANCE RESULTS

Analysis of variance provides a significance test for overall differences among means in each set, but does not give information about differences between particular pairs of means. A statistical test of differences between all pairs of means is provided by computing a separate Newman–Keuls comparison of ordered means (see Winer, 1971, pp. 215-218) for change variable means, country means, and change variable means within each of the nine countries. Since we are interested in patterns of rank-ordered means that apply to the entire set of dependent variables, as well as the findings for each individual variable, it is advantageous to present the country results of all 32 analyses in one table, and the change variable results of all 32 analyses in a second table with results for each significant country by change interaction provided in context.

Dependent Variable Means by Country

The country effects from the two-way analyses have a unique presentation advantage. For each dependent variable there are four separate two-way analyses of variance: country by type (domain) of change, country by initiator of change, country by objective of change, and country by involvement (role) in change. The four sets of country means produced by these analyses are identical except for trivial differences caused by variations in missing data. For simplicity, only one set of country means is presented for each dependent variable. Although the four analyses provided slight variations in the significance levels of the Newman–Keuls tests among means, the differences in outcomes were trivial. The strategy adopted was to report the differences obtained using the most conservative test.

Differences among country means obtained for the eight dependent variables are summarised in Table III. Countries are first listed in alphabetical order across the top of the table, with the number of teachers in that country's sample immediately below. Notice that the main body of the table contains one row of results for each dependent variable, and that each row contains two lines of data for each 'amount' variable and three lines of data for each valenced (negative/positive) variable. The first line provides the country names, and the last data line in each row (opposite 'Means') provides the mean score for that dependent variable listed in ascending order of size. A rank-order listing of means is required by the Newman-Keuls test of differences between all pairs of ordered means. Following statistical convention, a rank of 1 is assigned to the lowest mean and a rank of 9 to the highest.

The variables reported in the first two data rows measure the amount of teacher work life and student learning affected by the change without regard to their positive or negative impact, while the variables reported in the last six data rows all have scores with both negative and positive meanings. For these six 'valenced' variables, the percentage of teachers who gave a response with a negative valence was reported in the middle line of each data row opposite the '% Negative' label.

Alphabetical Countries:	Australia	Canada	China	England	Hungary	Israel	Netherlands	SouthAfrica	US-Michigan
Number of Cases:	50	65	50	27	34	57	116	37	50
Dependent Variables:	Rank=1	Rank=2	Rank=3	Rank=4	Rank=5	Rank=6	Rank=7	Rank=8	Rank=9
Q8A-amt: Amount of Work-Life Affected. Old Means=	Hungary 3.27	US-Michigan 3.58	Canada 3.71	Netherlands 3.77	England 3.78	China 3.84	Australia 4.06	South Africa 4.27	Israel 5.16
Q9A-amt: Amount of Student Learning Affected. Old Means=	Netherlands 3.26	Hungary 3.35	Australia 3.42	China 3.44	US-Michigan 3.74	Canada 3.80	England 3.85	South Africa 4.05	Israel 4.68
Q8A-val: Valenced Impact on Work-Life. %Negatives= / New Means= (Range -5 to +5)	South Africa 54% / -1.07	Australia 60% / -0.69	Canada 58% / -0.27	Netherlands 41% / 0.08	England 37% / 0.45	Hungary 27% / 0.87	US-Michigan 22% / 0.89	China 24% / 0.92	Israel 27% / 1.36
Q8F: Impact on Professional Development. %Negatives= / Means= (Range 1 Neg. to 3 Pos.)	Australia 74% / 1.51	South Africa 68% / 1.66	Canada 68% / 1.68	England 59% / 2.10	US-Michigan 44% / 2.26	Netherlands 35% / 2.45	Hungary 38% / 2.56	China 38% / 2.66	Israel 27% / 2.89
Q9A-val: Valenced Impact on Student Learning: %Negatives= / New Means= (Range -5 to +5)	Australia 78% / -0.48	Canada 67% / -0.11	Netherlands 55% / 0.58	England 53% / 0.64	Hungary 54% / 0.74	South Africa 54% / 0.77	England 38% / 0.90	Israel 37% / 1.25	China 36% / 1.48
Q10: Teacher Feeling About This Change. %Negatives= / Means= (Range 1 Neg to 6 Pos.)	Canada 56% / 3.36	Australia 54% / 3.48	China 20% / 4.22	South Africa 32% / 4.30	Hungary 24% / 4.32	Netherlands 21% / 4.32	US-Michigan 28% / 4.38	England 11% / 4.52	Israel 9% / 5.10
Q11A: Role in a Similar Future Change. %Negatives= / Means= (Range 10 Neg to 30 Pos)	China 86% / 16.78	Australia 54% / 19.08	South Africa 57% / 19.89	Hungary 24% / 22.50	England 17% / 22.69	Netherlands 12% / 25.00	Canada 18% / 25.08	US-Michigan 10% / 26.10	Israel 7% / 27.57
Q11B: Role in Any Future Change. %Negatives= / Means= (Range 1 Neg. to 3 Pos.)	Canada 42% / 1.77	Australia 34% / 1.88	England 26% / 1.93	Netherlands 14% / 2.10	Hungary 24% / 2.21	South Africa 19% / 2.30	China 6% / 2.30	US-Michigan 8% / 2.32	Israel 4% / 2.80

NOTE: Means underscored by the same line are NOT significantly different at the .05 level.

Table III. Dependent-variable means for countries: underlinings indicate significance of difference.

Each set of dependent-variable means in Table III is underscored by one or more lines to summarise the results of the Newman-Keuls comparison among all pairs of ordered country means. Means which are underscored by the same line are homogeneous, that is, they do not differ significantly.

Interpreting Table III Results by Variable

Results for Q8A-amt. The significance of differences among country means for Q8A-amt are summarised by underscore lines below the means. We can be 95% confident of two statements: first, since the line underscoring South Africa does not underscore Hungary, larger amounts of teacher work life are affected in South Africa than in Hungary; second, since the mean for Israel is not underscored, the amount of teacher work life affected in that country is greater than the amount affected in South Africa and all other countries. Observed differences in the means of pairs of countries not specifically mentioned in these two statements are underscored by the same line and, therefore, do not differ significantly. For interpretation purposes, the rank order of means underscored by the same line may be considered interchangeable.

Results for Q9A-amt. The significance of differences among Q9A-amt means are again summarised by underscore lines. The mean for South Africa is significantly higher than the mean for Hungary and the Netherlands, indicating that larger amounts of student learning are affected there. Once again, the mean for Israel is not underscored indicating that change affected more student learning in Israel than in any other country. Differences among all other pairs of means are not significant and their ranks may be interchanged.

Results for Q8A-val. Reading the Q8A-val underscores from left to right, we can be 95% confident that the Australian mean is lower than the means for all countries from England to Israel. Similarly, we can be 95% confident that the mean for South Africa is lower than the means for all countries from the USA to Israel, that the mean for Canada is lower than the means for all countries from the Netherlands to Israel, and that the mean for England is lower than the mean for Israel. However, the country means from the USA to Israel do not differ significantly. Again, the rank orders of means underscored by the same line are interchangeable.

The percentage of negative scores for Q8A-val ranges from 74% negative for Australia to only 27% negative for Israel. In general, the percentages reduce from left to right in the same order as the means, with two exceptions: South Africa (60%) versus Canada (68%), and Hungary (38%) versus the Netherlands (35%) versus China (42%). However, in

LeVerne Collet et al

both cases the means are underscored by the same line indicating there are only chance differences among them.

Two observations are of particular interest. First, negative effects of change on work life were reported by a strong majority of teachers in four countries (Australia, South Africa, Canada, and England), and large minorities (ranging from 35% to 44%) in four more countries (the USA, the Netherlands, Hungary and China). Even in Israel 27% of teachers reported negative effects on their work life. Second, the country means for Q8A-val ranged from a low of −1.07 for Australia to a high of +1.36 for Israel. In view of the extreme shift in the corresponding percentages from 74% to 27% negative, this is a surprisingly narrow range of mean scores. The combination of rather extreme percentage of negative effects and the narrow range of country mean scores occurred because most teachers received a Q8A-val score between −1 and +1. In other words, the average teacher in our study experienced a relatively small effect on work life whether it was positive or negative.

Results for Q8F. The percentage of teachers who responded to Q8F with a 1 (a negative impact) ranges from 54% for South Africa to only 5% for Israel. The percentage negatives neatly divide countries into two groups: on the left are three countries (South Africa, Australia, and Canada) where more than half of the teachers reported negative effects, and on the right are six countries (the Netherlands, England, Hungary, the USA, China and Israel) where less than half were negative. The mean scores exhibit the same pattern. The means for the first group all have negative valence, and the means for the second group all have positive valence. The underscore lines tell us that the means for all three countries in the bottom group are significantly lower than the means for all six countries in the top group. Within the bottom group there are no significant differences among country means or rank orders. In the top group, there are significant differences in means and ranks between the USA, China and Israel versus the Netherlands, and between Israel versus Hungary, England, and the Netherlands.

Results for Q9A-val. According to the percentage negatives for Q9A-val there are five countries (Australia, Canada, the Netherlands, Hungary, and South Africa) where a majority of teachers reported a negative impact of change on student learning, and four (England, the USA, Israel, and China) where a majority of teachers reported a positive impact. The order of decreasing percentages is consistent with the order of means except for the Netherlands, and there the shift in percentages is only 2%. The underscores tell us that the mean for bottom-ranked Australia is significantly lower than the means for the seven countries between the Netherlands and Israel, inclusively. On the other hand, the mean for second-lowest Canada differs significantly from only the top two ranks,

262

Israel and China. Since all other country means are underscored by the same line, difference among them is insignificant; therefore the rank orders within these homogeneous groups may be considered interchangeable.

The relative magnitude of the means and percentage of negatives here is similar to that for Q8A-val but shifted slightly in the positive direction. Such surprising combinations as 78% negatives in Australia but a mean of only -0.48 reflects the fact that the majority of teachers assigned scores that were either weak positive or very weak negative.

Results for Q10. The percentage of negatives for Q10 is much milder than for previous questions: a majority of teachers had negative feelings about the targeted change in only two countries (Canada and Australia), and even they had percentages in the mid-50s and means just barely below the zero point (3.5). In the remaining seven countries, negative percentages ranging from 32% to 9% were combined with positive means ranging from 4.22 in China to 5.10 in Israel, all indicating positive to very positive feelings about the change. The lines underscoring Q10 means tell us that the negative means for the bottom group (Canada and Australia) are significantly lower than all seven positive means for countries from China to Israel, inclusively, but do not differ from each other. However, the only significant difference within the positive-mean group is between China and Israel. Once again, if the ranks of countries underscored by the same line are considered homogeneous, the only change in rank order between Q10 and the previous questions is in the placement of China.

Results for Q11A. According to the Q11A scores, 86% of Chinese teachers and substantial majorities of teachers in Australia (58%) and South Africa (67%) were unwilling to serve in most similar-change roles, while less than 25% had this attitude in all other countries. The underscore lines divide the Q11A means into four groups. The mean for China is significantly lower than the means for all other countries. The means for Australia and South Africa are significantly lower than those for any of the six countries from Hungary (22.50) to Israel (27.57) inclusively. Means for Hungary and England are significantly lower than the means for the USA and Israel. Means for the Netherlands and Canada are overlapping members in each of the last two groups whose scores do not differ significantly from either of them. Considering the ranks of members of the same group to be interchangeable, the rank order of means is again similar to that of previous questions, except for the low placement of China and the relatively high placement of Canada.

Results for Q11B. Canada, Australia and England all have negative-valence means (less than 2.0) and substantial percentages (more than

25%) of teachers who had a negative reaction to participating in any new change (i.e. their response to this item was a 1). At the other extreme, only Israel had a very small proportion of negative responses (4%) and a mean large enough to indicate that a strong majority (at least 80%) of teachers responded with a 3, indicating willingness to participate in any future change. The underscore lines define four overlapping homogeneous groups. The lowest grouping contains the means for Canada, Australia, England, and the Netherlands. The second lowest group contains means for Australia, England, the Netherlands, and Hungary. The middle (second highest) group contains the means for England, the Netherlands, Hungary, South Africa, China, and the USA. The fourth and highest group contained only the mean for Israel, which was significantly higher than the mean for any other country. Within each of these homogeneous groups, the rank order of country means may be considered interchangeable.

Summary of Patterns in Table III

The rank orders of country means presented in Table III form a similar pattern for the valenced variables, except for China, whose low placement on willingness to participate in a similar change is an exception. When the Chinese exception is ignored and means underscored by the same line are considered to have similar values, the rank orders of the eight remaining country means exhibit a fairly consistent pattern. For every valenced variable the low group contains three countries (Australia, South Africa, and Canada) that consistently have the highest percentage of negative scores and low mean scores, usually with a negative valence, which occupy (or tie with) one of the first three ranks. The middle group contains four countries (England, the Netherlands, Hungary, and the USA) that tend to have smaller percentages of negative scores and mean scores with a mild positive valence, and either occupy (or tie with) the four middle ranks. The high group contains Israel, which consistently has the smallest percentage of negatives and a mean with a moderate to strong positive valence which occupies the highest rank.

In the earlier section outlining the locus of control hypothesis, the theoretical country rankings by locus expectation were: (1) Canada, (2) Australia, (3) South Africa, (4) England, (5) China, (6) the USA, (7) the Netherlands, (8) Hungary, and (9) Israel. When China is excluded, the bottom three ranks and the top rank either match or tie with the observed ranks in Table III for every valenced variable, and the middle ranks are roughly comparable. Even the Chinese result is less inconsistent than it seems. The mean for China is equal to or tied with its fifth-place 'internal' ranking for all valenced variables except Q11A, where it is significantly lowest. But this may not be a true contradiction because the young Chinese teachers may have considered several of the 10 listed roles to be the prerogative of experienced supervisory personnel. The overall country rankings support the locus of control hypothesis.

The need to add a valenced version of effects on teacher work life and student learning is documented by comparing the rank orders of the amount and valenced means. The effect is most easily seen by looking at extreme shifts in position. Examining work life data, for example, reveals that Australia and South Africa had the lowest valenced means (-1.07 and -0.69 respectively) but obtained higher amount means (4.06 and 4.27 respectively) than every country except Israel. This demonstrates that teachers in these two countries had *large* amounts of their work life affected, but the effect was usually in a *negative* direction. Countries in which the effect on work life was generally positive, such as Israel, achieved similar rankings on the amount and valenced scales. Notice that the valenced rankings are confirmed by percentages of negative scores of 74%, 60%, and 27% for Australia, South Africa, and Israel, respectively.

The amount versus valenced relationships for student learning present a similar pattern, but not quite as extreme. Canada, for example, was ranked sixth for amount means but second-lowest for valenced means, because 67% of teachers perceived that moderate amounts of student learning (3.80 out of 6.00) were affected in a negative direction.

The importance of using the new valenced scales in subsequent analyses is underlined by remembering that an important conceptual principle of this study was that the impact on work life was expected to be a major predictor of a teacher's affective (bad–good) response to change. One would expect a positive effect on most work-alteration variables to go with high teacher-affect scores, and a negative effect on most work life to go with low teacher-affect scores. This conceptual relationship argues for emphasising the valenced versions of effects on teacher work life and student learning in subsequent predictive analyses.

Dependent Variable Means by Change Categories

This section assesses the effects of four change variables (Q1 Domain or type of change; Q2, Initiator or source of change; Q3, Objective of change; and Q4, Involvement [role] in change) on each of the eight dependent variables, using two-way country by change analyses of variance. The results for the main effects of change-characteristics from these 32 analyses are summarised in Table IV, with each row by column 'cell' presenting the results for one analysis. The term 'main effects' refers to overall trends in the influence of a particular change variable as represented by differences among the marginal dependent-variable means for its three or four categories. For any one dependent variable the marginal category means for each change variable were computed by treating teachers from all nine countries as a single group.

In some of the 32 analyses reported in Table IV there was a significant interaction between countries and the change variable, which indicates that the rank order of category means for individual countries may differ significantly from the overall nine-country trend displayed in the marginal means. In Table IV, cells where a significant interaction occurred are flagged with the symbol **. In these cases, differences among results for individual countries are summarised in the text, with references to detailed explanations in the Appendix. Where there is no significant interaction, the overall trend expressed in the marginal means is interpreted as applying to all countries.

The layout of Table IV is similar to that of Table III, with the left-hand column identifying the eight dependent variables and the top (header) row identifying the four change variables. The second row of the table, immediately below the header row, lists the full label for the response categories within each change variable. An abbreviation of each category label is created using the first letter of each major word in the category name. For example, the category 'Management Practices' is abbreviated as MP. These abbreviated labels are listed in the first line of each data row of results in rank order of the corresponding category means. Once again, a series of underscore lines beneath the means summarises the results of the Newman–Keuls tests of the differences among all pairs of the ordered category means within each column.

The intent of the following discussion is to focus on patterns of change-influence across dependent variables, rather than the results for each dependent variable in isolation. For that reason, the results from Table IV are discussed column by column. To assist reader interpretation of the table, results for the first column are discussed in some detail, followed by more succinct presentations of results for subsequent columns.

Change-Characteristic Variables — Independent-Variable Categories

	Q1A. Domain or Type of Change	Q2. Initiator or Source of Change	Q3. Objective of Change	Q4. Involvement (Role) in Change
Categories	1. Management Practice 14%; 2. Teaching Practice 46%; 3. Learning Outcome 12%; 4. Student Experience 28%	1. Teacher Initiated 17%; 2. School Initiated 26%; 3. Community Initiated 09%; 4. Government Initiate 48%	1. Education Improve 44%; 2. Accountability/Eff. 23%; 3. Social Objective 33%	1. Low 16%; 2. Medium 53%; 3. High 31%

Dependent Variables:

Q8A-amt. Amount of Teacher Work-Life Affected. Old Category Means=
- Q1A: TP 3.91, SE 3.92, MP 4.08, LO 4.09
- Q2: GI 3.89, SI 4.04, TI 4.13, CI 4.19
- Q3: AE 3.84, EI 3.99, SO 4.03
- Q4: Med 3.80, Low 4.05, High 4.28; r=.124, p=.007

Q9A-amt. Amount of Student Learning Affected. Old Category Means=
- Q1A: MP 3.15, TP 3.71, SE 3.77, LO 4.05**
- Q2: GI 3.63, CI 3.77, SI 3.79, TI 3.82
- Q3: AE 3.45, SO 3.66, EI 3.85
- Q4: Low 3.34, Med 3.57, High 4.13**; r=.229, p=.000

Q8A-val. Valenced Impact On Teacher Work-Life. Percentage Negative= / New Category Means= Range: -5=V.Neg. to +5=V.Pos.
- Q1A: SE 55%/0.05, LO 48%/0.06, MP 55%/0.15, TP 41%/0.74
- Q2: GI 58%/-.08, CI 51%/0.34, SI 42%/0.68, TI 31%/0.98
- Q3: AE 59%/-.05, SO 52%/0.17, EI 39%/0.71
- Q4: Low 75%/-.96, Med 49%/0.44, High 31%/0.99; r=.310, p=.000

Q8F. Impact on Professional Development. Percentage Negative= / Category Means= Values: 1=Neg. to 3=Pos
- Q1A: MP 52%/1.88, LO 46%/1.89, SE 41%/2.02, TP 38%/2.16
- Q2: GI 47%/1.91, CI 44%/1.98, SI 41%/2.12, TI 30/2.29
- Q3: EI 43%/2.01, AE 40%/2.04, SO 42%/2.08
- Q4: Low 44%/1.82, Med 50%/1.90, High 26%/2.42; r=.216, p=.000

Q9A-val. Valenced Impact on Student Learning. Percentage Negative= / New Category Means= Range: -5=V Neg. to +5=V.Pos.
- Q1A: MP 71%/0.00, SE 60%/0.37, LO 50%/0.62, TP 42%/0.96
- Q2: CI 58%/0.24, GI 61%/0.29, SI 52%/0.61, TI 33%/1.53**
- Q3: AE 67%/-.02, SO 54%/0.58, EI 43%/0.97
- Q4: Low 82%/-.60, Med 50%/0.52, High 27%/1.40; r=.342, p=.000

Q10. Teacher Feeling About This Change. Percentage Negative= / Category Means= Range: 1=V.Neg. to 6=V.Pos.
- Q1A: SE 40%/3.82, MP 44%/3.85, LO 27%/4.20, TP 16%/4.59
- Q2: GI 44%/3.79, CI 36%/3.84, SI 27%/4.44, TI 09%/4.97**
- Q3: AE 41%/3.89, SO 32%/4.02, EI 19%/4.51**
- Q4: Low 65%/2.91, Med 29%/4.17, High 9%/4.91**; r=.447, p=.000

Q11A. Willingness to Take Roles in a Similar Change. Percentage Negative= / Category Means Range: 10 Neg. to 30 Pos.
- Q1A: MP 39%/20.5, LO 45%/20.6, SE 22%/23.8, TP 17%/23.8**
- Q2: GI 31%/22.0, TI 19%/23.4, SI 27%/23.8, CI 23%/24.2**
- Q3: SO 52%/21.8, AE 26%/22.1, EI 20%/24.0
- Q4: Low 48%/20.4, Med 24%/22.3, High 17%/25.0**; r=.280, p=.000

Q11B. Willingness to Take Roles in Any New Change. Percentage Negative= / Category Means Range: 1=Neg to 3=Pos
- Q1A: SE 24%/2.02, MP 18%/2.03, LO 20%/2.15, TP 15%/2.26
- Q2: CI 33%/1.88, GI 25%/2.04, SI 12%/2.28, TI 08%/2.43
- Q3: AE 23%/2.02, SO 21%/2.18, EI 14%/2.23
- Q4: Low 33%/1.82, Med 18%/2.16, High 14%/2.35**; r=.237, p=.000

*NOTE 1: Means underscored by the same line do NOT differ significantly. NOTE 2: ** indicates there is a significant interaction with country*

Table IV. Influence of change characteristics on the dependent variables as assessed by two-way ANOVAs (country by change) with a subsequent Newman–Keuls comparison of ordered means.

Results for Domain or Type of Change (Q1)

In Table IV, the results for type of change are displayed in column two. The four categories for type of change are listed immediately below the column title. The first letters of words in the category description (MP, TP, LO, and SE, respectively) are used to identify category outcomes in the body of the table. Before proceeding with a discussion of dependent-variable results, please notice the large differences in category response frequencies. Only 12% of the changes involved learning outcomes (e.g. statewide assessments), and 14% involved management practices, while 28% involved student experience and 46% involved teaching practices. These differences in frequency are reflected in the Newman-Keuls results and have important consequences whenever a significant interaction with country occurs. Categories with smaller nine-country frequencies often have very small response numbers in individual countries, and in some cases the category may fail to occur (i.e. $n = 0$). In general, smaller frequencies require larger differences from other means to be significant. To avoid unnecessary losses of statistical power, the results tabulated here represent a pair by pair computation of the significance of differences.

The amount of teacher work life and student learning affected, as shown in the first two data rows of Table IV, do not have the inherent bad–good valence shared by the three valenced work-alteration variables, and the three teacher-affect variables. Consequently, one would expect these two variables to produce somewhat different relationships among domain of change category means than would the six valenced variables below them. For these two variables, changes involving learning outcomes produced the largest means, and changes involving teaching practice the lowest or second lowest mean. Note, however, that the only significant difference for these two variables was the lower amount of student learning affected by changes in management practices than any other type of change. These outcomes agree with common-sense expectations. Changes in teaching practice would not usually involve large mandatory changes in what actually happened in the classroom or in what students learn, while changes in learning outcomes (e.g. student assessment) could have sweeping effects on both classroom behaviour and what students actually learn. Changes in management (e.g. a new grading and reporting system) could affect almost as much teacher work life as a change in learning outcomes (here the means are only 0.01 apart) but would be unlikely to have much effect on student learning.

The expected relationship among category means for valenced variables is almost diametrically opposite. Changes in teaching practice, because they are under the control of individual teachers, would produce positive reactions according to locus of control theory while changes in learning outcomes, such as student assessment, might be perceived as a threatening external judgement on teaching effectiveness and produce strong negative reactions. Changes in student experience (such as larger classes) or in management practice would tend to produce milder negative or positive responses between these extremes. This in fact appeared to happen. Teaching practice (TP) obtained the highest means, indicative of the strongest influence, for all three valenced work-alteration variables and all three teacher-affect variables. The percentage negatives generally tended to agree with this pattern.

There is evidence for the locus of control hypothesis in these results. Although the TP mean was not significantly higher than the other means in all cases, the fact that it was the highest mean for all six valenced dependent variables is itself highly significant. For any one variable, the probability of obtaining a highest TP mean by chance is 0.25; the probability of obtaining that result for all six valenced variables is 0.0002. This general finding strongly supports the locus of control prediction that changes in teacher practice would have the most positive impact on both the work life and teacher-affect variables. Unfortunately, the result does not support the expected superiority of management practice.

Notice that this finding might be affected by a significant interaction between countries and type of change for amount of student learning affected (Q9A-amt) and willingness to participate in a similar future change (Q11A). However, the country-by-country results for Q9A-amt and Q11A in Appendices A1 and A2, respectively, suggest that the significant interactions were due to changes in the magnitude of differences among means that do not affect their direction. Consequently, the finding of superior teaching practice scores for all valenced variables applies to all countries.

Results for Initiator or Source of Change (Q2)

In Table IV, the results documenting the effect of the initiator or source of a change on each of the six dependent variables appear in column three. From locus of control theory, one would expect teachers to respond more favourably as they gain more control over a change. Consequently, one would expect teacher-initiated changes and school-initiated changes to have more positive effects than changes that were initiated by the community or the government. Although the expected position of the community-initiated (CI) and school-initiated (SI) means is less certain, the probable ascending order is GI, CI, SI, TI.

The observed order of means in column three of Table IV is consistent with the locus of control prediction of greater teacher-initiated means than government-initiated means for all variables. Despite the fact that three of these differences were not statistically significant, the set of results provides moderate support for the locus of control theory. Notice, however, that we will need to examine initiator means country by country for the three variables having significant interactions: Q9A-val, Q10, and Q11A. Country-by-country results for these variables appear in Appendices A3, A4, and A5, respectively. For all three variables, the significant interaction was caused by the absence of teacher-initiated and community-initiated change in Australia and England. Nevertheless, it appears that teacher-initiated changes produce more positive results whenever they occur.

Results for Objective of Change (Q3)

The results for the objective of change analysis are summarised in the fourth column of Table IV. The locus of control hypothesis predicts the largest, most positive mean for education improvement (EI), with the accountability-efficiency (AE) and social objective (SO) means both lower and roughly equivalent.

Education improvement means were higher than the accountability and social objectives means for all variables except amount of work life affected (Q8A-amt) and impact on professional development. However, since both these exceptions were non-significant, they are considered non-supportive rather than contradictory. The rank order and percentage negatives for amount of student learning affected, valenced impact on teacher work life, valenced impact on student learning, willingness to participate in similar change, and willingness to participate in any future change are consistently in the hypothesised direction, with a significant difference for at least one pair of means for each variable.

A significant interaction for Q10 suggests that a similar finding for teacher feeling about this change may apply to most countries but not all. The country-by-country analysis in Appendix Table A6 demonstrates that in Australia and South Africa accountability changes produced more positive feelings. This reversal is understandable given the special conditions that make increased accountability highly desirable in these countries. Consequently, the overall pattern of results appears to support the locus of control hypothesis.

Results for Teacher Involvement in Change (Q4)

The effects of the degree of involvement in change on the six dependent variables appear in column 5, at the extreme right-hand side of Table IV. Notice that the categories in this case form a metric scale indicating increasing amounts of teacher involvement in the change. This property of the variable allows us to use both a correlation coefficient and the analysis of variance means to measure its effects. The locus of control hypothesis is not particularly relevant to the effects of level of involvement. Instead, we argue that increasing amounts of involvement in a change produce increasing feelings of ownership, which translate into an expectation of monotonically increasing dependent-variable means for the low, medium, and high involvement categories. Another way of expressing this expectation is to predict a significant positive correlation between level of involvement and each of the eight dependent variables.

Observe that, except for an insignificant low–medium reversal for amount of teacher work life affected, the ordered means of involvement categories is low, medium, and high for all eight dependent variables, and that the correlation coefficient is significantly positive for all eight variables. In addition, the percentage negatives for valenced variables form a confirming pattern, decreasing from low to medium to high, except for a small reversal of the low (44%) and medium (50%) categories for impact on professional development.

The effects of involvement were generally stronger, more uniform, and more pervasive than the effects of any other change variable. There was strong and consistent evidence that, averaged over countries, increasing amounts of teacher involvement produce corresponding positive increases in the amount of teacher work life and student learning affected; a more positive impact on teacher work life, professional development, and student learning; more positive teacher feelings about change, and greater willingness to participate in future change. However, the significant interaction of country and involvement for the amount of student learning affected, and for all three teacher-affect variables, suggests that the overall effect may not apply to all countries. Country by involvement interactions for amount of student learning affected, teacher feeling about this change, willingness to participate in a similar change, and willingness to participate in any future change are analysed in Appendix Tables A7, A8, A9, and A10, respectively. In most cases, the interaction is caused by country-to-country variations in the magnitude of the correlation, with the direction remaining positive. The only possible exceptions are for willingness to participate in similar change (Q11A) and willingness to participate in any change (Q11B), where England and Canada had non-significant negative correlations. Because the preponderance of changes in both countries were government initiations that forced teacher actions, these results are not considered contradictory. In conclusion, the general pattern of findings confirms that increased teacher involvement in a change leads to stronger, more positive results for every dependent variable.

SECTION 3: THE RELATIVE INFLUENCE OF CHANGE VARIABLES

The previous section examined the influence of the four change variables (type, initiator, objective, and involvement) on eight dependent variables, using two-way (country by change variable) analyses of variance. In that section, each of these 32 analyses was conducted in isolation. In the real world, however, all of the variables – country, age, gender, and the change variables (type, initiator, objective, and involvement) – affect the dependent variables in combination. The obvious corollary to these isolated findings is the first research question addressed by this section: (1) What happens to the relative influence of each of these independent (predictor) variables when all predictors are simultaneously present in a regression analysis?

Experience and common sense suggest that the influence of any one variable will be smaller within a set of predictors than when analysed separately. This occurs because of a common causality, in which one factor is a component of several different predictor variables. For example, the effect of countries overlaps with age, gender, and the change variables, because each country has a different distribution of these predictors. Some of the differences among country means for each dependent variable are due to the different pattern of predictors from country to country.

Another common causality was suggested by the results in the previous section. There was a considerable amount of evidence that the first three change variables (type, initiator, and objective) shared a 'locus of control' component. In general, locus of control theory and research suggests that the more control an individual (a teacher) has over an event (a change), the more positive his or her response will be in both attitude and behaviour. That is, changes perceived as being under remote external control would produce the least positive effects, and those perceived as under internal (personal) control would produce the most positive effects. This principle leads to a second research question: (2) Is there an internal versus external component within each of the three change variables, and, if so, what proportion of the total effect of change characteristics is accounted for by this component?

A complicating factor in this research is the role of involvement in change (Q4). At one level, it is clearly one of the characteristics of a change, and should be treated as one of the independent change variables that influence a teacher's work life and his/her affective response to change. On another level, it is a dependent variable that is, itself, influenced by the type, initiator, and objective of a change. In the latter case, it can be argued that involvement acts as an intervening variable that moderates the effect of the type, initiator, and objectives of a change on the teacher's work life and affective response. This argument gives rise to two additional research questions: (3) Is the level of a teacher's involvement influenced by the characteristics of the change, and (4) Does involvement moderate the relationship between change characteristics and the dependent variables?

Additional interests derive from research referenced in the introduction to Part Two which suggested that the characteristics of a change have a direct influence on a teacher's work life, and that these changes in work life influence the teacher's feelings about change. In the context of this section, this translates into two final research questions: (5) Do the alterations in a teacher's work produced by a change become the major influence on a teacher's affective response to change, and (6) Does the teacher's affective response to change then become the major predictor of their disposition towards future change?

Regression Procedure[2]

The overall regression analyses plan consisted of six successive stages derived from the flow of influence posited by Figure 1 at the beginning of Part Two. All regressions in this section were computed by treating teachers from all nine countries as a single sample with the effects of country assessed by dummy variables. Each successive stage of the analysis assessed the effects of adding one or more predictor set(s) to the regression equation. At stage 1, the baseline effects of context variables (country, age, and gender) were assessed. Locus of control was assessed at stage 2, change characteristics (type, initiator, and objective) at stage 3, teacher involvement at stage 4, work alterations at stage 5, and teacher feelings about the current change at stage 6. The six-stage regression plan is summarised in Figure 2.

Change in education			Teacher responses to the change			
Stage 1	Stage 2	Stage 3	Stage 4	Stage 5	Stage 6	
Context: Country Age Gender →	Theoretical: locus of control →	Characteristcs: Type/Domain Initiator Objective →	Teacher's involvement in the change →	Alterations in the teacher's work →	Teacher's affective response to alterations →	Teacher's disposition toward future change

Figure 2. Regression model derived from theoretical flow of influence.

The number of stages required to analyse a particular dependent variable was dictated by its position in the flow of influence chain. Thus, involvement required a three-stage regression analysis, each of the five work-alteration variables required a four-stage analysis, teacher feeling about the change required a five-stage analysis, and each of the two measures of teacher disposition toward future change required a six-stage analysis. Specific predictors and dependent variables are identified in the discussion of results.

REGRESSION RESULTS

The regression results for involvement and the five work-alteration variables are summarised in Table V and results for the three teacher affect variables in Table VI. In each table, the predictor variables are listed on the left side of the page in order of their forced entry into the regression. The dependent variable labels are listed in the header of the table above the columns of regression results. Except for the multiple R given in the second to last line of each column, the decimal numbers are R squared values that measure the proportion of dependent-variable variance accounted for by the predictor named on the left. Most of the R squared values in the table measure the proportion of variance accounted for by the labelled predictor within the overall regression. However, the decimal values opposite the 'Stage' labels are unique because they give the R square obtained using only the predictors up to and including that line. The number in parentheses immediately after each decimal number is the percentage of the overall prediction (multiple R squared) that is accounted for by each predictor. Immediately below the R squared for each change characteristic is its percentage contribution within the total for all characteristics, the combined effects of predictors 3, 4, 5, and 6.

The following commentary briefly summarises the results for each regression in Table V, followed immediately by the results for each regression in Table VI. Since we are primarily interested in themes that apply across data sets, the section will consider both statistical significance within regressions and the implied significance of redundant patterns. The following observations about patterns of findings that apply across dependent variables concentrate on relationships that are relevant to the research questions posed at the beginning of this section.

Summary of Patterns in Table V

Table V displays the regression results for six dependent variables measuring dimensions of teachers' work life. The following observations are relevant to our hypotheses.

1. The multiple Rs at the bottom of each column in Table V are all statistically significant but quite moderate, typically about .50 with R squared values of about 0.25, demonstrating that the regressions accounted for 25% of the dependent variable variance. The lower R for amount of work life affected (0.36) accounted for only 13% of its variance.

Dependent Variables →	Teacher Involvement Level	Amount Of Work-Life Affected	Amount Of Student Learning Affected	Valenced Impact On Work-Life	Valenced Impact On Student Learning	Impact On Professional Development
	Q4	Q8A-amt	Q9A-amt	Q8A-val	Q9A-val	Q8F
Predictor Sets:						
1.Country Effects	.1450**(65.0%)	.0863**(66.6%)	.0804**(36.6%)	.0542**(24.2%)	.0347**(13.4%)	.1131**(38.1%)
2. Demographic Effects						
Teacher Age·Experience	.0021 (0.92%)	.0003 (0.22%)	.0032 (1.45%)	.00460 (2.03%)	.0089◊◊(3.43%)	.0008 (0.26%)
	+.0001 (0.32%)	-.0000 (0.03%)	+.0003 (0.13%)	-.00075 (0.33%)	+.0004 (0.15%)	+.0001 (0.03%)
Teacher Gender (F=1,M=2)	-.0020 (0.91%)	-.0002 (0.19%)	-.0030 (1.37%)	+.00399 (1.78%)	-.0086* (3.3%)	-.0007 (0.24%)
Stage 1. Mult R Squared (1,2)	.1476**(66.2%)	.1019**(78.7%)	.1408**(64.1%)	.1581**(70.5%)	.1105**(42.8%)	.2749**(92.6%)
3. Locus of Control	.0080 (3.63%)	.0087 (6.69%)	.0061 (2.78%)	.0044 (1.97%)	.0175**(6.75%)	.0015 (0.50%)
% of R Squared (3,4,5,6)	10.65%	39.29%	11.15%	14.08%	32.25%	10.38%
Stage 2. Mult R Squared (1-3)	.1540**(69.0%)	.1091**(84.2%)	.1560**(71.0%)	.1725**(76.9%)	.1348**(52.2%)	.2769**(93.3%)
4. Type of Change	.0118◊ (5.27%)	.0053 (4.11%)	.0381**(17.3%)	.0064 (2.83%)	.0094 (3.63%)	.0018 (0.61%)
% of R Squared (3,4,5,6)	15.59%	24.13%	69.32%	20.28%	17.23%	12.69%
5. Initiator of Change	.0370**(16.6%)	.0025 (1.94%)	.0009 (0.39%)	.0097 (4.34%)	.0088 (3.42%)	.0071 (2.41%)
% of R Squared (3,4,5,6)	49.07%	11.39%	1.55%	31.04%	16.25%	50.07%
6. Objective of Change	.0094◊ (4.22%)	.0033 (2.55%)	.0042 (1.91%)	.0018 (0.79%)	.0145**(5.60%)	.0030 (1.01%)
% of R Squared (3,4,5,6)	12.49%	14.97%	7.63%	5.69%	27.16%	20.97%
R Squared: Combined (4,5,6)	.0591**(31.0%)	.0156 (12.0%)	.0440**(20.0%)	.0170 (7.59%)	.0357**(13.8%)	.0103 (3.48%)
% of R Squared (3,4,5,6)	91.61%	70.64%	80.11%	54.36%	65.56%	72.51%
R Squared: Combined (3 to 6)	.0754**(33.8%)	.0220 (17.0%)	.0549**(25.0%)	.0313◊ (14.0%)	.0544**(21.1%)	.0143 (4.81%)
Stage 3. Multiple R (1-6)	.47228	.35213	.45226	.43872	.44339	.53491
Stage 3. Mult R Squared (1-6)	.22305**	.1240**(95.8%)	.2045**(93.1%)	.1925**(85.9%)	.1966**(76.1%)	.2861**(96.4%)
7. Involvement Combination						
Involvement		.0055 (4.22%)	.0152**(6.93%)	.0317**(14.1%)	.0617**(23.9%)	.0106* (3.57%)
Pred.Involvement(Within-Country)		+.0041 (3.14%)	-.0127**(5.76%)	+.0317**(14.1%)	+.0281**(10.9%)	+.0037 (1.26%)
		+.0002 (0.16%)	-.0001 (0.06%)	-.0029 (1.31%)	+.0142**(5.49%)	+.0034 (1.14%)
All Change Components (3-7)	.0754**(33.8%)	.0276**(21.3%)	.0790**(35.9%)	.0661**(29.5%)	.1478**(57.2%)	.0218**(7.4%)
Stage 4. Multiple R (1-7)	.47228	.35981	.46879	.47346	.50823	.54471
Stage 4. Mult R Squared (1-7)	.22305**	.12946**	.21976**	.22416**	.25830**	.29671**

NOTE: Statistically significant values are flagged as follows: ◊ for (p≤.10), ◊◊ for (p≤.07), * for (p≤.05), and ** for (p≤.01).

Table V. Regression of six dependent variables on sets of predictor variables with the change in *R* squared and percentage of overall prediction accounted for by each set.

275

2. Country was a strong, statistically significant predictor of all six dependent variables. The variance accounted for by country ranged from a low of 3.5% for valenced impact on student learning to a high of 14.5% for involvement. The corresponding influence of country within these regressions was 13.4% and 65% respectively.

3. The four change characteristics together accounted for a significant 7.5% of the involvement variance and 33.8% of the overall prediction. Within change characteristics, initiator exercised 49% of the change-characteristic influence on involvement, type of change 15%, objective 12%, and locus of control 11%.

4. All change components (the four change characteristics plus involvement) combined to provide statistically significant contributions to the four-stage regressions for each of the five work-alteration variables.

5. Involvement was the most influential change component for the valenced impact on teacher work life, student learning, and professional development, and the second most influential for amount of work life and student learning affected.

6. Locus of control was the most influential change component for amount of work life accounted for, had second-place influence in predicting the valenced impact on student learning, and was a credible middle-rank predictor in the other regressions.

7. The relative influence of the remaining change characteristics shifted across dependent variables. Type of change had a strong influence on amount of student learning affected, objective of change strongly influenced valenced impact on student learning, and initiator had a second-rank influence on valenced impact on work life and professional development.

Summary of Patterns in Table VI

Table VI displays the regression results for three dependent variables measuring teachers' affective response to the change process. The following observations are relevant to our hypotheses.

1. The regressions for the teacher affect variables in Table VI are considerably stronger. The multiple R for teacher feeling about this change (0.74) accounted for 55% of its variance, while Rs of 0.69 and 0.55 accounted for 47% and 30% of the variance in willingness to participate in a similar change, and in any future change, respectively.

2. Country was again a strong, most influential predictor of participation in similar change and any future change, but accounted for only 3.8% of the prediction for teacher feelings about this change.

Dependent Variables →	Teacher Feeling About This Change	Willing To Participate In Similar Change	Willing To Participate In Any Change
Predictor Sets:	Variable Q10	Variable Q11A	Variable Q11B
1. Country Effects	.0210**(3.80%)	.1535**32.6%)	.0623**(20.5%)
2. Demographic Effects	.0031　(0.55%)	.0063◊　1.34%)	.0069　(2.26%)
Teacher Age/Experience	+.0021　(0.37%)	+.0061*　(1.30%)	+.0024　(0.80%)
Teacher Gender (F=1,M=2)	+.0008　(0.15%)	-.0003　(0.05%)	+.0041　(1.34%)
Stage 1. Multiple R Squared (1,2)	.1399**(25.28%)	.4079**(86.6%)	.1697**(55.9%)
3. Locus of Control	.0009　(0.17%)	.0025　(0.53%)	.0046　(1.52%)
% of (3,4,5,6) R Squared	3.97%	16.10%	41.18%
Stage 2. Multiple R Squared (1-6)	.1862**(33.6%)	.4197**(89.1%)	.1813**(59.7%)
4. Q1 Type of Change	.0089*　(1.60%)	.0027　(0.58%)	.0042　(1.37%)
% of (3,4,5,6) R Squared	38.25%	17.58%	36.99%
5. Q2 Initiator of Change	.0003　(0.07%)	.0024　(0.50%)	.00578　(1.90%)
% of (3,4,5,6) R Squared	1.68%	15.07%	51.52%
6. Q3 Objective of Change	.0001　(0.02%)	.0001　(0.01%)	.0013　(0.43%)
% of (3,4,5,6) R Squared	0.52%	0.32%	11.76%
R Square: Combined (4,5,6)	.0095　(1.72%)	.0055　(1.16%)	.0096　(3.17%)
% of (3,4,5,6) R Squared	40.97%	35.09%	85.74%
R Squared: Combined (3,4,5,6)	.0232*　(4.19%)	.0156　(3.31%)	.0112　(3.69%)
Stage 3. Multiple R Squared (1-6)	.2392**(43.2%)	.4277**(90.8%)	.2020**(66.5%)
7. Involvement Combination	.0207**(3.73%)	.0047　(1.01%)	.0001　(0.05%)
Involvement	+.0191**(3.46%)	+.0018　(0.38%)	-.0000　(0.01%)
Predicted Involvement (Within Country)	-.0000　(0.00%)	-.0041◊　(0.88%)	+.0001　(0.04%)
All Change R Squared (3,4,5,6,7)	.0423**(7.6%)	.0203*　(4.3%)	.0113　(3.7%)
Stage 4. Multiple R Squared (1-7)	.3250**(58.7%)	.4402**(93.5%)	.2125**(69.9%)
8. Total: Work-Alteration Variables	.2283**(41.3%)	.0052　(1.09%)	.0079　(2.61%)
Amount of Work-Life Affected	-.0013　(0.23%)	-.0004　(0.07%)	-.0000　(0.00%)
Amount of Student Learning Affected	+.0093**(1.68%)	+.0015　(0.32%)	+.0001　(0.03%)
Impact on Teacher Work-Life	+.0575**(10.4%)	+.0022　(0.46%)	+.0066*　(2.17%)
Impact on Student Learning	+.1024**(18.5%)	+.0004　(0.07%)	+.0002　(0.08%)
Impact on Professional Development	-.0009　(0.16%)	+.0008　(0.18%)	-.0008　(0.27%)
9. Predicted Work-Alteration Variables	.0000　(0.00%)	.0000　(0.00%)	.0000　(0.00%)
Stage 5. Multiple R (1-9)	.74386	.67847	.51564
Stage 5. Multiple R Squared (1-9)	.55333**	.4603**(97.8%)	.2659**(87.5%)
10. Feeling About Change (RSq.Change)		+.0106**(2.24%)	+.0379**(12.5%)
Stage 6. Multiple R (1-10)		.68622	.55117
Stage 6. Multiple R Squared		.47090**	.30379**

NOTE: *Statistically significant values are flagged as follows: ◊ for (p≤.10), ◊◊ for (p≤.07), * for (p≤.05), and ** for (p≤.01).*

Table VI. Regression of teacher affect on predictor sets with change in R squared and percentage of overall prediction accounted for by each set.

3. The four change components combined to contribute prediction influences of 7.6% for teacher feelings, 4.3% for similar change, and 3.7% for any future change.

4. Among change components, involvement had the strongest influence, type of change second, and locus of control third, for both teacher feelings and similar change. But the order of influence on any future change was initiator, locus of control, type, objective, and finally, involvement.

5. Demographics were significant for only two variables. Teacher gender was a significant negative predictor of the valenced impact on student learning in Table V: females perceived a stronger, more positive impact than males. Teacher age was a significant positive predictor of willingness to participate in a similar change in Table VI: older teachers were more likely to participate.

6. Within-country predicted involvement (Q4_predicted) had a negligible influence for most dependent variables, but was significant for valenced impact on student learning and marginally significant for willingness to participate in similar change.

7. In general, the last-entered predictor set was strongest for all valenced variables, and was particularly strong for teacher-affect variables. This finding provides support for the ordered relations posited by the chain of influence in Figure 2.

SECTION 4: SUMMARY AND DISCUSSION

The primary goal of the regression analysis was to determine the relative influence of the four change variables on the eight available dependent measures with the effects of relevant context variables controlled. This necessarily places major emphasis on the regression results, since they were the only analyses in which all variables were simultaneously present. However, the distributional data in Section 1 and the two-way analysis of variance data in Section 2 both have a direct bearing on the interpretation of regression outcomes. The intent of this section is to integrate all available analytic evidence to answer the research questions posed at the beginning of Section 3. In brief, these questions concerned: (1) the influence of change on the dependent variables when all predictors are present; (2) the influence of locus of control relative to other change characteristics; (3) the influence of change characteristics on the level of teacher involvement in the change; (4) the relative influence of locus of control, change characteristics, and involvement on dependent variables; (5) the effect of adding work-alteration variables as predictors of teacher feelings about change; and (6) the effect of adding teacher feelings about change as a predictor of teacher disposition towards future change. Each of these questions is closely related to an expanded flow-of-influence model of the effects of change.

Consequently, this discussion begins with an explication of the model and evidence of its validity. This is followed by discussions of the effects of context variables, the influence of change variables versus other predictors, the relative influence of change components, answers to the research questions, and theoretical support for the power of involvement.

THE CONCEPTUAL MODEL

Since the staged regression model was an operational definition of a conceptual flow of influence of changes in this study, we begin by defining an expanded model of the theoretical flow of influence from a within-country educational change, through successive measures of teacher responses (Figure 3). Beginning on the left-hand side of Figure 3, we see that changes in education occur within particular countries having different demographic distributions of teachers. The nature or characteristics of the change are defined by four measures: locus of control, type of change, initiator of change, and objective of change. Because locus of control was expected to be subsumed within the original three characteristics, regression stages 2 and 3 are combined here and treated as alternative characteristics of a change. Throughout this section the term 'change characteristics' refers to these four predictor sets: locus of control, type of change, initiator of change, and objective of change. In the interests of brevity, these characteristics are referred to as locus, type, initiator, and objective throughout the remainder of this discussion. The terms 'change variables' or 'change components' refer to the four change characteristics, plus involvement (the level of teacher involvement).

Change in education		Teacher responses to the change			
Context:	Characteristics: Stages 1 & 2	Stage 3	Stage 4	Stage 5	Stage 6
Country Demographics Age Gender	Locus of control Type of change Initiator of change Objective of change	Teacher's involvement in the change	Alterations in the teacher's work	Teacher's affective response to alterations	Teacher's disposition toward future change

Figure 3. Expanded model of the theoretical flow of influence in educational change.

In the model, each change is defined by a particular combination of change characteristics which is expected to heavily influence the level of teacher involvement at stage 3. Involvement now becomes the primary influence on work-alteration variables at stage 4, with change characteristics having a secondary direct influence because some of their effect flows through involvement. Note that involvement is partly a fifth descriptor of the change and partly a teacher response to the change, as illustrated by its intermediate placement in Figure 3. At stage 5 work alterations, like involvement before, become the primary influence on

279

teacher feelings about change, with involvement now taking a secondary role. Similarly, at stage 6, teacher feelings about the change become the primary influence on their disposition towards participation in future change. Given the central role of the model in determining the analysis performed and in the interpretation of results, evidence of its validity is of paramount importance.

Evidence of Model Validity

There is both logical and empirical evidence for the validity of the Figure 3 model. The logical explication of relationships will lead to a definition of expected outcomes. If the regression results are consistent with those expected outcomes, the model is said to have construct validity.

Logical Evidence

The flow of influence posited in Figure 3 is supported by the temporal sequence of the elements in the chain. The context in which the change occurred (the country and its demographic distribution of teachers) clearly existed prior to the change and had some influence on its characteristics. The characteristics of the change (locus, type, initiator, and objective) represent the 'nature' of the change; these would normally be known by a teacher at the time a change is announced. Except for the relatively rare case in which the respondent teacher participated in planning the change, teacher involvement could not occur until the change was implemented; and even planners are likely to experience the heaviest involvement during implementation. At the next stage, alterations in a teacher's work caused by a change will begin during implementation, but will not be fully known until the change is operational. Similarly, a teacher's feelings about a change will, of course, develop over time as the change occurs. But since, in our case, feelings were not measured until after the change had been operating for some time, the response should reflect the effect of completed work alterations. Although a teacher's disposition toward participation in future change is not temporally dependent on their feelings about the current change, the recency principle derived from the second law of associative learning suggests that these feelings would have a predominant influence even if previous experience with change had provoked different feelings. In summary, time linkages support the flow of influence defined by Figure 3.

Empirical Evidence: expectations and results

It was argued earlier that change variables would have both a direct effect on each dependent variable, and an indirect effect passed on through successive links in the chain. If indeed this happened, then the link immediately preceding a particular dependent measure would be especially strong since it contains both its own direct effect and the indirect effect of the preceding elements. Increased strength would also be predicted by the recency principle referred to earlier.

To check on the possibility that the presence of the locus of control variables detracted from the effects of change-category variables, new regressions omitting the locus of control predictors were run for every dependent variable. The predictor weights for change characteristics in these regressions were consistent with those recorded in Table V in all cases. It was concluded that the presence of locus of control variables did not reduce the influence of change characteristics, but rather added to it.

In a true chain of influence, the direct effects of a characteristic become weaker and the indirect effects stronger as the influence flows further along the chain. When this concept is applied to our staged regressions, it suggests the hypothesis that the last component added to a regression equation should be the most influential predictor, with a corollary reduction in the influence of previous predictors. Notice that this hypothesised last-entry relationship would not apply to the context variables, whose prime function is to provide a common baseline by controlling the effects of the non-manipulable country and demographic variables. Although context effects would not necessarily become smaller than those of the most recent predictor, a reduction in the magnitude of effects would be expected with each added predictor.

The last-entry hypothesis can be tested in Tables V and VI by comparing the changes in R squared values at each regression stage, which represent the last-added predictor(s), with the R squared values attributed to the same predictor(s) within the overall prediction. A quick review of the tabulated values reveals that the hypothesised greater value of the last-added R squared was confirmed in 13 out of a possible 13 instances. (Remember that the locus of control increment does not count because it is one of four change characteristics in Figure 3. The appropriate change in R squared for measuring the four-characteristic effect is the difference between the stage 3 and stage 1 values of R squared.) The smallest difference in paired R squared values occurs in the prediction of the amount of teacher work life affected, where the recently added change characteristics variables accounted for 2.20% of the variance within the overall prediction and a mere 2.21% as the last-added element. Although this is a trivial difference, it is in the hypothesised direction. In the other 12 instances the differences were much larger, and generally favoured the most recent by a two to one ratio.

Although the above result confirms the last-entry hypothesis, it provides only tangential evidence of the indirect effects of change; that is, evidence that the effects of change are indeed 'passed on' through sequentially dependent predictors. However, the stage 5 addition of five work-alteration variables as predictors of teacher feelings about change provides a unique opportunity for more compelling evidence. If the influence of change is indeed passed on, one would expect the work-alteration components most influenced by change variables to be the strongest predictors of teacher feelings about change. The combined effect of all five change variables (four change characteristics plus the involvement combination) can be computed by finding the difference between the R squared values at stage 4 and stage 1 in Table V. Change variables accounted for 2-3% of the variance in Q8A-amt (amount of work life affected) and Q8F (impact on professional development), 7-8% of the variance of Q9A-amt (amount of student learning affected) and Q8A-val (valenced impact on work life), and 15% of the variance of Q9A-val (valenced impact on student learning). Comparing these results with the work-alteration prediction weights in the second column of Table VI (regression of Q10: teacher feelings about this change), reveals that both 2-3% variables received small, insignificant negative prediction weights (-0.0013 & -0.0009), both 7-8% variables received significant positive prediction weights (+0.0093** & +0.0575**), while the 15% variable received the strongest, most positive prediction weight (+0.1024**). This is a rather close match of change influence to predictive strength. In combination with the previous support of the last-entry hypothesis, it provides strong evidence for the construct validity of the chain of influence modelled in Figure 3.

EFFECTS OF CONTEXT VARIABLES

As explained in the introduction, only three context variables met the criteria for inclusion in the cross-cultural analyses: teacher age, gender, and country of residence. Teacher age and gender appeared only in the regression analyses, so all evidence cited will come from information contained in Tables V and VI. The effects of country, on the other hand, will use information from the 32 analyses of variance summarised in Table III as well as distributional information from Table II to supplement information from the regressions in Tables V and VI.

Influence of Age

The age variable, which also represented the amount of teaching experience, was expected positively to influence most dependent variables. In the presence of the other predictors, age/experience had a significant positive influence on willingness to participate in a similar change and a positive near-significant regression weight for willingness to participate in any future change, but the influence of age on every other dependent variable was too weak to be confident of its real direction and magnitude. The different prediction weights of age for the two types of future change is probably a function of the more precise measurement scale for participation in similar change. That item asked teachers to indicate their willingness to perform each of ten different roles, each of which required different levels of commitment. The 'any change' item, on the other hand, required a yes–no answer regarding their willingness to participate. Since the 'similar change' item is more reliable and the result for the 'any change' item was in the same direction, it seems fair to conclude that older, more experienced teachers were more willing than younger, less experienced teachers to participate in a future change.

Influence of Gender

A review of the R squared values in Tables V and VI demonstrates that gender had larger influence weights than age for all dependent variables except 'similar change', and also that the direction of influence was more varied. However, gender had a significant prediction weight (beta weight) for only one dependent variable: a significant negative influence on the valenced impact of change on student learning. Female teachers indicated a stronger, more positive impact of change on student learning than male teachers. Gender did not significantly influence any other dependent variable.

Influence of Country

Personal demographics (age and gender) were expected to be significant predictors of most dependent variables. Since age and gender distributions were known to vary widely from country to country, we expected much of the between-country differences to be accounted for by the age and gender variables. We were therefore somewhat surprised when country remained a strong and significant predictor for all dependent variables after the effects of age and gender were removed. In all nine regressions reported in Tables V and VI, country accounted for almost all of the influence of the combined context variables and was generally the strongest single predictor.

The relative impact of most influential countries can be inferred from the pattern of analytic results. Israel was by far the strongest positive influence among the nine countries, with the USA a distant second. Israel achieved the highest analysis of variance means and the strongest positive regression weights for all eight dependent variables, while the moderately high means and regression weights for the USA were generally not quite significant. Australia and South Africa had impacts almost as strong as those of Israel, but the direction of influence changed according to variable function. They had high analysis of

283

variance means and strong positive prediction weights for the two unvalenced measures (amount of work life affected and amount of student learning affected), but had low means and strong negative prediction weights for the three valenced work-alteration measures (the impact on work life, student learning, and professional development). In short, these countries experienced strong negative effects of change on almost all of their work life and student learning activities. They also had similar low means and negative predictor weights for the three measures of teacher affect: feeling about the change, willingness to participate in a similar change, and willingness to participate in any future change. Three other countries, Canada, China, and England, had a pattern of effects similar to those of Australia and South Africa, but generally not quite as extreme in either the positive or negative direction, and therefore usually non-significant.

Summary of Context Effects

As predicted by the recency principle, the absolute influence of the combined context variables was reduced as each new predictor set was added to the regression equation. For example, context accounted for an average 18.3% of the variance in stage 1 regressions, 7.7% at stage 4, and 6.4% at stages 5 and 6. In the involvement regression and in all five work-alteration regressions, the effects of context were stronger than all other predictors combined. It was also the strongest predictor for both future change variables, but was second to work-alterations in predicting teacher feelings about change.

Unfortunately, there is circumstantial evidence from Table II that some of the effect of change variables (the primary focus of the entire study) is confounded with country effects. The first line of evidence comes from the fact that countries with strong negative prediction weights have combinations of change characteristics that were negatively perceived by most teachers. Examples include a preponderance of government-initiated change aimed at learning outcomes in Australia, and government-initiated change aimed at accomplishing desirable but painful social objectives in South Africa. On the other hand, Israel, which had a strong positive prediction weight, was characterised by changes initiated by teachers or the school and aimed at improving teaching or education in general. A related line of evidence comes from critically important characteristics of change that were absent or extremely rare in some countries. For example, changes involving learning outcomes did not occur in England or Hungary, and either teacher-initiated or community-initiated changes (or both) were extremely rare in Australia, England, Canada, and China. Consequently, one must conclude that many of the dependent-variable differences among countries would probably be reduced if there had been a uniform distribution of change characteristics. The corollary is that an equal distribution would undoubtedly produce more pronounced differences in the effects of change characteristic and hence stronger prediction weights. The practical implication is that only strong trends in the effects of change variables are likely to be reliable.

CHANGE VARIABLES VERSUS OTHER PREDICTORS

The five-stage regression was used to analyse teachers' feelings about the targeted change. In this analysis, change has both a direct and an indirect influence. The direct effect of change at stage 4 accounted for 18.5% of the variance and 34.4% of the overall prediction as opposed to 14.0% of the variance and 25.3% of the overall prediction, accounted for by context variables at stage 1. The indirect effects of change are passed through the five work-alteration measures which act as intervening variables. The combined effects of work-alterations account for 22.8% of the variance and 41.3% of the overall prediction. The proportion of this effect that can be attributed to the indirect influence of change cannot be measured directly, but the fact that the work-alteration variables most influenced by change have the strongest predictor weights at stage 5 suggest a strong indirect influence.

Six-stage regressions were used to analyse teacher willingness to participate in a similar change and any future change. The direct effect of the combined change components at stage 4 accounted for a relatively small 3.2% and 4.3% of variance, respectively. The comparative influences of 40.8% and 17.0% of the variance at stage 1 were considerably stronger. The stage 5 effects of the combined work-alteration variables accounted for an additional 2.0% and 5.3% of variance, while teacher feelings about the change at stage 6 accounted for an additional 1.1% and 3.8% of variance. Based on the previous argument, it seems likely that a substantial portion of both the work-alteration and teacher feeling effects are due to the indirect influence of change components.

In summary, the direct effects of the total change were relatively strong. In general, they accounted for about half as much variance as the powerful context variables, and for more than 30% of the overall prediction. This is almost definitely an underestimate of the real strength of change effects since evidence reviewed earlier in this section strongly suggested that a substantial portion of the effects of country (by far the strongest context component) was due to the confounded effects of change characteristics. A further enhancement of change effects in the five-stage and six-stage regressions was suggested by strong circumstantial evidence that the indirect effects of change were probably as strong or stronger than their direct effects. It therefore seems likely that the true influence of change components was much stronger than indicated by the direct effects tabulated in Tables V and VI.

RELATIVE INFLUENCE OF CHANGE COMPONENTS

The relative influence of individual change predictors within the combined effects of all change components can be summarised by averaging the R squared values across dependent variables. Again, separate computations are required for four-stage, five-stage, and six-stage regressions.

Within stage 4 regressions, effects are averaged across the five work-alteration variables. Teacher involvement accounted for 44.6% of the total effects, type of change for 21.8%, locus of control for 13.7%, initiator of change for 10.4%, and objective of change for 9.6%.

In the five-stage regression of teacher feelings about change, involvement accounted for 67.0% of the total direct influence of change, type of change for 28.8%, locus of control for 2.9%, initiator of change for 1.0%, and objective of change for only 0.3%.

In the six-stage regressions, the relative influence of individual predictors was so different for the two measures of disposition towards future change that they will not be averaged. The regression of willingness to participate in a similar change result was similar to that of previous regressions. Involvement accounted for 37.9% of the total influence of change, type of change for 21.8%, locus of control for 20.2%, initiator of change for 19.4%, and objective of change for 0.8%. In the regression of willingness to participate in any future change, the initiator of change accounted for 36.5% of the total effects, locus of control for 28.9%, type of change for 26.4%, objective of change for 8.2%, and involvement for a mere 0.8%.

In summary, for all dependent variables except participation in any future change, involvement was the most influential predictor, type of change was second, locus of control third, initiator of change fourth, and objective of change fifth. For the somewhat unreliable 'any change' variable, initiator was the most influential and involvement the least influential.

Responses to Research Questions

Section 3 began with a listing of the six research questions, and the early part of Section 4 focused on how these questions could be answered by the regression analyses. Although most of the questions have been answered in the context of previous discussions, it is useful to conclude with direct answers for each question.

(1) What happens to the influence of change variables when they are analysed in the presence of all other predictors?

The influence of change is reduced by the presence of context variables, but remains significant and important. There was, however, circumstantial evidence that some of the effects of change characteristics were confounded with the effects of country and that work-alteration variables and teacher feeling about the change provided additional indirect effects of change. Since both of these influences would supplement the strength of the change effects, it is likely that the real influence of change variables is considerably stronger than that reported here.

(2) What are the effects of locus of control variables?

Locus of control was not a significant predictor *within* the overall prediction of any dependent variable. However, it generally *did* provide a significant increase in prediction from stage 1 to stage 2. Since locus of control was the second-strongest predictor among change characteristics, a close second to type of change, it is judged to be a useful additional predictor. Contrary to theoretical expectation, it did not prove to be a 'common causality' that accounted for most of the effects of the original change characteristics (type, initiator, and objective), but it added to the effect of those characteristics rather than stealing some of their power.

(3) Is the level of a teacher's involvement influenced by the characteristics of the change?

This major question of this research focused on whether involvement was influenced by change characteristics (locus, type, initiator, and objective) and then acted as a conduit to 'pass along' those effects as an indirect influence of change characteristics on work-alteration variables. The fact that change characteristics accounted for a highly significant 33.8% of the overall prediction of involvement confirms their influence. The fact that involvement was subsequently the most influential change variable in predicting each of the five work-alteration variables is consistent with it being a conduit for an indirect influence of change characteristics, but does not fully confirm it. However, the evidence that work-alteration variables were a conduit for the indirect effects of change predictors in response 5, below, would seem to support a tentative confirmation of a similar function for involvement here.

The relative influences of various change characteristics on involvement are also of interest. The initiator of change has by far the strongest influence on teacher involvement; more than three times the influence of the next-highest factor. However, despite variations in achieved significance levels, locus of control, type of change, and objective of change account for proportions of variance so similar that they are essentially tied at a mild 4-5% influence on involvement variance. Finally, notice that in Table V the combined (4, 5, 6) and the combined (3, 4, 5, 6) effects are both greater than the summed influences of their individual components. This is not a statistical error: rather, it indicates a synergistic relationship among components such that the pattern of predictor results adds to predictive power of the combined individual components.

(4) Does involvement moderate the relationship between change characteristics and the dependent variables?

The relative influence of change variables was consistent for all dependent variables except willingness to participate in any future change. For all seven remaining variables involvement was by far the most influential predictor, second influence (about half as much) went to type of change, third place to locus of control, fourth place to initiator of change, and last place to the uniformly weak influence of the objective of change. The regression weights of change components in predicting the exception (willingness to participate in any future change) were all insignificant and below the 1% influence level. Change variables had a negligible effect on teachers' willingness to participate in any future change.

(5) Do the alterations in a teacher's work produced by change become the major influence on a teacher's affective response to change?

The addition of work-alteration variables as stage 5 predictors of teachers' feelings about the targeted change accounted for an additional 22.8% of the variance with only a small reduction in the direct influence of change. The similarity of the pattern of regression weights for work alterations to the predictive influence of change on each work-alteration variable provided evidence that these variables acted as conduits for the indirect effects of change.

(6) Does the teacher's affective response to change then become the major predictor of their disposition towards future change?

The addition of teacher feelings about change as a stage 6 predictor of willingness to participate in similar or any future change provided very significant additions to both predictions. There was not, however, any direct evidence to confirm teacher feelings as a conduit for the indirect effects of change.

THE POWER OF INVOLVEMENT

When both its direct and indirect effects are considered, teacher involvement was by far the most powerful of the four change variables in this study. When studied in isolation, increased involvement produced a significant linear increase in every dependent variable in the study. The more teachers participated in responsible and initiating roles in school change, the more positive they felt about the change, and the more willing they were to seriously engage in future change. Furthermore, this relationship applied in individual countries, although the magnitude of the effect varied. The only exceptions were possible reverse relations (negative correlations) with willingness to participate in future change in England and Canada. However, the correlation coefficients were not significant in either country and could be the result of sampling error. Further, involvement retained a significant positive relationship with dependent variables in the presence of a number of other powerful predictors.

The results of both the statistical analyses in Part Two and the qualitative information from teacher interviews presented in Part One call attention to the variations in levels and kinds of teacher involvement in school change, the resulting variations in teachers' reaction to that involvement, and the nature of its effect on teachers' work lives. It is useful to note that 31% of teachers spoke of a high level of involvement in their school's change through initiator, planner, or shared decision-making roles, while 53% took part in implementer or supporter roles, and 16% had no role or one of active resister to the change. Consequently, 31% of teachers reached a level of involvement promotive of the most positive consequences for their schools and themselves.

The involvement of teachers can easily be incorporated in most school change, and contains much potential for promoting positive work life outcomes and for generating receptiveness and positive feelings of teachers toward change itself. In this sense, involvement appears to function as a facilitating force toward constructive change, and as an antidote for individual and group resistance to change.

If facilitators of school change can welcome this reasoning and build it into their practice, they could become quite encouraged about successful outcomes of change efforts and the receptiveness of teachers to change. As the findings from this research indicate, the strongest contributor to positive change outcomes is the increased opportunity for teachers to become involved in important and responsible roles, with shared determination of the change. The foregoing does not represent a totally new ground of thought and professional practice, but an encouragement for new individual and organisational competencies and revised beliefs about human nature and change. It is important to note that school leaders who have acquired professional abilities in school organisation development can promote the human conditions and facilitate the actions of teacher involvement for bringing about changes in their own schools.

Notes

[1] In the context of this study, 'teaching practice' refers to teaching practices, not (as in England) to a period of training spent in schools.

[2] The statistical technique of multiple regression is designed to uncover the relative contributions of each independent variable to a dependent variable. Readers unfamiliar with the concept of regression are advised to move directly to the sections titled 'Summary of Patterns in Table V' and 'Summary of Patterns in Table VI' in Section 3.

[3] This result is likely to have arisen from different interpretations of 'learning outcomes' which, for English teachers, were 'part of the things I do' rather than 'add-on' standardised tests. These are interesting and important cross-cultural differences, and examples of the care needed in dealing with meanings assumed to be transferable. [Ed. (Pam Poppleton)]

References

Bavelas, J.B. (1978) *Personality: current theory and research*. Monterey: Brooks-Cole.

Rotter, J.B. (1966) *Generalized Expectancies for Internal vs. External Control of Reinforcement, Psychological Monographs*, 80 (whole No. 609).

Winer, B.J. (1971) *Statistical Principles in Experimental Design*, 2nd edn. New York: McGraw-Hill.

APPENDIX TO PART TWO

Interactions between
Country and Change Variables

A significant interaction between countries and a change variable indicates that there are differences in the relationship among category means from country to country. A significant interaction can be caused by two kinds of differences in the relationships among category means. The first, and most obvious, interaction involves contradictory patterns of outcomes in which there are statistically significant differences in the rank order of category means from country to country. Note that observed category means that are underscored by the same line are *not* significantly different and should be considered the probable result of sampling error.

The second, more subtle, cause of a significant interaction involves a change in only the magnitude of differences among category means from country to country, but not in the rank order of categories. The most difficult interpretation of this second type of interaction occurs when one or more countries have no significant differences among the category means while other countries will have significant differences. In these instances it is necessary to look closely at the actual value of scores within patterns of rank ordered category means. Determining the type of interaction requires a table that presents category means by country.

The following nine tables and associated narratives describe the influence of four characteristics of educational school change upon several aspects of the teachers' work life. For each one, general trend information is extracted and more exacting information is described from a Newman–Keuls test of significance within countries. In each table's row labelled Rank Order of Means, sets of three or four letters are arranged in the order of smallest to largest means in each country. The letters used are the first letters of the category names. Letters (means) underscored by the same line do *not* differ significantly from each other, and letters (means) not underscored by the same line *do* differ significantly from each other.

The use of two methods of analysis in Parts 1 and 2 was to demonstrate complementarity rather than to 'pick the winner'. All researchers have a preferred model of analysis in mind, and will have chosen it before proceeding any further or delaying the choice of method until they have some results to guide them. The method selected must be one that is compatible with previous experience and designed to answer the research questions posed. The details of how this worked out are to be found in the Appendix. In this case complementarity serves to illustrate the qualitative findings by the teacher's voice.

APPENDIX A1. Country by Domain Interaction for Variable Q9A-amt

This inquiry examines the effects of different types of school change on the extent to which student learning was affected in each of the nine countries. Country by country results are summarised in Table A1.

Table A1. Influence of Types of School Change on Student Learning by Country

Countries:	Aust.	Canada	China	England	Hungary	Israel	Neth.	S. Afr.	USA	All
Types of Change										
Management Practice	2.22	4.00	2.85	3.00	3.14	5.17	2.22	3.0	3.56	3.15
Teaching Practice	2.80	3.55	3.79	3.94	3.25	4.78	3.34	4.13	3.75	3.71
Learning Outcomes	4.33	N=1	3.90	----	----	3.67	3.26	4.60	3.89	4.85
Student Experience	3.20	3.83	3.25	3.86	3.71	4.50	3.39	4.00	3.75	3.77
Rank Order of Means	MTSL	TSM	MSTL	MST	MTS	LSTM	MLTS	MSTL	MTSL	MTSL
Total Each Country	3.42	3.80	3.44	3.85	3.35	4.68	3.26	4.05	3.74	3.69

NOTE: Means underscored by the same line are NOT significantly different at the .05 level.

Averaged across nine countries the mean amount of student learning affected by management practice was significantly lower than the means for student experience, and learning outcomes. This indicates a general trend favouring changes of teaching practice, student experience, and learning outcomes as having stronger effect on student learning than change of management practice. This appears to be the case despite a non-significant reversal in these changes in Israel.

In addition, results for England and the Netherlands indicated that the other changes were *significantly* stronger than changes in management practice. Also, results in Australia and South Africa showed that change in learning outcomes was *significantly* stronger than changes in teaching practice, student experience, or management practice.

Israel's total effect on student learning appears strongest among the nine countries (mean = 4.68). Of interest, the teachers in England and Hungary did not report any school change efforts in learning outcomes.

Thus, the essential finding here is that, although the magnitude of differences changes from country to country, changes in teaching practice, student experience, or learning outcomes are more likely to achieve effects on student learning than changes in management practice.

APPENDIX A2. Country by Domain Interaction for Variable Q11A

This inquiry examines the effects of different types of school change on the willingness of teachers to responsibly participate in 'another' change. Country by country results are summarised in Table A2.

Table A2. Influence of Types of School Change on Teachers' Willingness to Participate in Another Similar Change by Country

Countries	Aust.	Canada	China	England	Hungary	Israel	Neth.	S. Afr.	USA	All
Domain of Change										
Management Practice	17.78	22.00	16.00	23.50	19.86	26.83	N=1	12.00	26.56	20.56
Teaching Practice	20.70	21.45	17.57	22.65	23.75	27.72	24.85	23.27	25.05	23.84
Learning Outcomes	19.33	N=1	16.50	----	----	23.00	----	19.60	27.11	20.63
Student Experience	18.10	26.03	17.88	22.57	23.57	28.47	N=1	18.07	26.75	23.81
Rank Order of Means	MSLT	TMS	MLTS	STM	MST	LMTS	T	MSLT	TMSL	MLST
Total Each Country	19.08	24.75	16.93	22.69	22.65	27.57	25.00	19.89	26.10	22.92

NOTE: Means underscored by the same line are NOT significantly different at the .05 level.

Averaged across all nine countries the willingness means for teaching practice and student experience were significantly higher than the means for learning outcomes and management practice, but there were no significant differences between either the higher or lower pair of means. Within six of the nine countries there was a general trend for school changes in teaching practice to have a stronger effect on teachers' willingness to participate in a forthcoming new change activity than do school changes in school management or learning outcomes. This observed trend is confirmed as significant (.01) when the data from all nine countries are summed together. Non-significant reversals in this trend occur in Canada, England, and the USA; changes in teaching practice are roughly equivalent to other changes in these three countries.

Once again, it is of interest to note that the teachers in the Netherlands observed only one kind of change (teaching practice) and that two other countries, England, and Hungary, did not observe changes in learning outcomes.

APPENDIX A3. Country by Initiator Interaction for Variable Q9A-val

This inquiry examines the country by country effects of different initiating sources of school change on the valenced impact of change on student learning. Country by country results are summarised in Table A3. In this case, complementarity was achieved by the reporting of teachers' comments that were illustrative of the 'rich descriptions' referred to above.

Averaged across nine countries, the valenced student learning means for teacher-initiated change were significantly higher than the means for change initiated by any other source. There were no significant differences among the school, community, or government means. The trend for higher teacher-initiated means was supported in Hungary, the Netherlands, South Africa, and the USA, and partly supported by second-highest placements in Israel and China. But there was also a one-place reversal in China, where the community-initiated mean was significantly higher than the teacher, school, and government-initiated means. A similar (one-place) reversal in trend occurs in Israel, but it is non-significant. In Australia, Canada, and England, the number of teacher-initiated changes was too small to permit the calculation of a stable mean, so these countries do not contribute to the trend for higher teacher-initiated influence. Nevertheless, it is probably safe to conclude that teacher-initiated change has a stronger effect on student learning than government or school-initiated change wherever teacher initiation occurs. The effects of community-initiated change in Canada, China, and Israel will require additional research to clarify.

Table A3. Influence of Initiating Sources of Change on the Valenced Impact of Change on Student Learning by Country

Countries:	Aust.	Canada	China	England	Hungary	Israel	Neth.	S. Afr.	USA	All
Source of Change										
Teacher Initiated	(N=1)	(N=3)	1.95	(N=1)	1.20	1.36	0.85	1.64	2.68	1.53
School Initiated	1.07	-.0.20	0.28	1.50	0.86	1.33	-0.03	0.00	0.84	0.61
Community Initiated	(N=1)	0.19	3.10	(N=1)	-0.12	1.93	0.07	-1.16	0.00	0.24
Government Initiated	-0.71	-0.17	1.76	0.52	0.23	0.84	0.33	1.25	-0.11	0.29
Rank Order of Means	GS	SGC	SGTC	GS	CGST	GSTC	SCGT	CSGT	GCST	CGST
Total Each Country	3.45	3.36	4.22	4.52	4.28	5.09	4.26	4.30	4.38	4.17

NOTE: Means underscored by the same line are NOT significantly different at the .05 level.

APPENDIX A4. Country by Initiator Interaction for Variable Q10

This inquiry examines the effects of different initiating sources of school change on the feelings of teachers toward the change they experienced. Country by country results are summarised in Table A4.

Table A4. Influence of Initiating Source of School Change on Teachers' Feelings Toward the Change by Country

Countries:	Aust.	Canada	China	England	Hungary	Israel	Neth.	S. Afr.	USA	All
Source of Change										
Teacher Initiated	(N=1)	3.00	4.15	(N=1)	5.33	5.29	4.91	4.20	5.77	4.97
School Initiated	5.00	3..67	3.69	(N=2)	4.50	5.11	3.95	5.00	4.50	4.44
Community Initiated	(N=1)	3.73	4.50	(N=1)	2.80	4.67	4.00	2.60	4.13	3.79
Government Initiated	3.10	3.13	4.55	4.35	4.00	4.91	4.10	4.50	3.20	3.84
Rank Order of Means	GS	TGSC	STCG	G	CGST	CGST	SCGT	CTGS	GCST	CGST
Total Each Country	3.45	3.36	4.22	4.52	4.28	5.09	4.26	4.30	4.38	4.17

NOTE: Means underscored by the same line are NOT significantly different at the .05 level.

Averaged across nine countries, the mean feelings about change for teacher-initiated change was significantly higher than the mean for school-initiated change, which in turn was significantly higher than the means for community- or government-initiated change. Within individual countries, however, the nine-country trend applied to only

Hungary, Israel, and the USA. Canada, the Netherlands, and South Africa reported low ranked teacher-initiated change, while England reported only government-initiated change, and Australia reported only government- and school-initiated changes. In view of the combination of reverse results, and missing data, the superior power of teacher and school-initiated change in the nine-country data can *not* be confirmed as a trend that applies to most individual countries.

The total number of teachers who identified government sources of change (225) in comparison to changes by teachers (77) or schools (117) would seem to indicate a higher power of government sources to initiate and effect change.

APPENDIX A5. Country by Initiator Interaction for Variable Q11A

This inquiry examines the effects of different initiating sources of school change on the willingness of teachers to responsibly participate in 'another' similar change. Country by country results are summarised in Table A5.

Table A5. Influence of Initiating Source of School Change on Teachers' Willingness to Participate in a Similar Future Change by Country

Countries:	Aust.	Canada	China	England	Hungary	Israel	Neth.	S. Afr.	USA	All
Source of Change										
Teacher Initiated	(N=1)	(N=1)	16.85	(N=1)	23.50	28.14	25.50	18.20	26.54	23.40
School Initiated	23.83	24.58	16.62	23.00	22.36	28.03	(N=0)	15.00	27.07	23.81
Community Initiated	(N=1)	25.93	19.50	(N=1)	22.20	23.00	(N=1)	21.40	26.00	24.22
Govt. Initiated	17.90	25.18	16.59	22.77	21.29	26.64	25.75	21.65	24.87	21.96
Rank Order of Means	GS	SGC	GSTC	GS	GCST	CGST	TG	STCG	GCTS	GTSC
Total Each Country	18.94	25.08	16.78	22.69	22.31	27.53	25.57	19.89	26.10	22.88

NOTE: Means underscored by the same line are NOT significantly different at the .05 level.

Averaged across all nine countries, the willingness mean for community-initiated change was higher than the means for teacher- or school-initiated change, and significantly higher than the mean for government-initiated change. The results within individual countries, however, are erratic. No country exactly repeats the nine country trend, and seven countries have minor reversals in order. Australia and England, the two countries without reversals, report no teacher or community initiation. As before, the Netherlands does not report any school or community-initiated change. Given these mixed results and the large amount of missing data, no overall trend can be determined.

It is only in South Africa that a statistically significant difference (.05) occurred within a country, indicating that repeated community initiatives for school change are more likely to promote willing participation in a similar change than are changes initiated by the government sources. As on other previous occasions, the participation willingness of Israeli teachers is stronger than the willingness by teachers in all the other eight countries.

APPENDIX A6. Country by Objectives Interaction for Variable Q10

This inquiry examines the effects of different objectives of school change on the feelings of teachers toward the change they experienced. Country-by-country results are summarised in Table A6.

Table A6. **Influence of Objectives of School Change on Teachers' Feelings Toward the Change by Country**

Countries:	Aust.	Canada	China	England	Hungary	Israel	Neth.	S. Afr.	USA	All
Objective of Change										
Educational Practice	3.56	3.73	4.30	4.30	4.75	5.15	4.58	4.80	5.09	4.51
Social Objectives	3.13	3.25	4.50	4.20	4.67	4.58	4.44	3.92	4.40	4.02
Accountability/Efficiency	3.71	2.92	3.38	4.91	4.25	5.33	3.81	5.67	3.15	3.89
Rank Order of Means	SEA	ASE	AES	SEA	ASE	SEA	ASE	SEA	ASE	ASE
Total Each Country	3.48	3.35	4.23	4.54	4.65	5.04	4.36	4.30	4.38	4.21

NOTE: Means underscored by the same line are NOT significantly different at the .05 level.

Averaged across nine countries, the mean feeling about change for educational practice is significantly higher than the mean for social or accountability objectives. Within all nine countries there is a general trend for the objective of improvement of educational practice to promote the most or second most positive feelings about the change, more so than the two other objectives. This overall trend is confirmed at a significant level (.01) when the data from all nine countries are summed together.

Only two countries show statistically significant internal differences regarding the promotion of positive feelings toward the change experienced by their teachers. In the USA, the objective of improving education is a significantly stronger promoter of positive feelings about change than is the increasing of accountability, but not significantly stronger than achieving social objectives. In South Africa, accountability objectives produce significantly stronger feelings than social objectives. Objectives aimed at improving education produce feelings stronger than social objectives and weaker than accountability objectives, but are not significantly stronger or weaker. The same order of objective means was obtained in Australia, England, and Israel, but all differences among means in those countries were non-significant. China is the only country in which the social objective mean was larger than education objectives mean, and there the difference was small (0.2) and statistically insignificant.

The pattern of results described above suggests a cross-cultural trend for changes aimed at improvement of education to produce more positive teacher feelings than changes aimed at achieving a social objective. The effects of change aimed at improving accountability and efficiency may be the most strongly approved in Australia, China, England, Israel, and South Africa, but additional evidence will be needed before it can be confirmed as a trend.

APPENDIX A7. Country by Involvement Interaction for Variable Q9A-amt

This inquiry examines the effects of different levels of teacher involvement in school change on the amount of student learning affected in each of the nine countries. Country-by-country results are summarised in Table A7. It may be a matter for surprise that few comments were made about poor pupil behaviour, given reports in the media over the period. We did not seek to elicit these as we are aware of the tendency to sensationalise this aspect of secondary schooling in the press so that where they are missing it must be inferred that this was overplayed by the media.

Averaged over nine countries, the mean amount of student learning affected increased from low to medium to high teacher involvement levels with the high mean being significantly larger than the other two. Within all eight of the nine countries there is a general trend for those teachers who had higher involvement in school change to experience their students' learning as being more affected by the change than teachers who had low involvement. This trend was confirmed by a positive correlation between involvement and student learning in every country but the Netherlands where the correlation was essentially zero.

Table A7. **Influence of Teacher Involvement on the Amount of Student Learning Affected by a Change by Country**

Countries:		Aust.	Canada	China	England	Hungary	Israel	Neth.	S. Afr.	USA	All
Teacher Involvement											
Low Involvement		3.31	3.67	2.14	3.00	3.17	4.00	3.17	3.73	3.29	3.34
Medium Involvement		3.11	3.61	3.56	3.92	3.45	4.76	3.29	4.46	3.59	3.57
High Involvement		5.17	4.25	3.89	4.00	4.00	4.68	3.26	4.00	4.05	4.13
Rank Order of Means		MLH	MLH	LMH	LMH	LMH	LHM	LHM	LHM	LMH	LMH
Correlations:	r=	.224	.103	.475**	.204	.280	.045	-.031	.152	.200	.229**
Total Each Country		3.42	3.78	3.42	3.85	3.67	4.68	3.27	4.05	3.74	3.71

NOTE 1: Means underscored by the same line are NOT significantly different at the .05 level..
NOTE 2: Significance levels for correlations are: ◊ (p≤.10), * (p≤.05), ** (p≤.01)

Statistical significance within individual countries occurred in Australia, China, and Israel. Thus, the influence of teacher involvement on the amount of student learning affected is clearly more certain in these three countries than in any of the other six countries. In summary, higher involvement tends to affect a greater amount of learning in all countries except possibly the Netherlands.

It is of special interest that the teachers at the three levels of involvement in Israel experience a stronger effect of school change on their students' learning than do teachers in any of the other countries.

APPENDIX A8. Country by Involvement Interaction for Variable Q10

This inquiry examines the effects of different levels of teacher involvement in school change on the feelings of teachers toward the change they experienced. Country-by-country results are summarised in Table A8.

Table A8. Influence of Teacher Involvement on Feelings About School Change by Country

Countries:	Aust.	Canada	China	England	Hungary	Israel	Neth	S. Afr.	USA	All
Teacher Involvement										
Low Involvement	2.38	2.27	3.43	3.67	3.00	4.00	2.00	3.87	3.00	2.91
Medium Involvement	3.79	3.36	4.32	4.77	3.91	4.93	4.38	4.62	3.82	4.17
High Involvement	5.00	4.25	4.44	4.45	5.06	5.24	4.79	4.56	5.43	4.91
Rank Order of Means	LMH	LMH	LMH	LHM	LMH	LMH	LMH	LHM	LMH	LMH
Correlations:	r= .417**	.403**	.204	.064	.478**	.300*	.368**	.289◊	.515**	.425
Total Each Country	3.48	3.33	4.22	4.52	4.32	5.11	4.34	4.30	4.38	4.20

NOTE 1: Means underscored by the same line are NOT significantly different at the .05 level..
*NOTE 2: Significance levels for correlations are: ◊ (p≤.10), * (p≤.05), ** (p≤.01)*

Averaged across nine countries, the mean feeling of teachers towards the change they experienced increased significantly from low to medium to high involvement levels. Within all nine countries there is a definite trend for those teachers who had higher involvement in school change to feel more positively about the change than teachers who had lower involvement. Notice that high involvement produced the most positive feelings within each country except England and South Africa. This trend for more positive feelings with higher involvement was very significant when the data from all countries were summed together, and was confirmed by positive correlations between involvement and feelings in every country. Although the trend is common across countries, the strength of the relationship varies from very weak (r = .064) to mild (r = .204) in China to strong, statistically significant relationships (r = .289 to r = .515) in all the other countries.

Statistically significant relationships within individual countries take place in Australia, Canada, Hungary, Israel, Netherlands, South Africa ($p < .10$), and the USA. Thus, the influence of teacher involvement efforts on positive affect toward school change is more certain in these six countries than in the other three countries. In summary, higher involvement produces more positive feelings in all countries.

Once again, teachers in Israel, involved at either high, medium, or low levels of school change, tend to feel more positive about school changes than teachers in any of the other eight countries.

APPENDIX A9. Country by Involvement Interaction for Variable Q11A

This inquiry examines the effects of different levels of teacher involvement in school change on the willingness of teachers to responsibly participate in 'another' similar change. Country-by-country results are summarised in Table A9.

Table A9. Influence of Teacher Involvement on Willingness to Participate in a Similar Future Change by Country

Countries:	Aust.	Canada	China	England	Hungary	Israel	Neth.	S. Afr.	USA	All
Teacher Involvement										
Low Involvement	15.94	25.00	16.14	24.33	22.33	26.00	24.00	16.60	26.86	20.37
Medium Involvement	20.21	24.82	16.71	23.23	20.91	26.00	23.82	26.00	24.36	22.30
High Involvement	22.17	25.38	17.56	21.50	23.59	28.61	26.00	16.56	27.67	24.96
Rank Order of Means	LMH	MLH	LMH	HML	MLH	LMH	MLH	HLM	MLH	LMH
Correlations:	r= .416**	.005	.183	-.315	.217	.229◊	.227	.024	.117	.277**
Total Each Country	19.08	25.00	16.78	22.69	22.50	27.77	25.00	19.89	26.10	22.90

NOTE 1: Means underscored by the same line are NOT significantly different at the .05 level..
*NOTE 2: Significance levels for correlations are: ◊ (p≤.10), * (p≤.05), ** (p≤.01)*

Averaged across nine countries, the mean willingness of teachers to participate in a similar change increased uniformly and significantly from low to medium to high involvement levels. Within all nine countries in Table A9 there is a trend for teachers who had a higher involvement in school change to feel more willing to responsibly participate in 'another' change than teachers who had lower involvement. This trend is quite significant when the data from all countries are summed together, and is documented as a trend by positive correlations between involvement and willingness in eight of the nine countries. In England, the correlation is a substantially *negative* $(r = -.315)$ but, because only 27 teachers were interviewed, the correlation is not even mildly significant $(p > .10)$. Note also that the correlations in Table A9 are somewhat weaker than those in Table A8. Here, Canada and South Africa have very weak correlations, China and the USA weak correlations, Hungary and the Netherlands mild correlations, and more substantial correlations in only Australia and Israel.

Statistical significance within individual countries takes place in just three countries: Australia, Israel (correlation only), and South Africa (means only). The case with South Africa is of special interest, since it is medium involvement that appears to be more promotive of a readiness to participate in further school change than is high teacher involvement. In summary, higher involvement produces a greater willingness to participate in a similar change in all countries except England where there appears to be an opposite tendency.

In usual character, the extent of participation willingness by Israeli teachers is stronger at all three levels of school change involvement than in any other countries.

APPENDIX A10. Country by Involvement Interaction for Variable Q11B

This inquiry examines the effects of different levels of teacher involvement in school change on the willingness of teachers to participate in almost any kind of educational changes in the future. Country-by-country results are summarised in Table A10.

Averaged across nine countries, the mean willingness to participate in any future change increased uniformly and significantly from low to medium to high involvement. Within seven of the nine countries (without England and Israel) there is a general, though minimal, trend for teachers who had higher involvement in school change to feel more positively about participation in almost any kinds of future educational change. The overall trend is highly significant when the data from all countries are summed together.

Table A10. Influence of Teacher Involvement on Willingness to Participate in Any Kinds of Future Educational Changes

Countries:	Aust.	Canada	China	England	Hungary	Israel	Neth	S. Afr	USA	All
Teacher Involvement										
Low Involvement	1.56	1.80	2.00	2.00	2.00	(N=1)	1.33	2.00	1.86	1.82
Medium Involvement	2.00	1.82	2.29	1.92	2.18	2.57	2.14	2.85	2.18	2.16
High Involvement	2.17	1.69	2.56	1.91	2.29	2.91	2.17	2.62	2.35
Rank Order of Means	LMH	HLM	LMH	HML	LMH	MH	LMH	HLM	LMH	LMH
Correlations: r=	.2700	-.107	.293*	-.020	.050	.208	.1580	.144	.405**	.221**
Total Each Country	1.88	1.78	2.30	1.93	2.21	2.81	2.11	2.30	2.32	2.16

NOTE 1: Means underscored by the same line are NOT significantly different at the .05 level..
NOTE 2: Significance levels for correlations are: ◊ (p≤.10), * (p≤.05), ** (p≤.01)

Statistical significance within individual countries occurs in the Netherlands, the USA, and South Africa. Consequently, the influence of teacher involvement on future participation in change is most certain in these three countries rather than in any of the other six countries. In summary, higher involvement produces a greater willingness to participate in all countries except Canada and England where the trend is again slightly reversed.

Once again, the total extent of Israeli teachers' willingness to participate in future school change overshadows teachers in seven other countries at all three levels of involvement in school change (subject to reservations about the nature of the Israel sample).

Summary of Results for Interactions

Country-by-country results are examined whenever a significant interaction occurs in order to determine whether the nine-country trend presented in the previous section applies to all countries. The analyses of results from the 10 significant country by change-characteristic interactions that occurred in the 32 two-way analyses of variance reported earlier are summarised under four broad headings: missing data problems, interactions involving amount variables, reversals of trend, and trends for initiating source.

Missing Data Problems. There were two kinds of missing data problems. The first occurred when certain categories of change did not occur in some countries. The second was when a large number of scores for a particular dependent variable were missing in a country. We will deal with these one at a time.

Two change variables had categories that did not occur in some countries. The type (or domain) of change category 'learning outcomes' did not occur in Canada, England, and Hungary. The initiating source category 'teacher initiated' did not occur in Australia, Canada, and England; and its category 'community initiated' did not occur in Australia or England. The fact that these categories of change did not appear in our data is *not* to be taken as evidence that they do not occur. It is just that Australia, Canada, and England had all been undergoing a series of government-initiated reforms that tended to involve teaching practice rather than learning outcomes. These reforms were apparently uppermost in everyone's mind. The bottom line is that any trend involving learning outcomes must exclude Canada, England and Hungary, and any trend involving community-initiated or teacher-initiated change must exclude Australia and England, with Canada also excluded for teacher-initiated change. These latter exclusions are particularly unfortunate since teacher-initiated change is theoretically superior according to the locus of control hypothesis and learning outcomes is a theoretically inferior type of change.

Interactions Involving Amount Variables. Unlike the other six dependent variables, the amount of teacher work life affected and amount of student learning affected were unvalenced in the sense that they measured the number of work life activities or learning activities that were affected by a change without regard to whether the effect was positive or negative. A country's reversal from the nine-country trend for one of these variables might therefore have a different meaning from a reversal for a valenced variable, which is why these variables are discussed separately. A country by domain (type) of change interaction involving amount of work life affected was summarised in Table A1, but these results contained no significant reversal. A country by involvement interaction

301

involving amount of student learning affected was reported in Table A7 but again there was no significant reversal. In each of these cases the significant interaction was caused by the *magnitude* of differences between high and low category means from country to country. In Table A1, the Australian difference is 2.11, and the US difference 0.33. In Table A7, the Australian difference is 2.06 and the Netherlands difference is only 0.12. It appears reasonable to conjecture that reversals in *direction* do not occur with amount scores because they are more objective than the more emotion-laden valenced scores. It is particularly interesting that Australia had the largest difference in both cases; we shall have more to say about the special case in Australia in a subsequent section.

Reversals of Trend. A significant reversal of the trend defined by the relationship among the nine-country change-characteristic means for a dependent variable represents a contradiction in outcomes. There were only three such contradictions in these data. The first was a relatively mild contradiction in the country by domain (type) of change interaction for the valenced impact of change on teacher work life. In this situation the nine-country trend that teacher-initiated change had a stronger positive impact on teacher work life than any other initiating source was contradicted in China where community-initiated change produced more impact than any other initiating source.

The most important reversals occur in the country by involvement interactions for willingness to participate in a similar change (Table A9) and willingness to participate in any future change (Table A10). The nine-country trend for all involvement analyses is a linear increase in the dependent variable with increasing amounts of involvement. In England, the negative relationship between involvement and teacher attitude towards participation in a similar change may be explained by the fact that much English change was initiated by the government, with compliance expected and in some cases compelled. The extremely slight negative relationships in Canada and England for participation in *any* future change may have a similar explanation, but are small enough to simply be a product of sampling error.

Trends for Initiating Source. Because teacher-initiated change was clearly more internally controlled than, say, government-initiated change, the initiating sources variable was expected to be a strong test of the locus of control hypothesis. Unfortunately, a trend that applied to most countries could *not* be established for any of the three dependent variables (amount of student learning affected, teacher feelings toward change, and willingness to participate in a similar change) involved in a significant interaction between country and initiating source. One important reason for the failure to establish a trend is undoubtedly the very limited occurrence of teacher-initiated and community-initiated change in Australia, England, Canada, and the Netherlands. Because of these ambiguous results, it must be left for future research to determine the true effects of initiating source.

PART THREE

Putting It All Together

Review, Reflections and Realities

PAM POPPLETON, JOHN WILLIAMSON & ALLEN MENLO

This comparative study of reactions to educational change, by secondary teachers in different countries, was guided by questions that were posed in the Introduction to this book. We now have to summarise and evaluate the new realities of teachers' work lives, as we have found them in our extended investigations, by drawing together the main strands of evidence from each of the previous sections. We examine the evidence in relation to each of the research questions in turn, illustrated by a small number of cases that raise particular problems of interpretation, then move to consider other issues that have emerged including the contributions of the respective methods employed. Finally, we point to some conclusions that should help teachers and policy makers handle the processes of reform or restructuring that facilitate, rather than impede, the teachers' work.

REVIEW OF RESEARCH QUESTIONS

What is the Role Played by the Socio-political Context in which Changes Were Introduced?

The new reality is that the changes in teacher work life that have come about are a result of radical and wide-ranging government-initiated reforms. Not all countries were affected to the same extent, but, particularly in the more economically developed countries, changes were related to the spread of the market ideology versus education as a public service, the information revolution associated with the growth of new skills, and the operation of choice and diversity in increasingly multicultural societies. Generally, changes seen as most important by the teachers were those to do with curriculum and pupil assessment.

However, a variety of different reform contexts were mentioned by our respondents, of which the socio-political context was the one that best differentiated our countries one from the other by drawing them into groups. Table III (Part Two) shows that teachers in Australia, South Africa and Canada reported the greatest negative impact on their work lives. Together with England, these were all countries that were experiencing government-initiated and tightly controlled reform movements. England straddled the middle group occupied by the Netherlands, Hungary, and China while teachers in Israel and the USA reported the least negative impact (which is not the same as the strongest positive impact). With minor shifts, these are also the relative positions of the three groups from their accounts in Part Two. As Williamson & Poppleton point out, the nine-country accounts clearly indicate that teachers perceived there had been a significant impact on their work lives in the past decade, which mirrored the experiences of major upheavals in curricula, expectations for pedagogy and accountability to which they have had to respond. Similar groupings are also observable in the tendency towards negative effects on opportunities for professional development and changes in student learning. Interestingly, however, it is not possible to predict, on the basis of these features, either what the teachers felt about the change or their willingness to participate in future changes (Part Two, Section 3). Thus, at a descriptive level of analysis, the findings of both quantitative and qualitative treatments are broadly in agreement but the details of the analyses also show considerable variations on different criteria (see Appendix to Part Two, Table A2).

In a review of current educational reform movements, Torres (1998) defined three major phases:

(1) 1983-1991. A 'top-down, rational, scientific management approach where "experts" were called in to tell us what to do in our schools'.
(2) 1992-1996. 'The decentralisation of authority' accompanied by the growth of the private sector, supposedly to cater for parental choice.
(3) 1997 – ? Education as an industry treated as a profit-driven enterprise.

The periods defined in this way have not, in practice, been mutually exclusive and examples of each may be found co-existing today. However, they are recognisable in the accounts that teachers gave of the changes that have had the greatest impact on their working life in the references they made to 'experts', 'consumers' and 'producers' as ways of describing the dominant influence in each period, when the main socio-political issues have come from either local traditions and culture, demographic and industrial changes or, finally, the pressures of globalisation.

Other factors must also be taken into consideration. The somewhat ambivalent position of the English teachers on either side of the countries experiencing high and medium impact has to be seen in the context of time and the events before and after the changes of the British Education Reform Act of 1988 were initially introduced. The more favourable reactions towards the changes came as issues were clarified, new responsibilities defined and situations reassessed when the process of change moved into its second phase. Comparable changes over time were not available in other accounts and this points up the importance of following major reform programmes through until they are well established. We conclude that: *cross country comparisons are weakened if they are made in different phases of wide-ranging reforms for different countries and that educational systems matter. State policy is an important context for teaching and learning* (McLaughlin & Talbert, 1993). Unfortunately, many of our teachers in all countries were confused and ambivalent about how the systems worked. Educational systems do not have built-in mechanisms that are responsive to the anxieties and wishes of teachers who rely primarily on the mechanisms supplied by the school. *Schools need to consider carefully how such mechanisms can be introduced.*

How are Centrally Determined Objectives Incorporated into Schools' Programmes of Development?

The key to the incorporation of centrally determined objectives is the process of implementation and this, as the interview data shows, depends on the degree of acceptance or rejection by teachers of the nominated change. That, in turn, depends upon the extent to which there is prior consultation to explain the objective of the change, about which many teachers in all countries, with the possible exception of South Africa, were very uncertain. It also depends on the extent to which teachers were involved in monitoring the process. During the process we have been told that teacher feelings about the change were adversely affected by lack of communication and being kept 'in the dark' about where the next change was coming from, but a striking feature of responses to 'things that helped implementation' was the number of teachers who emphasised their own professionalism in making what they considered to be the appropriate decisions for their students in the areas of curriculum and pedagogy. It is here that the opportunities for innovation occur in presentations tailored to the students' level of understanding and it was central to most teachers' understanding and practice of professionalism. These are the less dramatic innovations being made by teachers, often on a day-to-day basis: *Teacher involvement can occur at different stages of reform: planning, implementation, and monitoring. Teachers may be included at one stage but not at another.*

It is worth remembering that the English study included a substantial section on the views of headteachers (or principals) who controlled the implementation process at school level, but who were treated as a separate group from other teachers. The mechanics of the implementation process should be discussed by all involved and recognition of this fact has led to the establishment of training courses in leadership skills for school heads whose functions differ in different countries: While the English head teacher was first and foremost regarded as an outstanding teacher, the school principal in many other countries was primarily an administrator and may never have taught.

In reviewing the findings of the Australian study, Churchill & Williamson remind us of two things: (a) some 'realities are less "new"' than others, and (b) in an era of widespread reform movements, major changes do not impact on teachers one at a time but come in multiples. They list a number of factors that co-existed simultaneously in Australia to form a useful guide for interpreting the findings across countries – dissatisfaction with educational systems, a myriad of change expectations, conflicts between organisational and professional goals, dissonance between levels of teacher expertise and professional freedom of judgement and the maintenance of distance and immunity. All these arose from the implementation of many change initiatives that were seen as inappropriate for the school and its students.

'Curriculum' is a contested concept cross-nationally. In continental Europe it indicates syllabuses based on traditional subject divisions that, in most cases, are centrally controlled by either federal or state governments. In England it tends to include pedagogy, or the methods used to teach the subject and an additional category of 'both' had to be added in order to code the English responses. Teachers in the USA, on the other hand, focused mainly on examples of a pedagogy that disturbed life little outside the classroom. Hence, the question posed in the title of Evers & Arató, 'What Has Change Got to Do with It?', and the conclusion that change is sometimes seen as a continuous and positive experience. Where no teachers presented as opponents of change per se, a change was likely to be perceived as part of a long-term strategy for the country's development in the twenty-first century.

The way in which the curriculum is conceived, developed and implemented, and the degree of consultation and autonomy granted to the teachers in the process, form important elements of the educational culture.

TEACHERS' PERCEPTIONS OF THEIR ROLE IN CHANGE: RESOURCE AND TRAINING NEEDS

Whether the change amounts to reform, restructuring or innovation, it frequently introduces a new layer of responsibilities into the teacher's work. Curriculum changes are often accompanied by new methods of assessment with which teachers have to become familiar together with new requirements for documentation and the keeping of pupil records. In every country experiencing curriculum reforms these additional duties were the most resented since they restricted the time available for teaching and preparing lessons. In a number of countries teachers had received little help in acquiring new assessment skills (Australia and England). Israel and China (PRC) were the two countries where teachers seemed least burdened by such requirements, but Australia produced 28 teachers (30% of the sample) who claimed to have acted as 'resisters' to the curriculum-based change and the associated testing programmes.

The analyses of teacher role in the nominated change offered in Part Two show that of all the factors leading to satisfactory implementation, the degree and nature of teacher involvement, was the most outstanding. The statistical analysis of the teachers' responses cannot show 'expectations', 'conflicts', 'dissatisfaction', 'dissonance', and 'inappropriateness'. It can, however, show diversity of responses. The authors of Part Two offer the following comments on their analysis.

THE POWER OF INVOLVEMENT

Teacher involvement was by far the most powerful of the four change variables in this study. When studied in isolation, increased involvement produced a significant linear increase in every dependent variable in the study. Furthermore, similar patterns of relationship were evident in individual countries, although the magnitude of the effect varied. The only exceptions were possible reverse relations (negative correlations) with willingness to participate in future change in England and Canada. However, the correlation coefficients were not significant in either country and could be the result of sampling error. Further involvement retained a significant positive relationship with dependent variables in the presence of a number of other powerful predictors.

Since involvement is one variable in this study that can appear with a change having many different characteristics, and since it has the potential to be manipulated by a change agent, it is important to understand the mechanisms by which involvement influences the responses of participants. Accordingly, we will share some conceptual and pragmatic speculations regarding this aspect of school change since it appears to contain much potential for promoting positive outcomes and for generating receptiveness and positive feelings for schools and their teachers. If understood more fully, teacher involvement would seem to be both a facilitating force towards constructive change and an antidote for individual and group resistance to change.

311

The Place of Teacher Involvement in School Change

Part Two of this study reports the quantitative data analyses of four aspects or characteristics of school change: the change's type, origin, objective, and level of teacher involvement. Of the four, it is the involvement of the teacher in the change that clearly demonstrates itself to have the strongest effect on the six selected areas of teacher work life across the nine countries. For instance, the more the teachers experience themselves as participating in responsible, initiating roles in school change then the more positive they feel about the change and the more willing they are to engage seriously in helping to bring about future changes, and the more they are professionally enhanced as educators. The less they are involved, the less productive and experientially rich and challenging are those dimensions of their work lives.

The results of the statistical analyses in Part Two and the more qualitative information from teacher interviews in Part One mutually call attention to the variations in level and kind of teacher involvement in school change and, also, the resulting variation in teachers' reactions to their involvement, and the consequences for the teachers' work lives. It is useful to note that 31% of all teachers spoke of a high level of involvement in their school's change through acting as initiator, planner, or in shared decision-making roles, while 53% took part in implementation or supporting; 31% of the teachers reached a level of involvement that promoted the most positive consequences for their schools and themselves.

General expectations of widespread resistance to change were anticipated on the part of those teachers who saw it as a destabilising influence on their work life. This was most frequently found in conjunction with reforms affecting curriculum and pedagogy and/or restructuring initiated by central governments and implemented under controlled conditions. Australia, England, Canada, and South Africa may be cited as pivotal cases where work alteration forces emanated from external change environments. Resistance was not so marked in other countries where change was seen as a stimulus and a challenge (e.g. Hungary, USA).

It is important to explore some brief conceptual and pragmatic speculations regarding the involvement aspect of school change since it appears to contain much potential for promoting positive work life outcomes and for generating receptiveness and positive feelings of teachers toward change itself. If more fully understood, teacher involvement in change would seem to present itself as both a facilitating force toward constructive change and as an antidote for individual and group resistance. These speculations may begin to respond to one of the major questions of the present study: how do the characteristics of a change influence its impact on the work life of teachers, and does the influence vary across different countries or cultures? Indeed, evidence reported earlier in this section suggests that it does vary across countries as 'the significant interaction of country and involvement for all three dependent variables suggests that the overall effect may not apply to all countries'. For some, the overall trends may be magnified, and for others it may be diminished, or even contradicted. Croll (1994) reminds us that 'a model of teachers as implementers of change draws a sharp distinction between the processes of policy making and policy execution and excludes teachers from the former', and the data here support this conclusion

Change, Resistance, and Involvement

Mainstream social-psychological literature on the dynamics of change suggests that resistance to change is a natural human phenomenon and that the self system tends to be resistant to change. Based on the proposition that persons resist change, books and manuals have been written for practitioners that advise them on how to reduce or eliminate resistance to change. However, results of earlier research and practice within the Consortium for Cross-Cultural Research in Education (Menlo, 1987, 1989) have led to a view about resistance to change that tends to see it as a more unusual phenomenon in the teacher's work life than most literature on the subject would lead us to believe. From this research, most adults were observed as seeking, rather than resisting, change in self and surroundings. What has been observed is that when adults expect a significant personal, social, or material loss to occur during, or following, an engagement with change, they are unlikely to participate in the change out of their concern with the expected loss. Thus, the expected loss is the target of the person's resistance, and not the change itself, since change is a major characteristic of all living systems and functions as an inherent drive for activity, curiosity, and search for betterment.

If facilitators of school change can welcome this reasoning and build it into their practice, they could become quite encouraged about successful outcomes of change efforts and the receptiveness of teachers to change. As the findings from the present research appear to indicate: *the strongest indicator of positive change outcomes is the increased opportunity for teachers to be involved in important and responsible roles, with a shared determination of the change.*

This is not a totally new area of thought and professional practice, but an encouragement towards newer individual and organisational competencies and revised beliefs about human nature and change expectations. Unfortunately, these competencies are apt to meet strong barriers in the shape of the additional responsibilities that come with opportunities for involvement. Issues related to 'responsibility enlargement' have been fully discussed by Neave (1992). Work overload, which is the frequent outcome of such developments, was often mentioned by teachers in all countries as a consequence of new methods of pupil assessment, the frequent meetings deemed necessary to implement the reforms and general administrative lag.

Such conditions tend to occur when reforms are introduced rapidly without thought being given to how they are to be implemented. A good example mentioned by one English teacher was the burden imposed on him by the requirement that every child should have 'hands-on' experience of computer usage and every teacher some training in the application of information technology to each subject in the new national curriculum. Since there were few teachers who even knew what IT meant at that time (and they were the ones given responsibility for implementing the reform) it was indeed, a case of 'the blind leading the blind'. Another classic English case was the failure adequately to train the hundreds of teachers who were required to mark A-level exam scripts for university entrance in the year 2002. If ever there were powerful pragmatic decisions to be made, these illustrate the need for the training of implementers in new skills and in foresight for the reformers.

Change at this level never 'just happens' but has to be worked out.

General or widespread resistance to change was anticipated on the part of those teachers who saw it as a destabilising influence on the work life. Resistance was not so marked in countries (Israel, PRC) where change was seen as appropriately focussed, stimulating and a challenge.

The beliefs that informed the whole school philosophy and ethos too often remained within the purlieu of the senior staff, unshared with more junior colleagues.

The Role of Higher Education in Facilitating and Evaluating School Change

No specific findings on the role of higher education institutions per se emerged from the survey, so must they be presumed missing from the teachers' general perspective? Remembering that teachers were not questioned specifically on this issue, comments occurred only if the interviewee felt strongly about it. Strangely, educators have themselves found it difficult to reconcile their precise roles, as these have expanded under the impetus of reforms to meet greatly increased demands from the general public in their work as teachers. But it was with reference to the role of the teacher's professional development that higher education became more important at a time of change when formalised schemes of new work were being introduced. The assumption is that 'higher education' was seen as a responsive, rather than an initiating agency as far as change was concerned and seemed remote from the core issues of the study.

In this area also, things are changing. Governments and other research and development agencies have begun to stress the importance of research-user perspectives, user-links and user-involvement for research support now and in the future. In England this takes the form of generous research grants for schools and universities for joint projects to overcome the gap between researchers and classroom practitioners that Hargreaves (1996, p. 4) saw as 'the fatal flaw in educational research'. Such projects have a research training function in addition to greater relevance in the social context.

METHODOLOGICAL ISSUES ARISING FROM THE STUDY

The outstanding position of Israeli teachers on practically every aspect of the work life covered in the study resisted a convincing explanation given the several social and political upheavals of the 1990s. One possibility is that a school is usually situated in a community (e.g. kibbutz) that allows a high degree of autonomy to the staff. A study of the structure of the Israeli survey, however, revealed an imbalance in the sampling that could well be an anomaly, that is, a high proportion of school administrators in the sample. Since planning and innovation are key activities of this group, it is not surprising that they described themselves as innovators of 50% of the reported changes, the overwhelming majority of which were centred on micro-school functions. It remains difficult to reconcile the overwhelmingly positive accounts of their work lives by teachers with 'a lack of movement towards the desperately needed improvement in the status of teachers even today' (Dror, 2002). Similarly to their colleagues in Poland (Leszczynska & Olek, 1997), some teachers saw themselves not so much as servants of the state as government officers themselves, responsible for initiating as well as implementing reforms. In China (PRC), also, we found that teachers were asked to mediate a major philosophical shift towards more individual development from a 'collective or group' perspective.

Collet et al (Part Two) summarise the effect of country on response pattern as follows:

Countries with low teacher response scores had a higher
incidence of management and accountability changes initiated
by government, while countries with high response scores had
teaching changes initiated by the teacher or the school.

The Israeli case suggests that the majority of teachers judge their work lives primarily in terms of ability to influence the day-to-day impact of the school environment, which defines the extent of involvement that can occur.

Reflections on Methodology

It was clear from the beginning that in our studies of change and the teacher's work life, we would be dealing with so many instances of multiple changes and social definitions in the teachers' responses in the interviews that we would need to employ both qualitative and quantitative methods of analysis. It is rare in any context to find the two approaches to data analysis based on one database. Phases one and two of this study look at the same database through different lenses. Can they be integrated or can we say in what ways they complement each other?

On the surface they look very different. Part One explored the whole range of responses given by the teachers, of both micro- and macro-social influences on their work life and produced nine country-based case studies. Part Two, on the other hand, took selected responses, now coded and aggregated, to explore cross-country similarities and differences as a guide to the effects on teachers of the policy-making process generally

These differences in approach may be seen in Part One (Figure 1, p. 17), by an interactive model that recognises the interdependence of the variables explored, and in Part Two, where Collet et al (Figure 1, p. 249) assume a linear path of influence from the nature of the change through to its implications and applications. Thus, the objectives of Part One were to report the perceptions and experiences themselves under conditions of change in different countries, whereas those of Part Two were to achieve a more precise, predictive cross-cultural analysis. These procedures are intrinsic to qualitative and quantitative methods of analysis respectively and may now be summarised in the context of the study as follows.

SUMMARY OF RESEARCH PROCEDURES

Data:
Teachers' perceptions of the most important change to have affected their work lives during the previous five years

Method and Instrumentation:
Small group interviews and Interview Schedule

Data Analysis:

Quantitative	Qualitative
12 major variables, pre-selected numerical measures allocated	Post-interview codings adopted and applied

Treatment:

Tables of percentage response to each item in each country	Distinguishing within-country patterns of meaning

Anaylsis:

2-way analysis of variance (between countries and items)	Between-country interpretation of pattern
Multiple regression (to predict teachers' response to change)	Interview responses

Aim:

To gain evidence of what works distilled from a large number of cases	To gain evidence of what does and what does not work from intimate knowledge of a small number of cases

Assumption:

There is one best way to implement change for teacher acceptance	There are a number of ways to maximise success

The Arguments:

A positivist paradigm –	A phenomonological paradigm –
'holds that behaviour can be explained through objective facts. Design and instrumentation persuade by showing how bias and error are eliminated. (Smith, 1983)	'there are multiple realities that are socially defined. Rich description persuades by showing that the researcher was immersed in the setting and giving the reader enough detail to make sense of the situation'. (Firestone, 1987)

Conclusions:

'While theoretically different, the results of the two methodologies can be complementary' (Firestone, 1987).

Figure 1. Summary of research procedures.

Complementarity was the outcome originally envisaged in employing the two methods on the same data. It has to be acknowledged, however, that the accounts differ in their objectives, techniques and style of reporting in ways that almost exclude cross-reference but each has integrity within its own parameters and each makes a valuable contribution to the study of educational change. Each also contributes to the ongoing discussions of the respective roles of qualitative and quantitative methods of enquiry in the field of comparative, cross-cultural studies, but the two remain side by side rather than offering an integrated view.

Where collaborative research is conducted by nine different researchers or groups of them in nine different countries, it is to be expected that personal and professional perspectives will show through in the results. The last 20 or so years have seen a vigorous methodological debate in educational research on the applicability of each method that still rages in the pages of the professional journals and is usually stated in theoretical terms as the positivist versus the phenomenological paradigm.

The Comparative Dimension

The study has revealed a sufficiently broad picture of anxieties on the part of teachers in the studied countries about the state of their educational systems compared to their relatively few references to the role of the school and its community in initiating and managing change. The old certainties based on values in education have given way to an instrumental view about the restricted role of schools in the production of citizens for a highly competitive market economy. This has been described as the 'diminished school' which has become more isolated and in which the teachers have, to an extent, been deprofessionalised. While our study gives partial support for this view, it does not support the wholesale deprofessionalisation hypothesis, which perhaps has been overplayed in the literature (Hoyle, 1980). Teachers asserted their professionalism as a last-ditch defence against the forces seeking to diminish schools and systems. This is particularly true of the older, more senior teachers whose curriculum base was being attacked and of the younger recruits who were asserting their independence.

There is still a belief that schools can be enhanced rather than diminished by adopting a critical perspective on change. The more freely that teachers can express this belief, the stronger the professional community will be.

CONCLUSIONS

There are few clear-cut answers to any of the research questions posed, but rather an invitation to interpret the findings in the light of both research and considered judgment. One theme that emerges strongly is the dominance in the teachers' eyes of central government in policy making and the relative powerlessness of the school community in the teachers' thinking. Careful perusal of the findings by educators in each country against the relevant social/political/economic background is a necessary first step to forging successful policies. Teachers will be attracted to, and stay with, schools that offer them opportunities to experiment and design appropriate programmes for their students. They will not stay in schools that load them with additional responsibilities and keep them away from their classrooms. They will also view with suspicion any suggestions that diminish schools in the eyes of school or parent. Projecting a positive view of the teacher's work life should not be too much to ask of administrators and politicians.

References

Croll, P. (1994) Teachers and Educational Policy: roles and models, *British Journal of Educational Studies*, 42, pp. 333-347.

Dror, Y. (2002) What Happened to the Status of Teachers in Israel? A Historical and Educational Survey. 'In Touch With MOFET', *The MOFET Institute Bulletin*, p. 17. Tel Aviv, Israel.

Firestone, W.A. (1987) Meaning in Method and the Rhetoric of Quantitative and Qualitative Research, *Educational Researcher*, 7, pp. 16-21.

Hargreaves, D.H. (1996) Teaching as a Research-based Profession: profession, possibilities and prospects, the Teacher Training Agency Annual Lecture, mimeo.

Hoyle, E. (1980) Professionalisation and Deprofessionalisation in Education, in E. Hoyle & J. Megarry (Eds) *World Yearbook of Education, Professional Development of* Teachers, pp. 42-54. London: Kogan.

Huse, E.F. (1980) *Organization Development and Change*. New York: West Publishing Company.

Leszczynska, E. & Olek, H. (1997) Polish Teachers: still faithful servants of the state? Paper presented at the European Conference on Educational Research, Frankfurt-am-Main, Germany, 24-27 September.

McLaughlin, M.W. & Talbert, J.E. (1993) *Contexts that Matter for Teaching and Learning*. Stanford: Center for Research on the Context of Secondary School Teaching, Stanford University.

Menlo, A. (1987) Everyday Truths and Effective School Administration, *International Schools Journal*, 14, pp. 23-31.

Menlo, A. (1989) The Beliefs of Management and the Management of Beliefs, *Organizational Development Journal*, 7(2), pp. 36-42.

Neave, G. (1992) *The Teaching Nation: prospects for teachers in the European Community*. Oxford: Pergamon Press.

Smith, J.K. (1983) Quantitative versus Qualitative Research: an attempt to clarify the issue, *Educational Researcher*, 3, pp. 6-13.

Torres, I.R. (1998) American Educational Reform from 1978 to 1998: a case study of institutional reform in a College District. PhD dissertation, University of California, Los Angeles.

history of rvt - long + broad

1 * promise of comparisons

description for cross comparisons

primarily for cross comparisons

~ some takes conf + little doth
to require best types

~ lugh on how relatedness

80's ~ types - pics given

snapshots types - country off

date soz but not enough

diffs in concep + meth
across countries both
pos + neg

2 *
Index descrips
comparative sio
cross case

Var in temporal +
comparative trend
Des or success varies

Broad but slashes of color
written sob will
Israeli engagement

involv'm
discourse
agency - thing desire - bus wonder
purpose, gov X out
volatility - can invest

1 3 levels
mag + purpose
+ between
state control
(voste ey's US, Eng
autonomy
exp, func
instit

3 * Part 2
demos
types of Δ - tly
not org

rvt + labor hovt
metos
norms + patterns
- rvt ind

Part 3
Good summary
some weave
some misses
acknowl lms.
of snapshot app

(strength of
involv'm)
contribution?
depth?

320

growing
res others were
mag of Δ

1 feelings